STOCKWELL-MUDD LIBRARIES

D0593607

The Making
of Ministers

Essays on Clergy Training Today

Edited by: KEITH R. BRIDSTON
DWIGHT W. CULVER

AUGSBURG PUBLISHING HOUSE • MINNEAPOLIS

THE MAKING OF MINISTERS
Copyright © 1964 Augsburg Publishing House
All rights reserved
Library of Congress Catalog Card No. 64-13435

Scripture quotations are from the Revised Standard Version of the
Bible, copyright 1946 and 1952 by the Division of Christian
Education of the National Council of Churches.

BV
4020
.B7

Manufactured in the United States of America

151980

To
Elizabeth
and
Margaret

CONTENTS

iv

Contents

INTRODUCTION

One of Søren Kierkegaard's biting critiques of "the present age" is entitled: *Of the Difference Between a Genius and an Apostle.* He suggests that whereas "genius is born," it is "otherwise with an Apostle. . . . An Apostle is not born; an Apostle is a man called and appointed by God, receiving a mission from him." On this basis Kierkegaard goes on to argue: "An apostle does not develop in such a way that he successively becomes what he is *kata dunamin.* For to become an Apostle is not preceded by any potential possibility; essentially every man is equally near to becoming one. An Apostle can never come to himself in such a way that he becomes conscious of his apostolic calling as a factor in the development of his life. Apostolic calling is a paradoxical factor, which from first to last in his life stands paradoxically outside his personal identity with himself as the definite person he is. . . . As a result of this call he does not become more intelligent, does not receive more imagination, a great acuteness of mind and so on."[1]

Without committing oneself to Kierkegaard's thesis, or

vii

even pressing the analogy too hard, would it be entirely inadmissible to make a similar analysis of the difference between a clergyman and a minister? Obviously in practice the two are the same. They are embodied in the same person. Yet it is easier to describe what a clergyman is, what is required of him, what his training should be, than to define a "minister." This might be thought simply a play on words. But it is more than that. For "clergyman" is basically a sociological definition relating to the role of a particular individual in society, a description of the function of a special member of a religious institution. On the basis of such a definition and description it should be relatively easy to discuss "The Making of Clergymen," including their educational training. We know what a clergyman is, we know what the institution requires, and we set about providing the appropriate equipment for that service. It is that simple.

But may it not be otherwise for the "minister"? Here we are dealing not with a social role or an institutional function but with a divine ordination. In this case the orientation is not primarily sociological but theological—"a holy calling" (2 Tim. 1:9). Thus, though the priest "chosen from among men is appointed to act on behalf of men in relation to God," it is not to be forgotten that "one does not take the honor upon himself, but he is called by God" (Heb. 5:1, 4). Does educational training qualify one for this "heavenly call" or even prepare one to fulfill it?

The title and subtitle of this book of essays reflect this paradoxical sociological-theological duality that every clergyman-minister embodies within himself. The various essayists indicate some of the reasons why that duality is not a comfortable one to encompass. That discomfort is felt both personally as a vocational tension and organizationally as an educational dilemma. Erik Erikson's psychiatric study,

Young Man Luther, illuminates the personal tensions which
arise out of the conflicts between institutional obligations
and individual convictions within the context of clerical
training: "No course of training invented specifically to in-
tensify neurotic strain in a young man like Martin could
have been more effective than the monastic training of his
day. . . . In this connection I am led to think of my own
profession: let me make the most of a strange parallel. Young
(and often not so young) psychoanalysts in training must un-
dergo a training procedure which demands a total and
central personal involvement, and which takes greater
chances with the individual's relation to himself and to those
who up to then have shared his life, than any other professional training except monkhood."[2] John Osborne's play,
Luther, successfully staged in London and New York, is a
brilliant presentation of Erikson's thesis, dramatically depict-
ing this excruciating vocational struggle—in this case, the
monk becoming the reformer. Erikson analytically and Osborne dramatically both vividly demonstrate the fact that
professional training may "prepare" a man for his vocation
in the most paradoxical manner—almost as though the technical preparation were chiefly intended to provoke the revolt
through which vocational integration is ultimately achieved.
Perhaps this dialectical relation of vocational realization and
professional preparation does not create such severe personal tensions in all. But who has undertaken theological
study who has not felt some of it?

If the corporate and individual, the sociological and theological, the human and divine elements of the ministry create private tensions within those who have this call and
calling, these polarities are no less effective in placing severe strains on theological education itself. Indeed, one may
doubt that any form of clergy training, any system of ministerial education, could be immune from it. Perhaps some

of the perplexities surrounding recent attempts to "reinte-
grate" theological training are a result of not recognizing
that "effective" training has this paradoxical polarity within
it: namely, that clergy training *can* mean the unmaking of
ministers, potentially at least. Furthermore, if it did not
have this potentiality, it would probably be ineffective training. As Erikson says: "Any indoctrination worth its ideological salt, also harbors dangers, which bring about the unmaking of some and the supreme transcendence of others."

In short, "the making of ministers" is a far more complicated question than it may at first appear. If the essays in
this book do nothing else, they should at least shake any
superficial assumptions about the ease with which one may
arrive at quick answers and easy solutions in this field of
professional education. Also they should indicate the multi-
dimensional character of the problems facing theological
educators today. For example, it is popularly assumed that
"the making of ministers" takes place in seminaries: a layman goes in and a priest comes out. However, even if we
were to say that clergy training is something narrower, more
technical, more functional than the making of ministers,
even clergy training in this more specialized sense could not
be exclusively consigned to the seminary. The educational
process alone is too subtle, too elusive, to be broken down
into neat blocks labeled: elementary, high school, college,
graduate, and professional. It has to be seen as a whole
in order to make any sense out of it as a whole, or out of
any of its constituent parts.

To a certain extent one might simply dismiss the question of the making of ministers as part of that great "mystery of godliness" mentioned in the Letter to Timothy in relation to his ministry. In effect, that is what Kierkegaard
does in relation to the "Apostle": "A genius and an Apostle
are qualitatively different, they are definitions which each

belong in their spheres: the sphere of immanence, and the sphere of transcendence." Unless one makes this absolute distinction, according to Kierkegaard, one gets caught in the dilemma of having to judge St. Paul's qualities as a philosopher, as a literary stylist, or, even, as a tent-maker. And, as S.K. remarks: "As a genius St. Paul cannot be compared with either Plato or Shakespeare . . . as a stylist his name is quite obscure—and as an upholsterer: well, I frankly admit I have no idea how to place him."

This witty *reductio ad absurdum* apparently resolves all problems of theological training in one stroke. For the apostle (or the minister) doesn't commend himself by his philosophical profundity, nor by his doctrinal understanding. "Is it the profundity, the excellence, the cleverness of the doctrine? Not at all! . . . *Divine authority is, qualitatively, the decisive factor*." Kierkegaard's ironic *reductio* is meant to lead us to a serious consideration of the ultimate and essential nature of ministerial authority. There is little doubt that the problem of authority is a real and pressing one for this generation of ministers and future ministers. Walter Wagoner's *Bachelor of Divinity* faithfully mirrors this contemporary ministerial anxiety.[3] If Kierkegaard's *reductio* helps to resolve that, or even suggests a way of resolution, it probably ought to be listened to with the greatest attentiveness.

But taking the religious ethos as it is and the churches as they are (which Kierkegaard refuses to do, and which is a part of his creative genius), the fact remains that even the true apostolic minister must be trained as a clergyman to serve the church at all. (Unless, of course, clerical leadership were done away with entirely—which some Christian communities have in fact done historically and in view of the present discussions of the ministry of the laity in the ecumenical movement may be at least admitted as an open option.) But taking the situation as it is and is likely to be for some time to come, the special "set-apart" ministry is made up of those who have been professionally trained as clergymen. The question then is perhaps not whether this training in itself can make ministers—let us, for the sake of argument, admit Kierkegaard's view that God alone does this—but whether this training can be given in such a way that ministers are not unmade in the process. Or to put it in another way, can the divine authority behind the ministerial call be kept in some kind of creative relation with the functional and institutional exigencies of the clerical calling? If so, can the training of clergy facilitate rather than negate this paradoxical relationship?

As may be seen, the essays in this symposium do not beg the challenging question which Kierkegaard raises. Behind all of them lies this unresolved, perhaps unresolvable, tension between divine ministerial authority and human clerical function. If they are focused on the concrete institutional and educational difficulties of effective clergy training, it may be argued on their behalf that this side of the equation, pedestrian as it may seem in comparison with the pyrotechnics which can be engendered in considering the purely theological and doctrinal aspects of the ministry, is the "flesh" of the subject, and without being taken seriously into account, any doctrine of the ministry or theory of theological education is inevitably bound to be docetic, and therefore unrealistic.

This may be the chief theological validity of the empirical approach to theological training which has been characteristic of the Study out of which these essays have arisen. The Lilly Endowment Study of Pre-Seminary Education, financed with a generous grant from the Lilly Endowment, Inc., of Indianapolis and sponsored by the American Association of Theological Schools and the National Association of Biblical Instructors (now the American Academy of Religion), began its work in 1961 under the commission to study the relation of pre-seminary and seminary education in the training of ministers. During the course of the Study it became increasingly apparent that the pre-seminary college preparation of ministerial students could not be arbitrarily marked off as a completely independent and self-contained stage in the process of theological education. No doubt the seminary curriculum depends on certain academic accomplishments and proficiencies on the part of its entering students. And there can be little question that a closer curricular integration between the work done in college and that done in seminary needs to be realized, particularly in recognizing the theology study done in college through departments of religion and philosophy. These matters are to be given concentrated attention in the final report of the Study. But what became increasingly clear is that the education of ministers is a total process of learning, maturation, and vocational integration which has no sharp beginnings (college is certainly not the start of it!) and no end, other than death itself. A minister is being educated before he has reached a decision to become a minister and he continues to be educated all through his ministry, as long as it goes on, and he does.

The Study was chartered to be empirical. Through correspondence, interviews, visits to colleges and seminaries and church offices, by means of questionnaires to seminarians (over 17,500 responses representing over 83% of the seminary student population in the United States and Canada), college teachers, and practicing ministers, on the basis of tape-recorded consultations in different regions of North America between college, seminary, and church agency representatives, a vast amount of "hard" empirical data has been accumulated and sifted. This is the basis of the final report of the Study. But precisely out of reflection on this data, and in particular out of the regional consultations, came the recognition that the "pre-seminary" period was only one segment of an educational continuum which was essentially indivisible. "You cannot divide the seamless coat of learning," said Alfred North Whitehead. This Study confirms the validity of that insight for ministerial education.

As has been said, the following essays are firstfruits of the Lilly Endowment Study of Pre-Seminary Education. Their appearance in this form, as a volume separate from the report proper, has two main purposes. In the first place, it provides the opportunity of offering to a wider reading public certain material which has been of great value to the Study but which would not be appropriate as a part of the final report. In the second place, and more importantly, it provides the broader and deeper contextual setting—educationally and theologically—for the Study's report, which by necessity must be more empirically oriented and more closely focused on the pre-seminary and seminary curricular relationship.

Taken as a whole, the essays make another important point. That is, the education or training of ministers is not just the introverted professional concern of a clerical caste within the religious community. It is the concern of the whole body. Laymen, for example, have the right, indeed the duty, to be intelligently informed about how their ministers are prepared for the tasks to which they, the laymen, call them. Not infrequently individual laymen, and congregations themselves, have a crucial role in continuing the education of their pastors, and this sometimes includes rectifying the deficiencies which more adequate training in college and seminary might have accomplished. In short, congregations are not only where ministry takes place but are themselves ministerial "schools" where all can learn and all can teach.

Paul L. Holmer strikes this note immediately in the opening survey when he asks, "What kind of pastors do we need?" —a question that no one who is at all concerned for the church and the ministry can fail to think about. He discusses three topics: "first, something about the aims of the minister of the Gospel; second, the educational means at our disposal today; third, why theological training, even though professional, must be indirect and somewhat tangential in orientation." Finally, he makes a plea for healing the "unfortunate breach between American church life and the seminaries" and suggests that one important means of achieving this would be by "a more active training of ministers in actual parish life" in which "the churches were clearly charged with a more active role and one which could not be delegated to the seminaries."

John A. Hutchison maintains that theology is a significant and reputable form of study. Against those who would restrict theological study to the adherents of a particular faith or those for whom theology as such is a pejorative term, he writes under the assumption that properly defined and carried out theology is a fit and honorable occupation for the human mind with massive historical precedent for according it a central place in liberal education. Describing the renewal of theological study in American higher education as a "significant but small" development, he maintains that prospects for the *departmental* study of religion in public higher education are not very bright. The difficulties of an *interdisciplinary* approach are noted. The treatment of religion as an aspect of *general education* courses appears to be better than the alternative of nothing at all. Hutchison is least impressed with the *extracurricular* approaches. His recommended strategy is to use whatever combination gives most promise of success in "restoring the study of religion to its integral place in liberal education." To these practical concerns he adds a forthright statement of the need for a Christian humanism as an organizing center for the liberal education of the future minister.

Robert Michaelsen provides a comprehensive and definitive survey of the tension that has existed between Christianity and the liberal arts. He traces the historical development which created in this century "a semi-professional caste in the religion curriculum," leading to an attitude which discouraged pre-ministerial students from majoring in the subject which they would get "later and better" in the seminary.

William Nicholls, addressing himself to the special situation of the Canadian universities, raises issues of equal concern throughout the rest of North America. He asserts that the modern university, whether church-related or not, will be secular if it is wholeheartedly academic. The academic study of religion is a secular undertaking in which the department of religion needs neither special privileges nor special restrictions. Although the "academic study of religion has nothing to do with the mission of the church," the Christian professor of religion is a missionary simply by his presence *if* he affirms the values of the university as a loyal colleague and a diligent researcher and teacher. We do not "love" the university if we are always seeking to alter it. A loyal member of an academic community works on secular presuppositions. Religion is a vital part of undergraduate liberal education, but specialized studies in religion at the undergraduate level seem more appropriate for prospective teachers than for those preparing for pastoral work.

Paul Ramsey presents the case for "academic responsibility of the highest order to and for the entire range of theological studies as a university discipline." His criticism of the A.A.T.S. Statement on Pre-Seminary Studies as based on a "God and . . . " viewpoint first appeared in *Theology Today* and has been widely cited by those who argue for more adequate theological studies in pre-seminary education. He would define as standard the beginning of serious study of religion in undergraduate college, making possible truly graduate work at the seminary level.

Ernest C. Colwell presents his criticism of the A.A.T.S. Statement on Pre-Seminary Studies and especially its failure to include the option of a religion major. He argues for a shorter list of *requirements* rather than a longer list of *recommendations*. Noting the failure of the seminaries to support collegiate departments of religion, he declares that "theological education can become graduate level education only when and if it relates its curriculum cooperatively and constructively to the curriculum of the college." More sanguine than Hutchison about trends in the American college with regard to adding instruction in religion, Colwell urges that seminaries hasten the expansion of undergraduate religion departments by establishing the admission requirement of a major in religion. He specifies the content of a desirable religion major and indicates how his proposed minimum specifications might sometimes be met by interdepartmental cooperation.

Martin E. Marty suggests putting first things first: The seminary is not the place for cultural disciplines and the liberal arts college is not the place for theological education, except for those who remain laymen or non-professional theologians. For the pre-seminarian, premature theological tantalization ordinarily leads to superficiality. "Premature ripeness produces a narcissism, a dilettantism, a fascination with religion at the expense of theological hard work." "Once theological education formally is undertaken, one violates liberal learning if pretense is made that it can be sustained in disciplined fashion or that theology can be done justice to if there are still assignments ahead in liberal learning."

Elwyn A. Smith stresses the disjunctions between undergraduate and seminary education. He maintains that the conflicting assumptions on which the teaching proceeds at two levels requires for their resolution a functional interpretation of the ministry and of the study of theology. He presents the case for a theologically oriented functionalism in ministerial education.

Gibson Winter is concerned about "the institutional crisis which has shaken Christianity" and notes the "discontinuity between the theological enterprise and the religious actuality." He maintains that theological education can no longer be thought of as preparation of a "set-apart" ministry. "Professional training has no relevance without institutions in which professionals may exercise their vocations." Noting the interdisciplinary character of true theological reflection and the "need for research on the total ministry in the actual world of our time," he questions whether the theological schools "can and will participate in the conversation of message and world through which Christ's mission is going forward."

Charles L. Taylor discusses the need for the minister to be a theologian "educated to awareness." He distinguishes between training for the moment and that education which makes the minister, in his entirety, a fit man. In the division of labor "it is well for the college to emphasize history, the social sciences, and the discoveries of this century about human behavior, while the theological school, building upon these, specializes in the study of the Christian faith itself." The equipment needed for the performance of different functions is reviewed.

C. Umhau Wolf suggests that the reshaping of the parish ministry needs a theological orientation and the establishment of prerequisites other than academic for professorships, especially in the seminary. Believing that the place to learn about the world is through the world of the parish, he urges seminary professors to gain parish experience before teaching and to seek a systematic renewal of this experience. He thinks that the choice between a graduate school of theology and a trade school is a false antithesis and recommends that academic excellence be attempted in different types of seminaries building on different student preparations.

Reuel L. Howe asserts that "if the church is to speak to the present generation, its ministry must be able to listen as well as to speak." In the absence of the needed dialogical images, he now finds widespread the monological misconception of communication. The preacher is regarded as a performer and the congregation as the audience. The teacher as a lecturer tends to answer questions that have not been asked. There are confusions in the image of the pastor arising from tensions introduced by the incomplete assimilation of new developments in psychoanalysis and psychiatry. An improved seminary curriculum would involve lay participation in training ministers and would be based on the recognition that "the Gospel is a saving event that occurs in human relations and not a body of knowledge for mere verbal transmission."

Malcolm Boyd identifies the ministerial task as achieving a "point of contact for the Gospel with contemporary man in mass culture by creating new images which possess meaning for him." However, he warns against the manipulative methods of Motivation Research. We are to use insight and care to avoid exploitation. We will be content to be known as evangelists rather than as persuaders.

Arnold S. Nash is not content to discuss the merits of the religion major for the pre-seminarian, but addresses himself to the "question behind the question." "Through the liberal arts and sciences as now understood the future ministerial student is taught a confused world view which challenges the basic tenets of the Gospel which he will be trained to preach." Nash protests the view of religion by which it is seen essentially as that which can be localized in a course or curriculum rather than as a standpoint or perspective from which knowledge in any field is seen and understood and appreciated. "We should put our stress on religion as that which holds things together, rather than as a substantive field of study."

This volume is presented to pastors, teachers, students, educators, administrators, laymen—"to read, mark, learn, and inwardly digest"—as an ecumenical offering "for the perfecting of the saints, for the work of the ministry, for the edifying of the body of Christ."

KEITH R. BRIDSTON

Professor of Systematic Theology
Pacific Lutheran Theological Seminary
Berkeley, Calif.

DWIGHT W. CULVER

Head, Department of Sociology
St. Olaf College, Northfield, Minn.

FOOTNOTES

1. Søren Kierkegaard, *The Present Age* (Harper Torchbooks, 1962).

2. Erik H. Erikson, *Young Man Luther* (New York: W. W. Norton Co., 1958).

3. W. D. Wagoner, *Bachelor of Divinity: Uncertain Servants in Seminary and Ministry* (New York: Association Press, 1963).

THE THEOLOGICAL ENTERPRISE

*An
Analysis*

CAN WE EDUCATE MINISTERS SCIENTIFICALLY?

PAUL L. HOLMER

What kind of pastors do we need? Scarcely anyone who has thought at all about church and ministers has failed to think about that question. And with the plethora of popular studies about why ministers leave their profession, why they have breakdowns, how their authority is now administrative, and even what kind of wives they need, it is not a difficult transition to that somewhat plain issue, namely, "what do we want in the minister, priest or pastor?" A little teaching in a theological seminary soon clues one into that plaintive and yearnful quest among the students too; for they are, almost to the man, everlastingly concerned with what they ought to be and what their future congregations will expect them to be. Most of them have felt a very high calling sometime or other; and they are often befuddled by the curriculum and the professors, also by wider acquaintanceship with churches and parishioners. They usually want to know what "this"—and it can be everything from church history to church societies, Greek exegesis to St. Augustine, raising money for the educational wing to divine metaphysics—has to do with being a working pastor and minister of the Gospel. It is very difficult to reply with cogency and aptness to such questions.

One is reminded in such a situation of what obtains also with the rationale for so-called liberal arts programs in our colleges. While almost everyone teaching in our colleges and universities would make a strong claim for the importance of liberal arts training, there is very little agreement upon what should be included in that pattern of courses and training. Where everything counts, nothing much seems to be decisive and telling; and there is little wonder that some "colleges of science, literature and the arts," where education is supposed to be liberal and not immediately professional, are derogatorily spoken of as being "schools of lost ambition." Once the liberal arts curriculum was modest and relatively tidy. It had its point of departure in things Greek and Roman, but now its curriculum is as inclusive as the scope of science and scholarship. Whereas once there was a fulcrum and an order to the subjects, now there is neither. As we all know so well, there is discipline and reason, shape and purpose, to any one science and branch of scholarship, but there seems to be very little of such to a whole curriculum. Here the politics of the college now produces the students' program. So, when he asks why he should take this or that requirement, there are no longer any apparently better reasons than the fact that the catalogue requires it.

The proliferation of fields of learning has almost paralleled the demands leveled against professionally trained personnel; and the ministry is no exception. Like doctors, teachers, and lawyers, the ministers of the Gospel too have foundered amid the corrosive effects of social change. Their authority seems not to be spiritual any longer and their roles are several and not singular. But these things have been noted elsewhere. I wish to comment in this chapter upon the problems of ordering our learning to educate and to train a minister of the Gospel. For the very shape and style of our sciences and branches of scholarship have changed very markedly in recent years, and these invite a host of considerations about the plausibility and aims of theological education. It is, therefore, appropriate to ask just how the multiplying of fields of study for ministers equips them for their tasks.

In what follows, I will discuss three topics: first, something about the aims of the minister of the Gospel; second, the educational means at our disposal today; third, why theological training, even though professional, must be indirect and somewhat tangential in orientation. Our concluding remarks will provide another evaluation of the minister's continuing tasks and their bearing upon conceptions of his education.

I

Two commanding ends-in-view present themselves as relevant to the education of every minister of the Gospel. On the one side, the theological, there is the account of God, the creation of the world, and all the rest of the claims that constitute the objective assertions of the Christian tradition. On the other side, there is the subtle business of learning everything by which to teach persons to intend the world as Christians. The former account is certainly distinctive and has to be learned with care and precision; the latter involves a host of matters by which persons are taught to acquire a distinctive Christian consciousness. Whereas the former is by and large intellectual-like, easily abbreviated and communicated, the latter is primarily a matter of human subjectivity and character. It is personal and intimate and not easily done for one another.

About the first, the theological teachings of the Christian

tradition. Certainly the past thirty-five years or so of Christian theology ought to have made it reasonably clear that the objective claims of the churches of Jesus Christ are no accident. It seemed to be true for a rather long while that many intellectuals believed that Christian theology was a world-view and nothing more. Because world-views have only a temporary appeal, depending upon a host of cultural and intellectual considerations, it was argued that they must be continually revised to fit evidence and need. Theology had even been construed sometimes as an ideology, i.e., as an aggregate of ideas, convictions, and beliefs stemming from the religious group called Christians. But Christian theology is neither another world-view nor an ideology; and hence it is not made up by interested individuals who compose it as they go nor is it cast up by vast and insinuating social energies as another cultural artifact.

For at the very least, the Gospel is the story delivered by the apostles and committed to the church concerning Jesus Christ, the Son of God who became man, that he might reconcile the world and men to God. The subject matter of Christian theology is that good news whereby "Immanuel," God with us, is proclaimed. Theologians have not made up this story nor do they even make up the meanings of it. For the past several decades many Christians have been chastened by a variety of historical and theological studies which have made very explicit that which it is to our embarrassment to have forgotten. For the Gospel does insist that Jesus did live among men and that he did accomplish by his life, death, and resurrection the redemption of men. This has already happened, and to this extent every preacher has to learn that story in order to be the ambassador and messenger of the redemption that has already taken place.

It is, of course, one thing to state the Gospel and quite

another to believe and trust in it. The Gospel is a message and a deliverance, it is written down, it is spoken among us, it is sung and proclaimed in a variety of ways. The principal function of theology is to help us become clear about what the Gospel is and what it means. Sometimes, therefore, it issues in sets of doctrines and beliefs, often even systematically arranged, but still the substance of theology is the Gospel of God, the good news in Christ Jesus.

We began by suggesting that every minister of the Gospel must certainly be taught that objective account. There are, of course, several forms which this account has taken. We will note each in turn. First, there is the Scriptural story. Whatever the intellectual difficulties involved, the Old and New Testaments are the cradle of the salvation story. It is part of the task of every theological seminary to teach its students to read those books with the intent of getting that story. Scripture is also many other things. It reflects the culture of the day, the ideas of the period and perhaps the taste of its audience; but these features of the Bible might well be shared with every other book of its time. To read it with the expressed purpose of ascertaining the proportions of its distinctive message is the way to read it for the minister. But there are also the creeds. These are also an expression of that Gospel stated first in Holy Writ. Creeds are a secondary expression and seemed to have been derived only where the Gospel and the Bible had already been preached. They also state the objective teachings of the faith and were probably first formulated as convenient devices to abbreviate and to communicate the teachings.

In addition to the above, there has been since earliest times something we call theology. Usually we refer to it as "dogmatic theology." It constitutes a third corpus of teaching, a little different in form from Scripture and creeds. Most dogmatic theology arises from interplay between the message of the church and all of the other ideologies and hypotheses, winds of fashion and conviction, that continually sweep our world. Theology is here a name for that intellectual and polemical work of Christian thinkers who make it their task to address the array of teachings by which men are often diverted, if not deluded, from what the Gospel defines as their principal pursuit. Dogmatic theology is not a substitute for Scripture nor for a creed, nor is theology an improvement upon either of them. Usually theology has the merit of focusing reflection upon something otherwise neglected or bringing to remembrance what might otherwise be forgotten. In a broad sense, it might be said that theology teaches us what the Gospel means when other views, maybe scientific or political, maybe cultural or mythological, seem to impinge or even overlap.

If theology remains responsible, it is certainly the case that it too keeps the objective proclamation of the Gospel before its hearer. Surely it is the responsibility of teachers of those who will dare the witnessing as ministers to make them aware of the Scripture, of the creeds and the confessions, and lastly, of the dogmatic theological traditions. These three together are the sesame to an acquaintanceship with the teachings that make up the good news. And nothing that will be subsequently said, even enthusiastically, can be understood as mitigating the rightful place of such objective teachings. The only excuse for ministers at all is not their continual trumpeting even if the sound is exalted; rather it is the message of God, a kind of breath of Scripture, which must be added to them. Like Ezekiel's wheels, which did not move unless the Spirit moved them, so too the ministers do not function as men of God until those magnificent teachings that moved Paul and Peter, Luther and Calvin, are in very firm command.

Sometimes it is believed that ministers are spiritual seers, expected to read profound truths off the face of current events and natural occurrences. But actually the ministry of Jesus Christ has relatively small use for seer-like spiritual leaders. It demands witnesses, not seers. And the expression "witness" is not misleading; for it was as witnesses of something which occurred among men that the Scriptural authors wrote. The rest of us are hearers of that witness, and we do not invent the story as we go along or adapt it to suit contemporary hearers.

It seems plausible now to say that there is a larger consensus among biblical scholars and among theologians about this redemptive story than there was several decades ago. There has been a strong renewal of enthusiasm for God-centered and tradition-honoring interpretations of Scripture and theology. But one ought not to make any inferences from consensus, for surely the Gospel is not truer because so many students of Christian lore and history have recently conceded that this objective claim is distinctive of the Christian faith. Nonetheless, we can be thankful for the new regard for the magisterial teachings of the church, for it is even upon these and not the social and psychological advantages of unity that the hope of ecumenical Christianity finally rests.

There seems to be little difficulty in conceiving ways to teach Scripture, creeds and confessions, and even theology. But more about this will be noted shortly when the consideration of the new means of our day will occupy our attention. There is, first, another matter to consider. For it is not enough to conceive of the minister's education with attention only to the objective teaching. The minister's responsibility is to put that teaching to work transforming men. Christian teaching indeed has some similarities with other bodies of discourse, but the dissimilarities are much more important. For the objective claims of the Christian faith must be put to the task of fashioning anew the consciousness of a man.

Perhaps a word of caution is in order here. By consciousness nothing terribly refined or precious is meant. In correction of an error, now of rather long standing, whereby consciousness has been described solely as the having of ideas, let it here be insisted that there is another and very plausible use of the term. By consciousness we mean the various ways each man has of intending the world. We are "conscious" when we smile, respond, love, think, attend to, hate, avoid, etc. Most people do intend the world in a variety of ways. Thus, an esthetically refined man has an esthetic consciousness when he discriminates beauty and disavows ugliness. He may or may not have ideas in some extraordinary sense, but that is really neither here nor there. Becoming a Christian is certainly also a matter of learning to intend the world as a Christian. It is not an exaggeration to say that the entire panoply of Christian doctrine has its "telos" in the reconstruction of a man's life. This marks off the teachings of the church from other objective bodies of discourse, though it does not deny that they can also be objectively studied and even communicated.

Nonetheless, a minister's task is also to teach others how to live the Christian life. To do this, it is necessary for him to understand that the decisive thing for most people is not the attacks and questions of science but the struggle against their all-too-human passions. For learning to live a life according to the Gospel is learning to grant sovereignty to the love of God. The spiritual confrontation of believers is not with abstract teachings except in the rarest of cases, and even here it would be well to look for the disguise of the passional conflict. This is why the scientific acumen respecting everything associated with the Christian faith is not always the great desideratum. For the scientific exercise of one's scientific learning, even about the things of faith, is not one's responsibility as a pastor. Here the issue is rather that everlasting evasion and compromise, the continual slipping away from the demands of God and Gospel; and most of this is done by practicing another kind of consciousness, that of this world, which comes naturally and without struggle and seems always to be fitting and proper. For the world supplies a vast number of stimuli to our passions and intentions, most of which do not lead us into the pattern provided by the new life in Jesus Christ.

Being a Christian is, thus, a matter of being conscious, and being conscious is a matter of intending the world. This is to say that being a Christian is to admit to a distinctive quality and way of intending the world. The point for which every pastor must be trained is to make it clear to his parishioners that the correct response to the theological teachings, including Scripture, creeds, and dogmas, is not simply an assent to these assertions, as one would assent to most truths, but rather a new way of intending and handling the world and all things. There is a strict correspondence between the objective teachings and the subject. To put the matter very strongly, it might be said that the teachings require the new way of life, for without the latter, the teachings too are nothing more than an ideology or one more *Weltanschauung*, albeit full of religious symbols.

It is not an optional matter. One of the marks of being a Christian is, of course, to have started on the process of becoming transformed by the renewal of one's mind and eschewing conformity to the ways of this world. And every pastor must be prepared to follow through on his teaching to this extent, for otherwise the very teachings are maligned. So, two kinds of pedagogy are in order: first, one must know what the Gospel is and be prepared to impart it via Scripture, worship, liturgy, theology, confessions, and whatever other means are appropriate; second, one must help everyone put these things to the use of creating and sustaining the Christian consciousness, the poise and style of the faithful life. The first kind of task involves a straightforward pedagogical manner, often even direct impartation; the other supposes some indirection and patience, perhaps such pedestrian virtues as temperance in judgment, exercise of authority, maybe through sacrifice and obedience. To everyone, in turn, it must be said that Christianity requires not only knowing, for then it would be a branch of knowledge and this it clearly is not; neither is it simply a move of the personality, an event within subjectivity, without an object or structure. Because faith involves both an objective and a subjective component, every minister of the Gospel must be prepared to treat both. Without either, Christianity is truncated; with both, faith becomes the new life, the eternal life, and withal the victory over the world.

II

If these are goals that must be met by the education of ministers, then the question is: What kind of means do we propose to meet them? The requisites seem simple—acquaintanceship with the kerygmatic stuff of the Christian tradition and some competence to deal with the vagaries of human subjectivity on behalf of that Gospel. But we will find that there are many difficulties.

Theological education has increasingly in the past one hundred or so years included the scientific study of almost the full range of Christian materials. For even longer, Western scholars have been studying and thinking about religious materials. It is quite obvious that we have acquired almost frightening dexterity in thinking about the Bible, about rites, customs, traditions, institutions, social environment, personages—in fact, about almost everything associated with

the Gospel and its origins and its subsequent history. Most
of these skills are relatively recent.

It is not amiss to assert, therefore, that the modern world
has witnessed a marked increase in the scope of relevant
knowledge about the Christian religion. We have added to
our store of historical information; we have created sociological, anthropological, political, and psychological ways
of construing materials old and new. More than this, the
past century and a half has meant a correction of earlier
errors, new accuracies in the prevailing methods of inquiry,
and an astonishing enlargement of available materials. But
there is even more. For the progress in knowledge concerning religious materials has paralleled the advances in the
natural sciences and other humanistic disciplines in a host
of other respects too. It has meant far greater internal con-
sistency, a general increase in the systematic connectedness
with other ideas, a better sense of proportion between the
parts of knowledge, an increase in the precision and the
depth of interpretative ideas brought to bear upon the vast
materials, and even more, emancipation from diverting confusions and irrelevancies. There can be no doubt that there
is intellectual progress in the field of religious studies. At
the very least it can be shown that there is now easily available a very intensive intellectual cultivation, even sophistication, respecting the Christian religion, and a more extensive diffusion of this sophistication among the masses of
men. But more should be said, too, for the cultivation of various kinds of studies, biblical and historical, philological and
others, which bear upon religious materials. This has been
so concentrated and so detailed, and has included nationals
of so many countries and periods, that such studies bid fair
to being exemplary instances of scholarly acumen and international objectivity.

The creation of a subtle and sophisticated cognitive way

of intending the world is one of the glories of our modern life. As time has gone by, more and more materials have been submitted to study. Things religious are now included. For it is quite clear that the intellectual's consciousness is quite pronounced and specialized too. From early Greek times to the present there has been a slow cumulative progress in such endeavors. Gradually area after area of human interest, natural events, social events, finally even psychological and religious phenomena, have been studied and known in a variety of ways. It has been the custom to proclaim all of this for the fact that new knowledge is continually being thereby produced. But another factor must also be noted, namely, that a new quality and kind of consciousness, a new way of intending the world, a new set of habits and dispositions, by which the world can be understood, handled, paid attention to, addressed, queried, is thereby introduced. When the knowledge itself is forgotten, as it so easily is, there is still the consciousness, the manner and way of attack and inquiry, which persists. The residue is a new temper, a qualification of outlook and orientation, which is an impersonal and objective, disinterested and detached attitude.

Modern theological instruction has participated very generously in this kind of study of Christian materials. The means provided by modern scholarship for the education of ministers are now, by and large, very much like the means of the intellectual life everywhere. Modern knowledge about Jesus, about the Scriptures, about the history of Christian ideas, the thought of Paul, the life of the early church, and a host of other matters, is increasingly abstract, impersonal, and neutral. This is necessary in order to keep such knowledge without bias and coloring and illuminative of the subject matter without distortion and passion.

But a major difficulty is all too apparent. For the thought

which grasps Christian materials in such a manner is a thought about Christianity; and the language which describes Christian materials in such a manner is a language about Christianity. Both are different from the thought or language which is imbued by Christian passion and which is dominated throughout by Christian categories. For the difference between a thought "about" and a thought "of," between the language "about" and the language "of," lies in the fact that the first fulfills a cognitive function and is not religious or Christian at all in the sense of either being actuated by a Christian motivation or fulfilling a Christian intent. If it is knowledge, it is neutral; and this does not mean that it is irreligious, but only that its purpose or place within a life history, which alone can be religious or irreligious, Christian or non-Christian, is indeterminate and undefined.

Most of modern scholarship, including that about Christian materials and hence the bulk of the contemporary theological seminary's curriculum, is in the "about" mode. Nowadays we can say with scholarly aplomb, "These are the facts, persons, ideas, claims, valuations that constitute the Christian religion." To a very remarkable degree, then, we can formulate in cognitive ways, easy to teach and lecture about, much of what we were earlier alluding to when we spoke about the objective material, the story of the Gospel. Rather should we say that it seems as though we could state it. For the moment let us consider one significant example.

Within the field of historical studies impinging upon subtle theological considerations, scholars have made what many consider very important contributions to our understanding of the historical person of Jesus Christ and the early milieu of the church. Certainly no finality has been claimed by responsible students for these researches, but our historical sense with respect to the early days of Christianity has clearly been enriched very considerably. Here, at any rate, it is tempting to set down these results of study as if they were means to progress in the Christian life itself. Who could deny the ambition of every Christian to know Jesus better? Isn't it also true that the more refined knowledge of our day, in contrast to fortuitous and inept sayings of another day, promises to be a step bringing the knower nearer to his Lord? But here we do have to pause, for what could even the maximum researchers finally accomplish? Suppose we knew enough to simulate the knowledge of a historical contemporary. Would we then know what to say about Jesus Christ? Would this successful quest for the historical Jesus solve all of the Christological questions? And the host of strange questions about his lordship, whether God really was in him, whether he was the Messiah, what significances his teaching should have—would these and more really be any closer to resolution? A little reflection will show us that his significance for our lives is not a matter of scholarship at all. Most of the issues we have cited were also disputable to his contemporaries. No kind of progress, cognitive or otherwise, has quite removed the challenge his life provided.

Here we come very close to the heart of the matter. For the historical founder of the faith of the Christians elicited from those who were his followers a language of faith, a thought of faith, which included an interpretation in which historical accuracy was not the deciding factor. That language of faith, of which the Bible is replete, was soon part of that faith, not just the expression thereof. In fact, that language of faith is itself faithful. The historical detail, be it little or encompassing, as well as his historical existence, be it known in part or in full, remains something of a "sign." And if one asks what a sign is, we need only remember that sometimes a sign is a publicly displayed notice of an activity which can be transacted within. So it is with a sign on a building or a sign which advertises something. Jesus Christ's historical character was the sign, and to know more of its detail is like knowing the sign better but never partaking in the activity which the sign invites. The language of faith was not in its earliest expressions one with the language about faith, even though the latter was then trivial by comparison to the present hour; and it is not now one with it either. The language of faith has always been an expression of passion, whether early or late. The language about the things of faith, even that about Jesus Christ, must, on the contrary, be passionless and disinterested. This is why Jesus considered as the sign has always revealed the intents and hearts of men by challenging them to an interpretation which is never made easy by historical research nor made more difficult by the passage of time.

This is to note an anomaly. For theological education is successful at imparting the language about Christian matters. It is in this mode that our education, even seminary education, addresses itself to Jesus Christ, who is the author and finisher of our faith. Put in other language, our seminary training has plenty of means at its disposal today—the entire panoply of objective learning about Christian matters. But most of it, if not all, is in the "about" mode. This is a rich and almost endless material, but its quantity does not change its quality. It remains heterogeneous to the language of the faith, however extensive it becomes.

The fact of the matter is that a man may believe all kinds of things about God, about Jesus of Nazareth, and even the future life without thereby becoming Christian or even religious. For it is not finally simply the set of beliefs which matters. The Christian faith is "how" we believe in God and "how" we take life as a consequence. The seminarian who has learned all that can be taught about these matters in an objective manner still has the hardest thing to learn. It is a moot point whether it even can be taught at all.

But this is to pre-judge matters a bit. Earlier we noted that a major desideratum for every minister of the Gospel was competence in Scripture, in the confessions and creeds of the church, and in the theological traditions. It turns out, almost disconcertingly, that each of these in turn can be thought "about." In fact, there is a vast literature about each of them in turn. But Scripture, creeds, and theology are also the language of faith. By learning about them, one does not necessarily learn to speak and to think with them, and yet this is the Christian aim. To learn the language of faith, to speak with Paul, and to sing with angels is not an idle bit of hymnody, for it comes very close to the essence of things. The minister needs to be taught the faith, not just about it; he needs the language of faith, not just more about it. The Gospel itself is not found in the language of scholarship about Jesus; it is found in the passion-ridden words of the apostles and the cradle which is the Scripture. It is found, too, in the confessions and in the striking theological and God-imbued words of St. Augustine, Luther, Calvin, Kierkegaard, Karl Barth, and numerous others.

This is not to deny significance to studies about any of these men and their works. What has been said does, however, focus our attention upon how peculiar the task of teaching men to be ministers of the Gospel really is. For the Gospel is not a product of our efforts nor an emergent from the life-history of even the most devout of Christian scholarship. Once men thought that they could teach others the Gospel by teaching non-dogmatically and even historically, hoping to encompass the Gospel as they spread their nets wide for the full range of facts. Our seminaries too have shared this optimistic view. We have studied everything non-theologically and non-dogmatically. Probably some persons have mistakenly believed that theology as the language of faith and of the church could be taught by the new sciences about Scripture, church, theology, and ritual. But this is an egregious error. However, it is no error to teach such subject matter, for at the very least it can be said that thought or language about religion is exactly like thought about anything else in being a tool, whose actual use for the Gospel or otherwise, for good or for evil, is not predetermined. But theology, here understood as the generic name for the language which encompasses and surveys all life and things in the light of Jesus Christ, has abandoned all abstract attitudes of impersonal objectivity and has become a reflective expression of a Christian person in the service of divine ends.

Modern learning about Christianity is very rapidly passing into that marketplace for ideas, the modern university. Insofar as it is truly knowledge, aloof, and disinterested, it is compatible with both faith and unfaith. So it is conceivable, if not widely illustrated, that both a Christian's language of faith, his theology, and a non-Christian's language and thought could well share a common core of knowledge about Christianity. Likewise, the common core of disinterested knowledge might be shared equally with irreligious and religious, with Jews, Christians, Mohammedans, and infidels. The point is that the radical differences between men that are marked by the adjectival expressions "Christian" and "non-Christian" are not ultimately due to differences of knowledge. The hope of unanimity for the race does not seem to lie in the progress of the sciences of religion. On the contrary, even the maximum sophistication about Jesus, shared equally by the race, does not seem to promise anything more than the satisfaction of the desire to know. The modern seminarian, though making use of what our ancestors would have deemed an extraordinary amount of reflection and an astounding range of odds and ends of knowledge, is not thereby immediately more Christian. Whether anyone is more religious than our ancestors is another issue; but certainly the business of coming to a decision of faith is today a very circuitous route, and the way is so beset with long and roundabout considerations, most of them recently introduced, which continue to postpone action that decision seldom seems to be effected by an education at all.

In short, this is to note that modern seminary education, if it shares to the fullest the enthusiasm for contemporary scientific study of everything connected with the Christian faith, still does not quite thereby include the language of faith. For in order to be educated in the Christian faith, one must speak that language and share its numerous usages. The Gospel is not about Jesus and God; instead, it is the judgment and evaluation of everybody and everything in the light of God in Christ. It supposes the passion that faith is, and it nowhere effects the transition from no faith to faith.

The means of seminary education are immediately incremental, then, to knowledge about all kinds of things and also to a virtuosity in the use of the language about Christianity. The aim of the education, I assume, is something else, most probably an accomplishment in the language of the faith. For accomplishment here would mean the intensification and purification of the Christian passion, its domination and sovereignty in judgments passed upon all things, the marked increase in the use of Christian awareness in the everyday relations of life, and above all, such a use of the language of faith as would elicit an ever-current renewal and deepening of the fundamental commitment of the person—every person who heard that witness—to the Christian Gospel. But this is only one side of the matter. Earlier we have noted that another aim of theological education is certainly to produce what the Roman Catholics have long called "the formation" of the seminarian. This was described as teaching him to intend the world as a Christian. However, one of the products of teaching "about" all of these divine matters is also the temper or consciousness that is appropriate. The quality of consciousness which so easily grows up with scholarship is the disinterested and somewhat conjectural and hypothetical temper of the scholar. It does not take much observation to note how quickly contemporary seminary students divide into almost natural groups. On the one side, there is the tiny minority who take to the seminary teaching with zest and ask for more of the same and are critical if they think the standards are not scientific and scholarly enough. On the other side, there is a group who do not respond very well, probably because they are not so academically and temperamentally suited, but this group also frequently includes those whose impatience is manifest and who insist that all of this stuff is irrelevant anyway to the vocation of the ministry.

It is not the purpose here to give consolation to the lazy and to the stupid. And for the many who believe that they know enough already and for whom seminary is a work of supererogation anyway, there is little that can be said. But those of us in responsible positions must also learn to keep our categories straight. There is a hiatus, a logical and psychological incommensurability, both between the language about faith, be it scholarly and learned, and the language of faith, on the one side, and between the consciousness created by scholarly interests and that which is typical of witnesses to the Christian way, those captivated and overpowered by the Christian pathos. Whereas the scholarly temper is tentative, hypothetical, and inquisitive, impelled by curiosity, the Christian temper is declaratory, categorical, and aggressive, urged onward by the need of men for salvation. Likewise, the language about faith is incomplete, probable, and dependent on evidence, whereas the language of faith is proclamatory, all-inclusive, and certain.

The hopes of educators for the ministry, therefore, have to be much more carefully grounded. The means proffered in the typical Protestant seminary are better calculated to make a man an expert on the religious materials. Those means are only slightly related both to the character formation which is the desideratum of the Christian enterprise and to the Gospel which gives reason to church, sermon, and the Christian life.

To this date, it seems that American seminaries have thought only spasmodically about curricular matters. In what follows, a brief excursus will be made into these areas with the express purpose of addressing the aforementioned difficulties.

III

The question is: How shall we educate ministers? If it is clear that a minister must know the Gospel (and via Bible, confessions and creeds, and theology) and must know how to teach the Gospel so that it will be used to sustain a Christian consciousness and way of intending the world, then how shall he be taught these things? The negative point is also clear, namely, that scholarly command of the thought of Paul is not the same as being possessed by that thought. Knowing about Paul is to know about Paul's language of faith, but this is but a third-person approximation. The task is to have a first-person command of the language and of the thought of faith. The minister must be a witness to God in Christ. However, the fact that he is a witness does not argue that a scholarly account, accurate to the last detail, is the witnessing medium. Useful though a scholarly account might be, it still is about the witness and not the witness it-self. The issue is something like learning to speak lovingly to one's beloved. If words are not there—all the courses on marriage and courtship, engagements and sex, will not sup-ply them. Being able to speak the language of affection is not quite the function of scholarship either, though this does not disparage the scholarly interest whatsoever.

Is this to say that Christianity cannot be taught? For centuries there has been lurking a threatening anti-intellec-tualism, and what has been said might seem to give sub-stance to such counsels of darkness. But another proposal or two might mitigate such counsels. For one thing, it must be asserted that Christianity is, in all instances, learned. Christianity is not a natural and sub-cultural phenomenon. There are no native and indigenous Christians, Christians by birth. And countries where Christians are counted by geographical location are using the term "Christian" as loosely and as irresponsibly as they would if they counted moral men by the same means. Christianity is in fact taught. It must be taught, because it is a peculiar message, and as Luther said, it was not thought up in the kitchen. The me-dium for teaching it has usually been the sermon and the liturgical and worship practices of the church. The Bible, the creeds and the confessions, and the ongoing theologi-cal discourse have been perennial in their power. But to teach about them is not to impart their Christian content. Christian teaching, whether of Bible, creed, or theology, has invariably been passionate, enthusiastic, aimed at the af-fections and needs of men and not at their curiosities and conjectural concerns. The context, therefore, must be right for the Bible, creeds, and theology. The assumption that one could move from the context of the church, where the consciousness of sin is supposed, where the need for God is the very reason for being there, to the academic hall, where that consciousness of sin is irrelevant, where only the need for learning has status—the assumption that one could move from one to the other without loss to the content is a mistaken one. The point is that the same words as those used in church lose their Christian meaning when the "how" of that context is gone. On the other hand, the "how" of the academic hall is peculiar too, though Christians certainly have less to learn from this context than they have from the church.

If a lover whispers words of affection to his beloved, these depend greatly upon their context. If such words are repeated aloud for the class in "Social Relations," they become legitimately objects of great curiosity. They mean quite differently as the context changes. The more that seminaries have become like other institutions of learning, and the more that professors of Christian studies have exploited the possibilities of studying Christianity disinterestedly, the wider the gulf between the church and the seminaries has become. For in one context the language is put to evangelical uses, in the other it is the subject of inquiry and the object of a variety of disquisitions. To insist that nothing is really changed because the same thing is being asserted in both contexts is to miss the issue altogether. It seems doubtful to me that the church can expect all of its ministers to weather such a demanding shift of climate in the interest of preparing for their service. Certainly there must be a large number of persons, otherwise qualified, who simply cannot make such a transition of temper from day to day and survive. Theological education is perhaps peculiar, and it behooves us all to think hard about it and about the hardships it requires in persons of dedication and conviction.

Christianity is also learned in another respect. The quality of temper that is the way of Christian consciousness is also an acquisition. But the learning here is not simply intellectual. Christianity is also a "how" and a "way," not only a view or a perspective. And learning to intend the world as a Christian is like learning to love, learning to care, and many other such important matters. Living as a Christian is also being put under the discipline, and this discipline is taxing and quite unlike the disciplines we otherwise meet. The point is that a minister of the Gospel must learn how to teach the Gospel so that the pragmatic effects of Christ's grace and life will be made clear. Everything here must be learned, for Christ is the way, the truth, and the life. To apprehend Jesus Christ without one's way of intending the world also being changed is to miss the Gospel. For the difference that the Gospel makes is to be found precisely in the "how" of the Christian's life and thought and language. This means that the language of faith is not an artifact cast up by the Christian tradition; instead, it is certainly an expression thereof, but more strongly, it is part of the performance of the Christian life. It is one with the Christian's way of intending the whole world. It means little if anything without the Christian's consciousness as its locus and context.

If both of these must be taught, how can we prepare ministers with such responsibilities? It seems that the present trends will not be abated, for certainly the scientific study of religious and Christian materials will go on and on. But increasingly it ought to be made clear that most of such study is also of purely scholarly interest. As time goes by, it will become increasingly difficult to include within any manageable curriculum even a fragment of the material that is available, and of the material included it will certainly be necessary to allow every student his own choice according to his inclinations and talents. The point is that the professional requisites of the minister are and will be principally the two noted before—competence respecting the objective Gospel and some know-how respecting the passions and subjectivities of his parishioners. Students ought to be told just that so that they will recognize that Christianity is served only indirectly by such teaching. They will have to effect the transition themselves, for more learning will never do it. Their task, if thus learned, is to bring the faith to the learning. Or in another context, the learning is a tool awaiting its Christian ordering and use. Perhaps there will always be a significant group whose faith will be powerful enough to carry them through to new and significant responsibilities of assimilating modern knowledge to Christian uses. Perhaps there will be quite a few ministers of the Gospel, so talented and so dedicated, who will be able to press the new and better knowledge of Christian Scripture, history, and theology concomitantly to a more effective use of these things for the enlightenment of the conscience, the intensification of the soul's ardor, and even the communion of the individual with God. Then it would be very clear that such training would mean an advance in the Christian economy.

However, there are others for whom the knowledge and kind of academic training may be another indifference, perhaps even a temptation to be overcome or a problem to be resolved. Here the church must take new and bold steps. For one thing, we must explore the feasibility of shortening the course of ministerial study. There seems to be no good reason to require seven years of advanced work for the ministerial student. Certainly a four-year course leading to the Bachelor of Divinity degree would be sufficient. Ministerial training is not a deeper and deeper penetration into the field, and we have lost rather than gained by analogizing the training with that of other professions. Long terms of study ought to be required of scholars in the field of religious studies, for it is becoming increasingly clear that a short-term preparation is downright absurd. But a minister is not a scholar; he is a preacher and witness to God in Christ and ought not to be intimidated by such alien academic standards. Nonetheless, requisites ought to be met. These requisites have been lost sight of in our day of enlightenment and non-dogmatic reflection. The church ought to be encouraged to work out once more standards of excellence which are indigenous to the Gospel and the calling of the faith.

Perhaps the same embarrassment would once again ensue. For the church seems ill-prepared today to declare itself in such arenas. The matter of certifying preparation has fallen to the seminaries in one group after another, and often because the seminaries have been looked upon as the arm of the church, eminently qualified to ascertain preparedness. But the seminaries too have had their vicissitudes, and their own criteria for excellence have undergone a subtle change. Though I am not asking here for domination of church in academic matters, I am suggesting that the oddness of the Gospel's requirements has not easily passed through the channels of seminary protocol either. Perhaps this matter ought to be addressed indirectly too.

Is it not time to consider anew a more active training of ministers in actual parish life? It seems to me that most ministerial candidates need both academic exposure and an active internship program under the most scrupulous direction. They need an opportunity to put their understanding of the Gospel to immediate use. Furthermore, they need on-the-spot correction. Most of the inchoate religious life in this country is perpetrated by well-meaning and religiously earnest persons. The enormous breach between theological studies and the practices of the churches is allowed to perpetuate itself because no devices are proffered by which to close the gap. Church life often goes on unguided and untouched by the theological "teleology" which is its genius and life. Often, too, theological students are studying materials which they can seldom orient to the requirements of believers' lives. This is not a proposal to press all theological studies into immediate use or all churches into theological arenas. But it is to say that a more active internship and actual use of the seminary tools must be conceived. The minister charged with the responsibility of guiding such a young man ought to be his director and also carry a very active relation to the young man's seminary. It is not enough either simply to have a seminarian working with an older man, for then he frequently becomes simply the flunkie charged with doing what no one else wants to do. The program must be so conceived as to make the minister an active agent in the process of converting the learning of the seminary into the language of the pulpit and the pew. More than this, such a man ought also to be charged to do what seminaries find increasingly difficult, namely make clear the bearing of theology upon the task of evangelizing the world.

As matters now stand, seminaries are becoming more and more like universities. It seems ridiculous to ask them to reverse themselves. Just as modern schools of medicine have gradually come to share almost completely the sciences and their non-utilitarian curricula, so too the seminaries have come to be more and more like liberal arts colleges, where the learning is best when it is least professional. No amount of tinkering with combinations of the course offerings will make much difference, and certainly no plan to force the professors to be practical is going to help. Neither will the strengthening of the so-called practical departments do very much to help. The undeniable fact is that the methods of teaching, of understanding, and of construing the subject matter have changed, subtly but surely. There has been no single turning point and no overt crisis, but the change has taken place. The disinterested and detached style of handling even Christian materials is standard for our teachers, our pupils, and our schools. The only way to address this situation is to make it clear to seminarians that what transforms the words of Scripture into the Gospel is not more scholarship, and more learning, but it is faith.

The creation of an active core of clinicians, who would mediate between the more abstract learning of the seminaries and the needs of the body of Christ, will not be easy. It will demand not more academic theology, addressed to the issues of science and scholarship, but more churchly theology, addressed to the conditions of unbelief and human sin. The seminarians will need then at least two years' exposure to the rigors of church discipline, a kind born of the expressed non-academic disposition to have them taught by the Gospel, both in speech and in manner. And through devices like these, an active two-year internship with constant correction and where an immediate use of exegesis, of theology, of history, will be bent to the task of making the Gospel clear, perhaps once again the education of the minister in the life of faith will become lively and explicit.

More than this is to be gained however. The unfortunate breach between American church life and the seminaries will probably begin to heal. Almost every American theological institution rings with hearty criticism of the trivial practices of the churches, the noise of the solemn assemblies, and the inane theology of the ministers. Yet most of those young men who are so hearty in their condemnation either quit altogether or they quickly conform themselves. If the churches were clearly charged with a more active role and one which could not be delegated to the seminaries, then perhaps the responsibility to make what is a third-person language about faith actually a first-person expression would no longer simply belong to the individual; instead it would be a part of the teaching ministry of the church of Jesus Christ.

I. COLLEGE PREPARATION

Cultivation

of

Christians

Albion
College
Library

LIBERAL ARTS AS A FOUNDATION FOR SCHOLARSHIP IN RELIGION

JOHN A. HUTCHISON

I

What is the relation of theology to liberal education? If the future minister is acknowledged to be a man as well as a clergyman, the question is imperative. It is so for the good reason that liberal education is that form or aspect of education which is addressed to man as such, its aim being the fulfillment or realization of his humanity. Hence liberal education stands in contrast to, and in tension with, those forms and aspects of education whose function is technical or professional, whose aim is not the realization of humanity but the acquisition and development of special skills or bodies of knowledge for some specific ulterior and instrumental purpose. Surely it is a gross betrayal of both theology and liberal education to assume in advance of discussion, as so often is done in contemporary discussion, that theological study has a solely or principally professional aim. This essay will raise the question of theological study and liberal education in twentieth century America, arguing that the relation is hu-

manistic and that it is fundamentally important to both par-
ties. Incidentally, one clear corollary of our argument is
that the legitimate professional goals of theological education will be furthered better if it is treated as a liberal study
and not simply or primarily as a professional or pre-profes-
sional study.

The terms "theology" and "theological study" are here
used to designate the study of religion in critical and comprehensive form. I shall further assume that theology is a
significant and reputable form of study. Surely religion is a
pervasive and significant fact of man's experience—as general and important in its occurrence as art, politics, or language—and therefore free, critical study aiming at understanding is a fundamental aspect of liberal education. It may
well turn out that the area of human experience designated
by religion has a further significance—that it has a transcen-
dent reference or reality. Religious people often argue that
this is the case, but religion is *at least* a pervasive and significant form of human experience; and this is its claim to
inclusion in liberal studies and education. The further claims,
whether of an affirmative or negative sort, as well as the
critical adjudication of these claims, may simply be indicated here as agenda for theological study.

These innocent assertions concerning the nature of theology involve by clear implication bitter controversy with at
least two equal and opposite groups of opponents. First are
those theologians and religious adherents who assume that
theological study must be limited to those of a particular
faith, and that theology is that faith's effort at self-under-
standing. This assumption is fatal to theological study in
a free and pluralistic society and academic community. What
modern university could undertake theological study on this
basis? Indeed the operation of this assumption in the past
has been a major factor in creating the present academic

hostility to theology. While I cannot take time to argue the case, I shall assume here that theological study can and by right ought to be open to all serious inquirers and that properly it is intellectually as free as any other form of liberal study.

The second group of opponents are those ignorant and bigoted academics for whom theology as such is a pejorative term. They continue to be a group of considerable importance in American higher education, particularly among the older members of faculties and administrations. It is beyond the bounds of our present discussion to launch an attack or counterattack against these anti-theologians. Suffice it here to assert the counterassumption from which this essay is written, namely, that theological study properly defined and carried out is not only a fit and honorable occupation for the adult human mind, but there is massive historical precedent for according it a central place in liberal education.

It may illuminate the contemporary American issues to glance at the ways in which men of other times and places in human history have construed the relation of theology to education. It is no excessive historical generalization to assert that religion is the mother of education and that through most of human history education has continued to live within the household of faith. In the primitive and archaic cultures of mankind, education involved religious elements in its auspices and its content. This relation has continued in many of the non-Western cultural traditions of mankind. Illustrations from China, India, and Japan come readily to mind.

In the West similar relations have obtained from ancient Greece and ancient Israel to the present or at least to the recent past. The first professional teachers of the West, the Greek Sophists, were significantly involved in the critical study of religion. The archetypal teacher, Socrates, was in this respect both Sophist and anti-Sophist; he studied religion with a view both to criticism and to reconstruction. Surely the view of mind and man taught—and incarnated —by Socrates included fundamental religious elements. So too the philosophy of Plato (and somewhat more questionably that of Aristotle) involved religious elements. Plato's Academy, the first liberal arts college of the Western world, included theological study as an important and necessary ingredient of the curriculum. Among the many other illustrations of theological study as an element of liberal education there is space only to mention the medieval university where theology was queen of the sciences.

The modern period of Western history has been marked, indeed defined, by the massive secularization of all aspects of human culture. Nowhere has this process of secularization been more in evidence than in higher education. Hence for many readers the illustrations of the previous paragraph may seem, in a libelous phrase, to be of merely historical significance. However, other men in this time of crisis will seek from the past, guidance and suggestions for present action.

II

Contemporary America or indeed the whole contemporary world is in the midst of what may be termed an educational revolution. To be sure, the contemporary world has been hit by so many radical and violent changes that the term revolution has become trivial. Yet the plain, unmistakable fact is that of all the vast and violent changes of the twentieth century, it may well turn out that the most radical is the educational revolution. It may be said to consist of the operation of two assumptions. The first of these is in contrast to the traditional assumption of education as the privilege of the aristocratic few and postulates that education (in-

cluding higher education) is a basic human right; the sec-
and assumption is that education in action can remake both
man and the world. These assumptions may be true or false,
or a garbled mixture of truth and falsehood; but the important fact is that they are, as the phrase goes, operative,
and their operation in the minds and hearts of millions of
men in all parts of the world constitutes the educational
revolution.

The practical import of these observations for the present
discussion is the existence of a vast and ever-increasing
flood of students in American higher education. The enrollment figures for American higher education graphically
characterize the revolutionary situation. In the past, in America and elsewhere, fewer than 5% of the college age-group
of the population was given higher education. Beginning
with World War II the figures began to rise until now almost
40% of the age-group in America goes to college; and the
figures will surely go well over 50% within another decade.
In absolute numbers the figure stands today at an unprecedented 3,000,000 and this is expected to double during the
next decade. The large and plain fact, then, is that an enormously larger number of human beings is today participating in higher education, and this education is playing an
enormously larger part in their whole lives and in the common life of their society. Incidentally in America and elsewhere an ever-increasing percentage of this education is
public and tax-supported; and there is every indication that
this percentage will continue to rise for the foreseeable
future. The question implicit for us in these vast movements
is the role of theological study in this emergent higher educational pattern.

One other development in contemporary higher education is pertinent—though we must immediately add that it
is of different order of magnitude from the educational rev-

olution. It is the revitalization of theological study in American colleges and universities during the past two or three decades, largely as a result of the contemporary renaissance of theology associated with such names as Barth, Niebuhr, and Tillich. This revitalization has taken the form of the founding of departments of religion (why "religion" rather than "theology" constitutes an interesting question) in many colleges and universities as well as the reorganization and revitalization of previously existing departments. The result has been a new vigor as well as a higher intellectual quality of theological study. Yet two limitations must be kept clearly in mind. First, this movement has been largely limited to denominational and independent institutions of higher education. Its impact upon public higher education has been minimal. Second, it is in the whole picture of American higher education a relatively very small movement. This may be seen from faculty statistics. According to a recent survey there are approximately 3,000 teachers of religion in accredited American colleges and universities, and the number will increase to 4,500 in a decade—figures identical, incidentally, with teachers of philosophy. These numbers may be compared with the 12,000-15,000 teachers of history and English literature. The revival of theological study in American higher education is a significant but small development.

III

We come now to the central question of what part theological study can and will play in liberal education in the decade ahead. Powerful forces both on and off the campus continue to push it out of the picture. In the vastly increased educational activity of the coming decade what part can and will be played by the study of religion?

Speaking generally, four strategies may be observed at

the present time. Religion is studied (1) departmentally, (2) interdepartmentally or in multidisciplinary programs, (3) as an aspect of general education courses and programs, and (4) in various extracurricular projects and activities.

The departmental approach to the study of religion has the obvious strength of recognizing theological study as a discipline alongside the other disciplines of the curriculum. Paul Ramsey has forcefully stated the advantages and strengths of this approach. (See below, pages 91-114.) We might also add the practical point that in the liberal arts faculty and curriculum, what is everybody's business is nobody's. The departmental study of religion makes this subject matter distinctly somebody's business.

Two weaknesses, one intellectual and the other practical in nature, must also be noted in the departmental approach to the study of religion. Intellectually, religion presents the unique spectacle of an aspect of human experience which is inherently related to other aspects and areas. Hence to coop religion up in a department studied by itself in antiseptic specialization is to do great violence to it. So the late Alexander Miller in his *Faith and Learning* argued from the inherent nature of religion (or at least of Christian faith) to multidisciplinary forms of study in the humanities and social sciences.

The practical objection to departmental study of religion is even more powerful. As previously noted, an ever higher percentage of all-American higher education will take place in public tax-supported institutions. This essay is written in a state where the figure now moves from two-thirds toward three-quarters. In tax-supported higher education, departmental study of religion is often illegal or unconstitutional, and even more often, publicly inadvisable. In many states a department of religion in the state university or college would be prevented by powerful ecclesiastical groups from performing its free and critical task in the study of religion. Educational administrators are not often outstanding in their courage to resist such groups. Hence, in general, the prospects for the departmental study of religion in public higher education are frankly not very bright.

To be sure, there are welcome exceptions to this rule. A few tax-supported institutions, such as the University of North Carolina, have departments of religion. However, it is notable that the University of Massachusetts does not, nor do any of the branches of the University of California. There are also notable and successful structures such as the School of Religion at the University of Iowa where departmental study of religion takes place in excellent and successful fashion.

The second or interdisciplinary approach to the study of religion brings to the task the skills, experience, and knowledge of a wide variety of intellectual disciplines, and departments ranging from philosophy, history, and literature through such social sciences as psychology, anthropology, and sociology. The strengths and weaknesses of this approach are precisely the opposite of the departmental approach. It does emphasize in a notable way the interaction of religious faith with many notable aspects of human experience and culture, yet it leaves the study of religion to the mercy of a coalition of various specialists, and to the changing fortunes of faculty politics with their alliances and coalitions, their truces and wars. In point of realistic fact, it is an approach which is possible where the first approach is out of the question—and one adds in which some excellent intellectual work is done

The third approach, namely the study of religion as an aspect of general education courses or programs, bears close relation to the second. Sometimes the two overlap in the same curriculum. The general education movement is surely the most important curricular development in American liberal education since the coming of the elective system. It may be regarded as a response to the weaknesses of the latter, which in its extreme forms defined a liberal education as the successful completion of a series of fifteen to twenty specialized courses whose only relation was contiguity or succession. General education—whether in its Columbia, Chicago, or Harvard forms—or in any other form—has sought to move away from specialization toward generality, or in other words toward a consideration of mind and knowledge taken in inclusive and integral unity. It has sought this objective by a variety of methods, ranging from a systematic consideration of philosophic categories of knowledge to a study of practical human problems which cut across the lines of disciplines and departments. A hardy perennial in general education is the great books or humanities course, which by the study of great books in the Western tradition manages to cut across departmental lines and to focus attention on the whole humane tradition of the West. In many ways, and in many varying degrees of success, such courses and programs have compensated for the massive specialization of modern knowledge by focusing attention upon the humane values which have been the unifying perspective of our whole cultural tradition.

General education has involved religion in at least two significant ways. First and most obviously, great books courses have almost invariably included the study of great religious texts such as the Bible (or selected books of the Bible) or Augustine's *Confessions*. Dante's *Divine Comedy* and Milton's *Paradise Lost* are also recurring items in such academic syllabi. To study these documents with any degree of perceptiveness is to be involved in the study of religion.

A slightly more subtle religious implication is also involved in general education in many of its forms. Religious experience is inherently synoptic or integrative in nature. So true is this assertion that the statement tends to become convertible; thus any synoptic or integrative experience tends to take on religious quality. Hence also in negative form, any movement toward specialization is inherently a movement away from the religious quality of experience. Indeed, it may be taken as an educational prescription that if we wish to avoid religious issues, we need only chop the mind's life into a series of specialized bits of knowledge.

So it is that the concern of general education with integrative or synoptic ideas has inevitably raised religious issues, or at least issues of undeniably religious significance. Hence it may be said that general education has, sometimes unwittingly and even in spite of itself, asked religious questions. Often it has had no clear answers to these questions. Yet, in education as elsewhere, questions must precede their answers. To this extent general education has been a gain over those specialized forms of education where the deepest and widest human questions never even are asked.

It is easy enough to belabor the weaknesses, both educational and religious, of general education. Often it has led to superficial acquaintance with vast bodies of material. Yet, as one wise educator has remarked, while the first reading of any great book is bound to be superficial there must be a first reading. Often, too, the concern of general education with theological study has been depressing in its superficiality, brevity, and ignorance. Yet, the general conclusion seems entirely justified that this treatment is far superior to the alternative of nothing at all.

The fourth approach, namely that of extracurricular projects and activities, is clearly the least effective. Taken alone, it may be regarded as a last resort to which many students in American colleges and universities are driven by the lack of any curricular resources for theological study. As a supplement and reinforcement for curricular study, such extra-curricular projects have often demonstrated great value. They are of enormous variety both in themselves and in their relation to the curricular core of the educational process. Keeping in mind the influence which extracurricular factors often have upon the actual outcome of education, we must at least conclude that this is a valuable resource.

Which one or combination of these approaches to the study of religion shall we select and use in any particular situation? The general answer is that we must use whatever combination gives most promise of success in restoring and sustaining the study of religion to its integral place in liberal education. The forces of the academic world aligned against this objective are of such strength that we shall need all the resources we can muster.

IV

Beyond all the issues of strategy and tactics lies a fundamental question of principle, namely, what is the relation of humanism to faith? The goal of liberal education is the development and fulfillment of man's highest and most distinctively human powers. It is in a word a humanistic goal. But what is the relation of this humanistic ideal to religious faith, and more specifically to the Christian faith whose center is not man but God?

Often humanism and faith have been viewed as enemies. Throughout the modern period Christian theology has shied away from humanism, for reasons both good and bad. For the past century the term "humanism" has been preempted by a somewhat odd group of dissident liberal minds who have been unable to "believe in God" but determined to "believe in man." Opposition to this humanism has preoccupied much of theology. Yet even when the proper and traditional meaning of humanism as the cultivation and fulfillment of human excellence in all its manifold forms is restored, there is still a genuine tension between humanism and faith. As Karl Barth has remarked, to say "God" is not simply to shout "Man" in a loud voice. Or to put the matter in terms of man, to assert that man is a bridge to be passed over and to call man an end or goal are different and perhaps incompatible views. A profound tension persists between humanism and faith.

Yet the inexorable and tragic facts of the twentieth-century world making for dehumanization are leading to a revaluation of this relation. The twentieth century is marked by a struggle which can only be termed as that of Man versus Anti-man. It is so whether we refer to the hard dehumanization of totalitarian societies which grind the face off their members, or the soft dehumanization of the free societies which condition them off by the subtler arts of the persuaders. The result is shockingly similar in both cases. *Brave New World* and *1984* loom as ominous possibilities in both cases.

In our tortured time we are coming to see that while God and Man are clearly not equivalent terms, there is a close and significant relation between them. As André Malraux remarked, in the nineteenth century God died, and in the twentieth, man died. Paul Tillich points more affirmatively to the same relation in his repeated assertion that man is the question to which God is the answer. Whatever one's particular formulation, there appears to be a significant relation between the basic convictions of faith and the values which form the content of humanism. By some such process of reasoning we are led to see the significance and relevance of the term "Christian humanism."

To be sure, Christianity is not unique among the faiths and philosophies of mankind in producing its own distinctive brand of humanism. We shall not be false to the situation to imagine a conversation in which man asks, "Who am I?" "What must I do and be to be genuinely human?" and in which the various faiths and philosophies make their distinctive and characteristic replies. There are differences and even incompatibilities among the answers; but there are common elements as well. In brief, there are different humanisms—Christian, Jewish, Buddhist, agnostic, and perhaps many more as well. Yet these different humanisms may be characterized as different variations on a basic theme.

Such a humanism, of whatever variety, has particular pertinence as a guiding ideal for contemporary liberal education. On the one hand, contemporary liberal education desperately needs some organizing center. Yet it equally needs the foundation of basic human values. Conversely, the basic convictions of religious faith need wider and more significant expression than is often accorded them in institutional or organized religion. In other words, Christian faith (as well as other civilized faiths) needs the expression and application provided by liberal education.

Such lofty utterances seem unrelated to the prosaic details of educational practice—or of ecclesiastical practice, for that matter. Yet our religion and our education need such a faith to lift them above momentary whims and caprices and give them enduring significance. The future minister whose education and well-being are the center of these studies needs the orientation of Christian humanism.

RELIGION IN THE
UNDERGRADUATE CURRICULUM

ROBERT MICHAELSEN

I

It is well to recall . . . that liberal education originated independently of Christianity, that it later developed in response to historical forces (such as the revival of the classics and the birth of modern science) which had nothing directly to do with Christianity, and that its main objectives have often appeared to be opposed to Christian ideals. . . . It is on the whole, *secular,* deep-rooted in this worldly concerns and aims. . . . It is *uncommitted* to anything beyond an amorphous humanism as an explanation of the meaning of existence.[1]

The story of religion in American higher education might be told in terms of interaction between the liberal and the Christian motifs. These motifs sometimes blend together in apparent harmony, sometimes complement each other in creative tension, and sometimes go their own separate ways in open or covert opposition to each other. As our story develops, subsidiary motifs appear with increasing vocationalism, professionalism, and specialization.

The initial, and for many years primary, objective of liberal and Christian education was that of raising up good

43

servants of church and civil society, God and country. The prototype is Harvard, founded to produce a literate ministry, and, incidentally, a literate congregation. The manner of doing this was through the classical curriculum— the study of medieval arts and philosophies (the liberal arts) and the languages and literature of learning. Though founded primarily to educate men for the ministry, Harvard was not a professional divinity school. It was taken for granted by the founders and directors of the college "that a minister should have the same liberal education as any other scholar."[2]

Still the attempt to fuse the classical and the Christian is obvious. Hebrew was prominent among the learned languages, and readings from the Hebrew Bible were required daily of the freshman class. (Students in Harvard's early years even received some training in Aramaic and Syriac.) Studies in divinity—catechetical, biblical, and the scientific study of theology—were a regular part of the academic diet. The students were thoroughly grounded in the theological system. (The *Marrow of Sacred Theology* by William Ames, the English Puritan, was the primary text of catechetical theology.) Students were trained not only to read the Bible in the original languages, but to interpret it in accordance with accepted hermeneutical standards. By the time they had finished their course they were prepared to handle any major theological issue in the scientific fashion of the day. This was true of all students whether they were headed for the ministry or not, since it was assumed that all educated citizens of the commonwealth should be theologically literate. Many men who had chosen the ministry as a profession stayed on for the M.A. degree, a course largely individual in nature and consisting of further grounding in theology.

While not a professional theological seminary, the college

was suffused with a religious purpose. "The course," says Professor Morison, "was more deeply impregnated with religion than any liberal college today." Christ was the foundation and the end. *In Christi Gloriam,* inscribed on the college seal of 1650, expressed the fundamental purpose of the founders. *Veritas* meant divine truth.[3]

The purpose and the methodology were almost the same at New England's second college, Yale. This institution was founded by Connecticut ministers in 1701 "for the educating and instructing of youth in good literature, arts, and sciences; that so by the blessings of the Almighty God they may be better fitted for publick Imployment, both in Church and Civil State." "Suitable youth," future ministers and magistrates alike, were to receive "Liberal" and "Religious Education . . . under ye blessing of God."[4]

II

More than a century later, in 1828, the faculty of Yale College issued a carefully prepared report in defense of the traditional liberal arts curriculum. This report received the approval of the Yale Corporation and was widely circulated. It kept Yale on an even keel for another half century and was very influential among the new colleges that were founded in such prolific numbers during this period.

The Yale curriculum of 1828 evidenced the continued coalescing of the liberal arts and the Christian strains. The biblical languages and biblical study continued to be required. The liberal arts course was capped in the senior year with required courses in moral philosophy, natural theology, and the evidences of Christianity. These courses were thought to round off the student's education, to be a final preparation for his entry into the world, and to provide a rationally defensible and impregnable *Weltanschauung* by which to live.

At least one of these courses was usually taught by the president of the college and the others by the college preacher. The texts used for many years were three books by the Anglican clergyman, William Paley: *The Principles of Moral and Political Philosophy* (1785), *The View of the Evidences of Christianity* (1794), and *Natural Theology* (1802). These works presented a careful and detailed defense of the Christian system in the language and metaphor of the Age of Reason. They were used at Yale for more than sixty years.[5]

"To recount the vacillations and vicissitudes of the small college curricula of the past century," wrote the president of Reed College, William T. Foster, in 1911, "is mainly to trace the influence of radical Harvard and conservative Yale."[6] What Foster had in mind was Yale's continuing defense of the classical liberal arts curriculum, largely prescribed, and Harvard's early advocacy of the elective and the broadened curriculum, especially under President Eliot after 1869. Through the Civil War, however, both institutions clung to the long-established pattern of the liberal arts, the biblical languages, and the capstone course or courses in moral philosophy, theology, and Christian evidences.

During this period hundreds of colleges were founded— most of them by churches as nurseries for ministers. Nearly all of them instituted some form of the classical liberal arts curriculum, together with the biblical languages and a senior capstone course. Like early Harvard, they were not primarily seminaries, and their courses were not primarily professional in nature, although the training of ministers was the chief purpose for their establishment. Few of them could duplicate seventeenth century Harvard in the number of Oriental languages offered or in the depth and thoroughness of theological study, but they almost universally provided study in New Testament Greek, some regular Bible study, and some sort of philosophical-theological statement and defense of the faith. The course or courses on various aspects of the evidences of Christianity became a part, and in most instances a required part, of the curricula of most of the colleges of early nineteenth century America. (This was true also of most of the state schools.) As at Yale, the most commonly used textbooks were those written by Paley, with Bishop Butler's *Analogy* running a close second.[7]

Nevertheless, strong pressures for change were developing. Some called for a more practical education, protesting against the "dead" languages of the past and the courses which seemed to have little relevance to the workaday world. (Such a protest stimulated the Yale Report of 1828.) Others felt the thrill of a developing scientific and critical spirit which was being so vigorously expressed in European universities, especially those of Germany. Some were not pleased with the "sectarianism" of the denominational school and, while they recognized the desirability of some *Weltanschauung* course, they ruled out the specifics of Christian theology. Furthermore, this was an age when theology was suspect, not only among the cultured despisers of religion, but even in some of the religious communities themselves—especially those like the Methodists and the Baptists, the rough-and-ready variety characterized by strong experiential and practical emphases and no small amount of anti-intellectualism.

In this environment the study of theology gradually disappeared from the college curriculum. This trend was augmented by the establishment of the professional theological school—a development of considerable significance to the future of the liberal arts college as well as the study of theology and religion.

One of the earliest of the seminaries, Andover, was founded in 1808 when the defenders of orthodox Calvinism in New England became convinced that Harvard was no longer safe because the Hollis Chair of Divinity was now occupied by a man of Unitarian persuasion. At about the same time Princeton Theological Seminary was founded by leaders of the Presbyterian Church who were no longer satisfied with the orthodoxy of the instructors at Princeton College. The seminary was to be located at Princeton on the condition that it be allowed to use certain of the college's facilities and that the college not "establish a professorship of theology as long as the seminary remained at Princeton."[8]

The concern of the orthodox to hold their own and the bitter sectarianism that resulted caused some educators to make careful provision that religious instruction be kept from the college curriculum and prompted some state legislatures to pass acts specifically prohibiting religious instruction in the public schools and in some instances even prohibiting the establishment of theological departments in state universities—and in one instance even in private colleges.[9]

Two of the great educational leaders of the nineteenth century, Thomas Jefferson (the University of Virginia) and Henry P. Tappan (the University of Michigan), envisioned a situation in which, while theology would not be an integral part of the university curriculum, theological faculties would locate adjacent to the university and there make use of the facilities and resources of the university and be available for instruction in various aspects of theology. Such a plan might have proved beneficial to both theological education and the developing university system, but the vision never became a reality as the denominational theological school and the university went their separate ways.

The establishment of the denominational theological seminary separated from the college or university and the gradual removal of the study of theology from the main current of American academic development (and intellectual life) were to have far-reaching consequences before the end of the century.[10]

III

American higher education underwent a revolutionary development in the period between the Civil War and World War I. The prescribed curriculum was replaced by the elective system in institution after institution. Curriculum offerings multiplied many times. Degree programs were developed in the sciences and the professions. The classical curriculum declined. Modern languages tended to replace the ancient languages, especially at the undergraduate level. Graduate and professional education developed in dramatic fashion and, in turn, produced marked changes in the liberal arts curriculum. A new spirit permeated the system—the spirit of science, the critical and investigative spirit which had found such full expression in the German universities. American higher education felt the full effects of the intellectual and scientific revolution of the nineteenth century.

What were the results for the study of religion? The Christian Evidences course was replaced by courses in philosophy or psychology. The study of theology disappeared almost entirely from the curriculum, except in the professional school or the colleges of the more conservative churches. The number of required courses in religion dropped perceptibly. Bible study continued to be important, but the results of historical-critical studies in biblical literature and history began to appear. Senior *Weltanschauung* courses, where they continued to be required in the Christian liberal arts colleges, were modified in an effort to deal with the intellectual and scientific revolution. And the critical-scientific method was applied to the study of religion in an impressive fashion at a few developing graduate institutions.

By the early twentieth century the required Christian Evidences course had almost entirely disappeared. Paley and Butler no longer satisfied the needs of the age. A few substitutes were tried. One of the most popular was George T. Fischer's *The Grounds of Theistic and Christian Belief,* first published in 1883. Fischer was professor of ecclesiastical history in Yale College. His book was designed to counteract the "unfortunate" influences of the German higher criticism and the theory of evolution. He too endeavored to establish the truth of Christianity, but he appealed more to "internal or moral" evidences than to "external proofs from miracles" and thus differed from Paley.[11]

At Harvard, where the elective system had been introduced under President Eliot, Butler and Paley had disappeared at the college level by 1880. "Christian Evidences" was relegated to the divinity school and courses in French, English, and German philosophy, and a special course in the philosophy of evolution appeared at the undergraduate level.

Biblical studies continued to be emphasized in the church-controlled or church-related institutions. However, even there certain changes occurred. English Bible gradually replaced the study of the Bible in the original languages. The amount of required work in Bible declined and in some instances biblical study became wholly elective or an option along with two or three other areas in meeting a requirement. And the influence of the historical-critical method appeared.[12]

Courses in Bible were offered as electives in many non-church institutions. The University of North Carolina, for example, as late as 1875 required attendance for three years at lectures on the Bible. By 1890, however, this requirement had disappeared, although the catalogue for 1890-91 indicated that students were expected to attend Sunday school classes in Bible. In 1902 Bible courses were offered through the Y.M.C.A. These courses continued to be offered for many years, and while not required by the faculty and administration, students were encouraged to attend them.

The offering of Bible courses or lectures through extra-university agencies and with some sort of recognition or sanction by the university came to be a common practice at various universities beginning in the late nineteenth century. Courses in the English Bible open to all students in all divisions of the university were offered at the University of Chicago in 1905-06 at 8:30 A.M. on Sundays. "The aim of these courses," according to the catalogue, was "to guide the students into a study of the Bible which shall be at the same time thoroughly scientific and spiritually helpful."[13]

Denominational Bible courses were developed at many state universities. The most widespread efforts in this period were made by the Disciples of Christ, who established "Bible Chairs" at the Universities of Michigan, Virginia, Kansas, and Texas between 1893 and 1904 and a Bible College at the University of Missouri in 1896.

One of the most significant developments in this period was the application of the scientific method to the study of religion. The blossoming of language studies in the late nineteenth century made possible an examination of the sources on an unprecedented scale. The study of Assyrian, Egyptian, and Babylonian paved the way for the study of the roots of biblical religion. Arabic opened the Muslim world to American scholars. Sanskrit made possible a coming to grips with the religions of ancient India. Linguistic study, combined with the use of the critical methodology of scientific history, led to the science of the History of Religion or Comparative Religion. The developing social sciences—especially anthropology and psychology—also made available new findings and techniques for the study of religion.

Major programs in the History of Religion or Comparative Religion, and in the languages and literature pertinent to these areas, were developed at such institutions as Harvard, Brown, Pennsylvania, and Chicago. While the History of Religion or Comparative Religion flourished in these universities, it did not catch on immediately in most colleges and universities.[14] This development was to come later in the century and then rarely involving more than courses of an elementary nature.

At the turn of the century a number of competent academicians turned their attention to the applications of the methods of the developing science of psychology to the study of religion. The psychology of religion showed promise of becoming a fruitful discipline and an important part of the curriculum in the college and university. However, the discipline failed to develop in quite the fashion that might have been anticipated in the early twentieth century. Much of the interest generated was channeled off in the more "practical" directions of pastoral psychology and religious education. Moreover, developments within the whole field of psychological studies were not conducive to the advance of the psychology of religion. On the one hand, the impact of Sigmund Freud greatly accelerated interest in the psychopathological aspects of human experience. On the other hand, as Behaviorism came to dominate psychology proper, the study of religion almost entirely ceased to be an area of concern. Thus the early promise of the psychology of religion was never fully realized, and while the subject did show up in the curriculum in religion from time to time, it never occupied a central place.[15]

The university system brought increasing specialization which in turn affected the college course where there developed the system of majors and minors and an increasing professional and vocational emphasis. This tended to become the source of unity insofar as there was one at the undergraduate level. The elective system made for a proliferation of courses and an increasing fragmentation. Both the liberal arts course and the study of religion suffered in the process. A major in religion became possible but almost exclusively in the church-related institutions and there chiefly as a pre- or semi-professional course.

The most common course in religion well into the twentieth century was the Bible course. Where there were departments they were likely to be Bible departments or departments of biblical literature or biblical literature and history. This was true where courses were available in tax-supported institutions as well as in church-related and independent colleges.[16]

Courses which reflected the influence of certain distinctive trends in American Protestantism appeared in the curriculum in religion in the early twentieth century. Among these was a whole group of courses with a social emphasis such as "Applied Christianity," "Christian Sociology," and "The Social Teachings of the Hebrew Prophets," all developing out of the context of the Social Gospel Movement. Francis Greenwood Peabody, one of the early proponents of the Social Gospel who became Plummer Professor of Christian Morals at Harvard in 1886 and was dean of the Harvard Divinity School from 1900 to 1907, is reported to have been "the first teacher in the United States to demand and create a permanent place for systematic Christian social ethics as a university discipline in a liberal education as well as in professional theological education." His courses were offered in both the College and the Divinity School at Harvard. Figures for 1903 indicate that 127 students from outside the Divinity School took his course on "The Practical Ethics of Social Reform." Peabody founded the Department of Social Ethics in Harvard in 1906.[17]

Professor George D. Herron, radical Social Gospel leader of the late nineteenth century, instituted a department of applied Christianity at Iowa College (Grinnell) with the announced purpose of attempting "to apply the principles revealed by the Great Teacher to the political, social, and religious problems of the present age."[18] This department developed into something of a division of social sciences and social work under Herron's leadership. The department continued in existence at Grinnell for forty years after Herron's forced exit from the scene at the turn of the century. Similar courses in applied Christianity appeared at other institutions.

A movement in a practical or semi-professional direction is evident in the rapid expansion of courses in religious education, especially in the 1920's. A survey in the mid-1920's disclosed that of 293 colleges of the "evangelical" denominations, a total of 235 courses were being offered in religious education. Over eighty percent of the institutions surveyed listed such courses. In some instances even a major was possible.[19]

The course in religious education frequently showed the influence of the philosophy of progressive education with its roots in the instrumentalism of John Dewey and his followers. This philosophy was anti-theological in nature; its ardent proponents in effect ruled out the study of religion or theology as valid content areas, stressing instead the "life-centered" course and a curriculum under secular control. Values were to be discovered in and through immediate experience. Experimentalism and the scientific method were stressed.

There were some institutions which resisted the fragmentation and specialization (and indirectly at least the instrumentalism, naturalism, and scientism of the progressive education movement) of the early twentieth century and which initiated or continued a curricular program in which religion played a central role. These institutions were of two types: (1) those which attempted to continue the historical liberal arts and Christian curriculum and (2) those which built their curricula almost entirely around a biblical core with little regard for the liberal arts. The institutions in the first category were chiefly those with conservative theological ties, rooted in a religious tradition which had been little affected by the anti-theological trends of the late nineteenth and early twentieth centuries. This was true especially of Roman Catholic, Lutheran, and Reformed colleges. The second type was the Bible college, a new type of institution which developed under conservative or fundamentalist auspices in reaction to the intellectual revolution of the late nineteenth century. The curricula of such institutions were both Bible-centered and functional or vocational in nature with little liberal arts emphasis. It was designed to elicit and elucidate the truth of the Bible, not facts *about* the Bible. Thus the approach was catechetical and evangelical, rather than critical and cultural. The Bible college also had as its prime purpose the training of men and women for some type of Christian vocation.[20]

Tax-supported colleges and universities grew at a phenomenal rate in the early decades of the twentieth century (and this growth continues unabated at the present time). The state school perhaps best evidenced the characteristics of an age of increasing specialization and fragmentation. The choice of courses and professional programs was likely to be extensive. New offerings appeared frequently in answer to the needs and desires of the constituency. While courses in Bible or religion were often among those available as options to the students, few state institutions developed anything approaching a well-rounded program in religious studies. The courses that were available were usually offered in departments other than religion, such as English or philosophy, or in semi-independent or independent institutions such as Bible chairs, denominational foundations, and schools of religion. Here and there a department of Bible or biblical literature or religion existed.

Perhaps the most significant curricular development in the state college and university in the early decades of the century was the establishment of the independent or semi-independent Bible chair or school of religion. We have already alluded to the activities of the Disciples of Christ in this regard. Professor Charles Foster Kent of Yale spearheaded a movement which also had as its goal the creation of schools of religion in state universities. He was the leading figure in the founding of the National Council of Schools of Religion in 1923. One of the primary purposes of this organization was to assist in the selection and education of well-qualified students who might become available to teach in schools of religion in state universities. A few such schools were started, but the movement lost momentum after Kent's death in the early twenties. The National Council of Schools of Religion became the National Council on Religion in Higher Education in 1924. Kent's idea of schools of religion was quietly dropped and the selection and education of students to teach in such schools ceased to be of importance. The Council turned its attention to the selection and assistance of well-qualified students who might teach not only religion but any of the major subjects in any college or university.

One of the most significant of the schools of religion founded in the 1920's was that established at the State Uni-

versity of Iowa under the leadership of Dr. O. D. Foster
and Professor M. Willard Lampe. From its beginnings in
1927 the curricular offerings of this school, which were
taught by Jewish, Roman Catholic, and Protestant professors, were a regular part of both the College of Liberal Arts
and the Graduate College. The School was legally incor-
porated and received most of its financial support from non-
tax sources. However, most of the state schools tended to
develop in such a fashion as to provide for the study of almost
everything except religion.[21]

IV

While the fragmentation of higher education continued
on into this century, many educators called for a halt, at
the undergraduate level at least. The elective system was
modified. Required courses reappeared and the general education course was introduced. This was a course designed
to present a "core" to the student, to ground him in some
aspect of his heritage, and to provide some sort of integration for his education. The nature and purposes of a college education and, in particular, a liberal education were
the objects of much discussion. This resulted in some instances in a reaffirmation of some form of the humanistic
and liberal arts tradition of the past.

This reaffirmation of the liberal arts tradition had certain
effects on the curricular offerings in religion. The course in
Bible reappeared, or was modified, now as a course in which
the cultural and literary values of the Bible were stressed.
The classics of the Judaeo-Christian tradition were rediscov-
ered and sometimes, along with the Graeco-Roman classics,
formed the base of the core course.

Perhaps religion was, after all, one of the liberal arts;
perhaps it had an important place in the liberating process
of education, in helping the student to develop a critical

mind and to find viable answers to life's most pressing problems. On the other hand, perhaps religion demanded too much with its concern for ultimate loyalties.

The mood of the Protestant Christian community underwent considerable change in this period: from a non- or anti-theological bias to a renewed concern for theology; from a highly individualistic and personalistic understanding of religion to a renewed interest in the community of faith; from a bland form of universalism to an attempt to wrestle with "the scandal of particularity." The mood of the twenties and thirties was captured and illustrated in a statement by Patrick Murphy Malin, made in 1941 when he was president of the National Council on Religion in Higher Education. "Religion—to whose advancement in the field of higher education our Council . . . is dedicated—is for us, whatever our differences, a search; it is the conscious search for all that can be known about man and the universe. . . . To this indispensable religious search, all ways of knowing are tributary. . . . the religious seeker should . . . persist in his inquiry to the very end, changing his particular beliefs as often and as drastically as evidence requires. This comprehensive and endless discovery is necessarily at bottom individual and free."[22]

Where such a mood prevailed any and all study would seem to have been religiously relevant and the specific study of religion as a community of faith and as point of view would have been geared toward the growth of the individual. Such a mood appeared to coincide with the mood of liberal education which, as Professor Harbison observed, "is *uncommitted* to anything beyond amorphous humanism as an explanation of the meaning of existence."[23]

But even as Malin penned his words in 1941 a change in mood was developing in the form of the theological renaissance of the thirties and forties which produced a renewed appreciation of the Judaeo-Christian tradition. Theologians affirmed the uniqueness of God's revelation in Jesus Christ and turned now to the Bible and the theological writings of Christianity as a means of gaining further understanding of that revelation. Now the Bible was seen not merely as a work of great cultural and literary value but as the Word of God or the profoundest written expression of the Word of God. Here and there teachers in the colleges and universities sought to present it in its theological context. Here and there a religion department or program sought to expose students to the richness of their religious and even theological heritage, not only that these students might be helped to make intelligent choices as free individuals, but also that they might come to grips with the claims of the major religious tradition of the West, with what one teacher of religion in a liberal arts college has called the "rugged uniqueness of Christianity."[24]

Once again tension between the ideals of a liberal education and the confessions of the Christian community became evident. The realities of the modern world made it quite clear that there could be no return to the early days when the Christian confession had been the *raison d'être* and the source of unity in the college.[25] Nevertheless, that confession could no longer be ignored or treated lightly by those who would do justice to the past or the present.

There is striking evidence of a general overhauling of the curricular program in religion in the 1940's resulting in a fuller program, and the establishment of departments of religion in a number of colleges and universities. There is little evidence that the amount of required work in religion increased significantly, but the courses in religion did become more popular among the electives chosen by students. There is further evidence of an effort to make these courses more relevant to the total liberal arts program; more cultural in nature, less professional, less "practical," less isolated. Finally, as suggested, there is clear indication of a rebirth of interest in theology and concern with the religious tradition of the West as courses in Bible became less of the history and literature variety and more centered in the context of the Bible and courses in Christian classics and Christian thought appeared.

These trends can be illustrated by allusion to developments in the disciplines of the history of religion and the philosophy of religion, and by brief histories of curricular changes in three major institutions. The history of religion enjoyed a certain vogue in the early part of the century because of its stress upon a scientific and objective approach. The philosophy of religion also fitted into the mood of objectivity and the stress upon beginning *de novo* in the search for truth. In some instances the two disciplines were brought together as religions were set side by side and an effort was made to ascertain by rational and scientific means the truth values present in each. Stress was placed upon the continuity of Christianity with other religions and upon the similarities among all religions. The philosophical approach was preferred over the theological because of the apparent exclusiveness and a priori commitments involved in the latter. By the 1940's, however, it had become apparent that no religion could be understood apart from its own context, assumptions, and claims and that no individual could approach this subject—or any subject—*de novo*. It could no longer be assumed or granted that the man of no faith was better fitted to understand religion or a religion than was the man of obvious commitment. The history of religion, which outside of a few graduate programs had become something of an armchair and synthetic enterprise now demanded first-hand contact where possible and a careful confrontation with sources and historical and cultural context and perhaps, above all, a taking of *homo religiosus* with profound seriousness. The philosophy of religion suffered a certain displacement as it fell between a growing interest in theology, on the one hand—note the increased use of "philosophical theology"—and a developing concern with language analysis in philosophy proper, on the other.[26]

We have chosen Princeton University, the University of North Carolina, and Stanford University to illustrate more specifically some of the trends suggested above. Developments at Princeton are surely among the more interesting and significant. As late as 1900, courses in Bible were required of both freshmen and sophomores, and into this century the president of the college still gave instruction in philosophy or ethics that was essentially religious in content and outlook. By 1910 the Bible course had disappeared as had the department of biblical literature. Only two courses in religion appeared in the 1920-21 catalogue: Philosophy of Religion and the Ethics of Christianity. In the early 1930's a special faculty committee was authorized to study religious education in the University. A report was submitted to the faculty in 1935. It is a significant document in the history of the study of religion. After distinguishing between the study of religion and the practice of it, the report called for the restoration of the study of religion to the curriculum as an academic discipline. This was understood to mean a critical approach using the historical method. The committee indicated that the primary objective of such an approach should be "an understanding of what the religious forces *themselves* are. . . ." The report suggested further that "no comparative study of religion should be attempted until one religion has been thoroughly mastered," and it implied that this one religion should be Christianity, or that the one religious tradition should be the Hebrew-Christian. This was suggested, not out of any particular sectarian bias, but because it was judged better to begin with "the central religious force in the culture of which we are a product."

Specifically, the report called for the initiation of a program by the introduction of two courses: (1) the Development of the Religious Thought of the Hebrews, and (2) Religious Thought in the Gospels. The faculty of the college recommended and the trustees approved the introduction of these courses at the junior level and the institution of a standing committee of the faculty to act in lieu of a department. This committee, under the chairmanship of Professor T. M. Greene, who had played an important role in formulating the report, selected Dr. George Thomas to teach the courses which were first offered in 1939-40 under the heading "Religious History." This designation was changed to "Religion" in 1942. The number of courses increased steadily and in 1944-45 plans for study in "Religion and History" and "Religion and Philosophy" were introduced. The faculty of the University granted the program departmental status and approved a major in religion in 1946. By 1950 courses were being offered in non-Western religions and the interdepartmental programs included "Religion and Literature" and "Religion and American Civilization" as well as "Religion and History" and "Religion and Philosophy." After augmenting the faculty of the department further, a graduate program leading to the Ph.D. degree in religion was announced in 1955.

The Princeton program in religion has followed quite closely the mandate of the original report. Christianity or the Hebrew-Christian tradition has received the greatest amount of attention. Course descriptions suggest the primacy of the historical method with the greatest attention being given, however, to religious thought, and Christian thought in particular, rather than institutional history or phenomenology. The department has offered, however, an increasing number of courses in non-Christian religions and probably offers at the undergraduate level as full a coverage of non-Western religions as any department in this country.[27]

Developments at two other institutions illustrate the effects of the theological renaissance of the thirties and forties.

While there were courses offered in Religion and Bible in various departments at the University of North Carolina, there was no well-structured curricular program in religion until the establishment of a Department of Religion in 1947 under the chairmanship of Professor Arnold Nash. It was immediately announced that the "first function" of the Department was "to help the students to understand the origin, development, and the significance of the Judaic-Christian tradition." Courses were listed in three areas: "(1) Biblical literature, history and theology; (2) the history of religion in Western civilization; (3) the implications of Christianity for the thought and practice of the day."[28]

For many years the chaplain taught most of the courses in religion offered at Stanford University. David Charles Gardner occupied this position from early in the century until 1936, when he was succeeded by David Elton Trueblood, who was appointed Chaplain and Professor of the Philosophy of Religion. Only one course was offered in Gardner's last year, "The Background of Christianity." Under Trueblood's leadership the curricular offerings in religion were considerably expanded and religion was listed as a separate department in the School of Humanities. "The study of religion," the departmental statement indicated under Trueblood, "is conducted in the spirit of objective inquiry. . . . The instruction is designed to aid the general student in the double task of understanding the roots of our civilization and facing the problems of the modern world."[29]

After Trueblood's departure in the late 1940's religion became a special program rather than a department in Humanities and the descriptive statement was changed to read:

> The purpose of the program is to introduce students to the world view of Biblical Religion as it has been developed and interpreted in the Western tradition and has been related to Western society. Study is systematic, historical, and comparative, with a double intention: to enable students critically to appraise the religious tradition in which they stand, and to supply them with the intellectual basis for a personal judgment.[30]

Thus one can see in the developments at Princeton, North Carolina, and Stanford a significant increase in both the historical and the theological study of the religious tradition of the West. Both the liberal arts and the Christian motifs are evident as the designers and teachers of these curricular programs sought to relate their work to the history of Western culture and to the leading philosophical and social issues of our age, and as they sought further to state and elucidate the central affirmations of the Christian or the Judaeo-Christian tradition and to make these relevant for our own times.

Since 1940 departments of religion or programs in religious studies have been introduced in a significant number of institutions and radical changes have been made in others. This has occurred in private and public institutions alike: in the Ivy League schools and in the tax-supported teachers colleges. A comparison of college and university curricular programs in religion with those in the standard disciplines from art to zoology would indicate that religion is still far from receiving the amount of attention that it might receive as a field of inquiry and a legitimate academic discipline. Nevertheless, the contrast with the situation a generation ago is obvious.

V

It is a truism to say that religion is a complex area, a commonplace to recognize that the study of religion is beset with many difficulties. The academician who maintains that religion should be studied like any other subject may be on the right track, but, other than maintaining a principle for which most teachers and scholars in the field would argue, his assertion is not greatly helpful. It does apparently rule out the obviously practical or professional course—and the trend of the past generation is definitely away from such courses. But it leaves unanswered the most crucial question of all: What *is* the discipline of religion? That there is a phenomenon called religion, most observers would not deny. But the study of such a phenomenon involves various disciplines including linguistics, archaeology, history, sociology, anthropology, psychology, philosophy and—in the Western tradition, at least—theology. Furthermore, because of the very nature of religion, questions of the relationship between the purely descriptive and the normative, between the objective and the existential, are perhaps more real in this area than in any other.

The complexity of the field is evident in the various curricular approaches to it—some involving a department and some not, some taking the discipline of theology quite seriously and others ignoring it or actually ruling it out, some concentrating on the West and especially Christianity and others giving considerable attention to non-Western religions. This complexity is also evident in the rationale for the study of religion. We have alluded to the tension between Christianity and the liberal arts. We might also refer to other and related tensions—between the professional and the academic, the practical and the intellectual, the existential and the objective. Historically, the curriculum in religion has been heavily influenced by a context of professionalism and practicality. Early colleges such as Harvard and Yale were founded for the preparing of a literate ministry, and although the original curricula were quite academic in character, the study of theology came to be increasingly professional. Curricular programs in religion came to be manned by men trained largely in such professional programs. One of the more obvious results was that the undergraduate curriculum in religion tended to become a pale reflection of the seminary curriculum, designed especially for the pre-ministerial student. It was because of this semi-professional caste in the religion curriculum that there developed in the twentieth century an attitude which discouraged pre-ministerial students from majoring in the subject. They would get all of that later (and better) in the seminary. (This attitude was given encouragement by the American Association of Theological Schools in the 1930's and 1940's.) For whom and for what end, then, was the curricular program in religion? Practical and personal goals continued to play a large role as they had in the capstone courses of the nineteenth century: to prepare the students to meet the problems of life. On the other hand, many saw in the scientific approach a way of lifting the study of religion to the academic and intellectual level at which it belonged if it was to be a legitimate college or university function. Still, this rarefied, highly intellectual, and specialized atmosphere seemed to be beyond the ken of most ordinary mortals. The psychology of religion veered in the direction of pastoral psychology—an approach with considerable practical and personal implications. And the demanding discipline of the history of religions remained the competence of but a few especially hardy souls. More recently, the prevailing rationale has seemed to combine a stress on the broadly academic and cultural—religion as a part of the liberal arts or as one of the humanities—and the theological.

While these complexities continue unabated, one can conclude that teachers and scholars in this field are coming to grips with them in a more significant fashion than previously and that the study of religion is showing real signs of coming of age. Curricular developments of the recent past would tend to substantiate this.

We have seen that in some major institutions religion is receiving more attention as a field of academic study than ever before. In these and other institutions it is being approached on a broad scale as a thoroughly legitimate subject within the liberal arts complex. In some instances, this breadth has been achieved through both a departmental structure and an interdepartmental approach which pulls together the relevant aspects of various disciplines vis-à-vis religion. Such a program is built around a core of specialists—biblical scholars, church historians and historians of religion, and theologians. At the same time, it utilizes the skills and work of scholars in related disciplines or fields. It seeks to take full advantage of one of the significant developments of the recent past: the increasing amount of attention being given to the various aspects of religion by scholars in such related disciplines. In a few universities —such as Princeton, Brown, Southern California, and the State University of Iowa, for example—these programs have been extended to or expanded at the graduate level, thus making possible, to an extent not realized earlier, graduate study in religion apart from a seminary faculty.

While this discussion has concentrated largely on developments within the Protestant Christian community and within the private college and university, it would not be fair to conclude that there have been no significant developments in the study of religion within the Roman Catholic Christian community (or the Jewish community) or within the tax-supported colleges and universities. One has the impression that there is considerable ferment today in the study of religion in Catholic colleges and universities—as seen for example in the expansion of the curricular program at Marquette University, or in developments at the Catholic University of America. Furthermore, one of the more significant trends of recent times can be seen in the involvement of an increasing number of Catholic and Jewish scholars in curricular programs in religion in both private and tax-supported institutions. This is another indication of a growing recognition of the richness and depth of the field of religion; the study of such a field increases in value and validity as scholars of various religious traditions engage in it together.

A professor at a state university observed a generation ago that the curriculum of his institution covered "nearly every conceivable subject (except theology)."[31] While this might have been typical of state universities in 1929, in recent years even theology has received some attention in some state institutions. Furthermore, the study—in some way or other—of religion now takes place in a great majority of tax-supported schools. The number of departments is not large and the number of fully developed curricular programs in this area is even smaller. Nevertheless, here and there such programs do exist, and there are very real signs that an increasing amount of significant work in religion (and even theology) is being done in such institutions.

We began this survey with a recognition of the tension that has existed historically between Christianity and the liberal arts. This tension has continued to exist down to the present time. The trend of the present does not appear to be so much an effort completely to relax the tension as an effort to make it more fruitful and creative by bringing it directly into the curriculum of the college and university and especially into the curricular program in religion. Thus the student might both learn about his heritage and come to grips with it existentially as he faces the major decisions of his own life.

FOOTNOTES

1. E. Harrison Harbison, "Liberal Education and Christian Education," in *The Christian Idea of Education*, edited by Edmund Fuller (New Haven: Yale University Press, 1960), pp. 60-61.

2. Samuel Eliot Morison, *Harvard College in the Seventeenth Century* (Cambridge: Harvard University Press, 1936), Pt. I, p. 165.

3. Samuel Eliot Morison, *The Founding of Harvard College* (Cambridge: Harvard University Press, 1935), pp. 247 ff.

4. Franklin Bowditch Dexter, *Documentary History of Yale University* (New Haven: Yale University Press, 1960), pp. 17 and 27.

5. Ralph Henry Gabriel, *Religion and Learning at Yale* (New Haven: Yale University Press, 1958), Chs. 6 & 7.

6. *Administration of the College Curriculum* (Boston: Houghton-Mifflin Co., 1911), p. 129.

7. James Orval Filbeck, *The Christian Evidence Movement* (Kansas City, Missouri: The Old Paths Book Club, 1946).
For an account of the role of the college president in the teaching of these courses see George P. Schmidt, *The Old Time College President* (New York: Columbia University Press, 1930), Ch. IV.

8. Thomas Jefferson Wertenbaker, *Princeton 1746-1896*. (Princeton: Princeton University Press, 1946), pp. 148 f. (For the full story see Ch. IV.)

9. Samuel Windsor Brown, *The Secularization of American Education* (New York: Teachers College, Columbia University, 1912), Ch. VI.
In 1835 the Illinois legislature approved an act to incorporate Illinois College, Alton College, McKendrie College, and Jonesboro College. This act prohibited the establishment of a theological department in any of the colleges. Although the prohibition was removed in 1841, the original action is indicative of an anti-theological and anti-sectarian sentiment. (Charles Henry Rammelkamp, *Illinois College, A Centennial History, 1829-1929*, New Haven: Yale University Press, 1928, p. 67.) At about this time, Rammelkamp points out, a committee of the Presbyterian Synod of Illinois charged "that the professors had departed from their appropriate duties and invaded the province of the theological seminary . . ." (p. 125). Thus Illinois College was prevented from teaching theology because of pressures from both church and state.

10. "An unexpected consequence of Andover's concern for ministerial and missionary training under proper theological auspices," asserts Professor Geroge H. Williams, "was the setting of a disastrous pattern in American education . . ." This "was the first step on the long road which led to the destruction of the college as a school of liberal arts. What theology began, law and medicine continued." (*The Harvard Divinity School: Its Place in Harvard University and in American Culture*, Boston: The Beacon Press, 1954, p. 5.)

11. Fischer's work was used as early as 1887 at the College of Wooster where it was required of all juniors. It was still being used there in 1901. It was also used at the turn of the century in a number of other institutions including Williams, Knox, Hamilton, Kenyon, Rutgers, Muhlenberg, and Furman.
Filbeck, *op. cit.*, pp. 129-132.

12. For example, the Iowa College (Grinnell) catalogue for 1892-93 indicated that all seniors would be required to take two hours of English Bible per week and that the Bible would "be studied from the spiritual *and* from the critical standpoint, as literature *and* as Word of God." Here is a clear illustration of the coalescing of criticism and apologetics, the attempt to pull together the liberal arts motif and the Christian point of view (p. 42. Emphasis added).

13. Two courses were listed for the year 1905-06: "The History of the Priest System," taught by William Rainey Harper, President of the University and distinguished Orientalist; and "The Life of Paul," by Shailer Mathews, Professor of New Testament. (*The Register of the University of Chicago*, 1905-06, p. 134.)

14. Professor Morris Jastrow of the University of Pennsylvania lamented—early in the century—that "there is scarcely a single American college in which the study [of the history of religion] has been accorded a place—even in the most modest proportions." (*The Study of Religion*, New York: Scribner's, 1901, p. 352.)

15. See Orlo Strunk, Jr., "The Present State of the Psychology of Religion," *Journal of Bible and Religion*, Vol. XXV (Oct., 1957), pp. 287-292; and Edward L. Schaub, "The Present Status of the Psychology of Religion," *The Journal of Religion*, Vol. II (July, 1922), pp. 362-379.
The names associated with the early development of the psychology of religion include William James, G. S. Hall, E. D. Starbuck, and J. H. Leuba. Hall developed the Clark school in which both Starbuck and Leuba were trained.

16. Willard E. Uphaus and M. Tegue Hipps found in 1923-24 that 184 of 269 denominational and independent institutions surveyed had some such Bible department. Other departments included: religion, 61; religious education, 54; and evidences of religion, 21. Of the courses examined, the study of Bible was most common, ethics next, followed by religious education, and then history, philosophy, and psychology of religion. ("Undergraduate Courses in Religion at Denominational and Independent Colleges and Universities of America," Bulletin VI of the National Council on Religion in Higher Education, no date.)
Edward Sterling Boyer studied fifteen "typical church colleges" later in the 1920's. He discovered that 568 semester hours were offered in all aspects of religion, 245 in Bible, 165 in religion, and 158 in religious education (*Religion in American Colleges*, Nashville: Abingdon Press, 1930).
Charles Foster Kent and Millar Burrows surveyed the undergraduate courses in religion at 181 tax-supported institutions in the academic year 1922-23. They discovered "that the courses in Biblical literature and history are far in the lead . . ." (Bulletin IV of the National Council on Religion in Higher Education, no date.) They also discovered very few distinct departments—the courses in biblical literature being offered either in departments other than religion or Bible or by independent or semi-independent Bible chairs.

17. Levering Reynolds, Jr., "The Later Years (1880-1953)," *The Harvard Divinity School*, *op. cit.*, pp. 174 and 180; James Fored, "Social Ethics, 1905-1929," *The Development of Harvard University, 1869-1929*, ed. by Samuel Eliot Morison (Cambridge: Harvard University Press, 1930), p. 223.

18. Catalogue of Iowa College, 1893-94, p. 45.

19. Theron C. McGee, *Religious Education in Certain Evangelical Colleges*, Philadelphia, 1928.
Religious education courses were also offered in state universities in the same period.
(Herbert L. Searles, *The Place of the Study of Religion in the State Universities of the United States*, a thesis submitted for the degree of Doctor of Philosophy in the Department of Philosophy and Psychology in the State University, Iowa City: June 1925, Appendix 1.)

20. See Frank E. Gaebelein, *Christian Education in a Democracy* (the report of the National Association of Evangelicals for United Action), New York: Oxford University Press, 1951, esp. Ch. VII, "A New Form of American Education." Gaebelein points out that well over a hundred such institutions have been founded since late in the nineteenth century.

21. Ernest Bernbaum, professor of English literature at the University of Illinois, observed, in his *Idea of a State University* (1929), that the curriculum at the University of Illinois had developed within the lifetime of one man from very meager beginnings until

it had reached the point where it covered "nearly every conceivable subject (except theology)." What he wrote about Illinois appears to have been true of many of the other state universities of the period as well. There was much sentiment for religion but little creative and concerted effort to provide for its serious study. (The Bernbaum essay is reproduced in *Of Time and Truth*, edited by Fred W. Lorch, New York: The Dryden Press, Inc., 1946, pp. 167-180. See also the perceptive comments of Norman Foerster in *The American State University*, Chapel Hill: The University of North Carolina Press, 1937, especially pp. 126 and 263.)

22. Introduction to *Two Decades: The Story of the National Council on Religion in Higher Education*, Bulletin XI, May 1941, p. 5-6. This emphasis on the free search by the individual had been approved by the fellows of the National Council in a statement of purpose in 1934. The document, according to Thornton W. Merriam and Martha H. Biehle, "stated that the Council, without demanding credal or ideological conformity, did expect the fellows to be in the forefront of efforts to change theology, social processes and institutions, and the methods and aims of higher education, when such changes would promote the religious growth of individuals" (p. 28).

23. *Op. cit.*, Note No. 1 supra.

24. The phrase is used by Professor Clyde Holbrook in a manuscript made available to the author.

25. "Whatever one's views," said the framers of the Harvard report, *General Education in a Free Society*, "religion is not now for most colleges or universities a practical source of intellectual unity" (Cambridge: Harvard University Press, 1945, p. 39).

26. See George F. Thomas, "The History of Religion in the Universities," *The Journal of Bible and Religion*, Vol. XVII (April, 1949), pp. 102-110.

27. "Princeton University Report of the Special Committee of the Faculty on Religious Education," April 11, 1935. Official Registers of Princeton University, 1930-1960. Correspondence with the chairman of the department, Professor Paul Ramsey.

28. *The University of North Carolina Record*, March 20, 1948, Number 436, p. 289.

29. Statement in the *Stanford Register*, 1945-56, p. 389.

30. *Bulletin*, Stanford University, 9th series, No. 43 (1955-56), p. 219. The influence of Professor Alexander Miller is evident as two things occurred: (1) a greater theological stress ("the world view of Biblical religion"), and (2) an intense effort to relate the courses in religion and especially the Christian faith to the total enterprise of the university. One of the courses offered by Professor Miller, for example, was "the Christian Faith and University Education." He also developed courses in Christian political theories and Christianity and contemporary society. For a fuller statement of what occurred at Stanford under Miller's leadership see his book *Faith and Learning* (New York: Association Press, 1960).

31. See Note 21.

THE ROLE OF A DEPARTMENT OF RELIGION IN A CANADIAN UNIVERSITY

WILLIAM NICHOLLS

The Canadian provincial university corresponds perhaps most closely with the state universities of the United States, as an institution very largely maintained by public funds, including in the Canadian case a rising proportion of federal money, and so far as religious matters are concerned maintaining the separation of church and state in a manner that results in the universities having a secular character. However, in Canada, as in the United States, such universities are not the only kind; only three universities, strictly speaking, fit the description, and each of these has its own peculiarities from the point of view of our present inquiry, so that not a little of what I have to say must be understood as arising rather directly from the conditions which prevail in the University of British Columbia. However, as I shall try to show, universities of this kind are a very important phenomenon, and other kinds of universities resemble them in respect of religious matters more than might be expected from a concentration upon the constitutional differences. On the other hand, I should not like any observations in the present essay to be understood as an attempt to influence decisions which similar universities may later have to make on their own account.

In general, Canadian universities seem to become more secular the farther west they are situated. In the Maritimes and in Eastern Canada, which were settled first, universities and colleges mostly began upon a religious foundation and are associated with one of the churches. For example, as might be expected, many such universities have a Roman Catholic foundation, while others owe their origin to the Anglican Church or to churches which later united to form the United Church of Canada. For such universities it has naturally been traditional to include religious instruction, sometimes compulsorily, in the undergraduate curriculum, and to associate theological colleges closely with the university itself. However, such instruction has often followed the lines of the official teaching of the church concerned. Other foundations in the east, of more recent date, whether private or public, have tried to keep clear of religious affiliations. The universities of the three western provinces, which belong to a period when religion was felt to be an obstacle to the free examination of academic questions, expressly exclude sectarian influence. The University of British Columbia had in its University Act until 1963 the requirement that (1) "The University shall be strictly non-sectarian in principle, and no religious creed or dogma shall be taught," and (2) "No religious test shall be required of any professor, teacher, lecturer or student, etc. . . ." (In a revision of the Act, passed by the Legislative Assembly in 1963, the word "taught" was significantly altered to "inculcated," precisely in order to remove doubts about the legality of the academic study and teaching of religion.) On the other hand, as elsewhere in Canada, theological colleges of various denominations are affiliated with the University, are represented on its senate, and have the legal right to confer degrees in theology!

The exact intention of the framers of the earlier Act is a debatable matter, and its meaning has not been tested in the courts. It need not be understood as ruling out religion, or its study, as such, but rather the influence of sectarian strife upon the calm detachment proper to academic studies, and particularly the use of university courses for the propagation of the views of any particular religious group. Historically, it is natural to guess that the liberal rationalist ideology played a certain part in the shaping of these provisions, but if that is indeed the case, no direct reference is made to the matter in the Act, and it hardly seems necessary to take it into account in the construction to be put upon the Act in practice. However, the inclusion of these clauses in the Act did have the important result that for many years the University felt itself debarred from introducing any courses in religion. Only within the last few years did the growing conviction of a substantial proportion of the faculty and administration, that a university which ignored the study of religion lacked something necessary to a university worthy of the name, lead to the reconsideration of the implications of the Act and the introduction of courses in religion on an academic and non-sectarian basis. Similar courses have been, or apparently soon will be, introduced in the other provincial universities.

However, the establishment of these courses, and the building up of the structure of a department to handle them, is evidently still to some extent a controversial matter, inasmuch as some regret these steps and consider them to have been retrograde. Both in the faculty, particularly among those whose discipline is in the physical sciences, and in the administration, a significant minority continues to reflect the influences which led to the inclusion of the clauses referred to in the Act, and indeed a more pervasive distrust of even the academic and detached study of religion as likely to be at best a waste of time and money, and at worst a source of illusion, of the propagation of myth for truth. Religion does not conform to the favored paradigm of the physical sciences, and therefore it cannot be a source of truth. Academic people, it is evidently contended, have no business studying such things. Thus, though it seems clear that in Canada at least the balance of academic opinion is in favor of the introduction of such studies, the debate continues, and its terms remain of practical interest to those concerned with the education of undergraduates in religious matters.

Universities such as I have described may rightly be asked to remember that the problem of the study of religion is not a new one. Both in Britain and the United States, in a number of universities whose reputation for academic excellence stands second to none, the question of the study of religion has been faced and answered. In institutions like Oxford and Cambridge, where theology formed part of the traditional curriculum, its study has been revolutionized in the twentieth century by the thoroughgoing application of the critical method, and experience gained there has likewise been applied in newer universities, whose original charter, like that of the North American foundations here discussed, seemed to exclude the study of religion, with the result that flourishing departments have grown up on an academic basis acceptable to all. Moreover, contemporary Western interest in the non-Christian religions of the East has opened up a new field of academic study, and it is hard to believe that this field falls outside the province of the university. The nineteenth century fear of sectarian strife may seem to have somewhat less basis in an age when Christians are drawn together by the ecumenical movement. It would be impossible today to carry on the academic study of Christianity without entering a scholarly community composed of members of many denominations. Likewise, Christians as a whole are interested in, and Christian scholars take part in, the study of the religions that have arisen outside our own Western culture.

Indeed, the case for the establishment of departments of religion in this type of university, which seems to me to be overwhelming, has nothing to do with the contest between "religionists" and "secularists" as such. The question is about the proper role of the university. A university that omits to study anything so important to mankind and its history as religion is clearly shirking part of its own role and risking the justified charge that it is content to be less than a true university. Nor can it be doubted that religion is, at least in part, amenable to academic study. It is here that the important and substantial question arises, and on this point there will be differences of opinion, not only between secularists and believers of various kinds, but among believers themselves. I have said that it cannot be doubted that religion is, at least in part, amenable to academic study. The question is: How far and over what areas is religion amenable to this type of inquiry? Specifically, what is the secular university to do with the truth-claims of the religions? Can it apply the detached and critical methods of academic study to religion, without implicitly or openly denying the claim to truth contained in it? And can religion be properly studied if that claim to truth, to saving truth indeed, is ignored or treated as an academic question, when in fact it is a question of an order very different from the academic? Perhaps even a "religionist" might prefer to keep his beliefs isolated from that sort of treatment.

Now, my contention is that the special traditions of universities, whether they are churchly or secular, are largely irrelevant to this problem, which arises wherever religion is studied in a genuinely academic spirit. To the extent that church-related colleges and universities understand their studies in the way characteristic of our time, the problems I have described will arise for them too. Moreover, it is obvious that the same man, without fundamental alteration in his academic procedures, whether in teaching or in research, may find himself professing the study of religion at one time in a church college and at another time in a secular university. Such indeed has been my own experience during the time I have been in Canada. The problem religion raises for the academic person is simply the reflection of the whole problem of religion in an age which has been characterized by many, by no means all of whom have been non- or anti-Christian, as irreligious, or more precisely nonreligious. It is the academic procedures, with their built-in scepticism and empiricism, which are characteristic of our time, and not the religious ways of thinking which seem to be challenged by them. In other words, the secular university is simply the modern university as such, and church-related universities will be just as "secular" in fact if they are wholeheartedly academic. One is reminded of the remark attributed to Dr. C. F. Weizsaecker, that the task of the Christian scientist is to render the hypothesis of God increasingly superfluous in his own discipline.

It may fairly be claimed, then, that to profess the study of religion in a secular university such as I have described is to be confronted in a typical form with some of the most important problems which face the church today. There is something essentially "healthy" for the Christian to be dragged out of the ghetto in which he is apt to live intellectually, and to be forced to realize that the problems confronting religion in our scientific and secular world are not external problems, to be met by a strategy of "getting religion into the university," but internal ones, which touch the believer himself. Getting religion into the university may prove comparatively simple, unless there is a concentration of prejudice in powerful quarters. The real problems may arise only after you have got it there, and become—as you must if you are to be honest in the reasons you have used to justify its presence—a loyal member of an academic community that lives and works on secular presuppositions. The church that thinks it has scored a victory when it has got religion into a secular university may be reminded that as a result the secular university has got some religious people drawn into its own very powerful life, and it is not only or necessarily the university which will be changed.

It is a commonplace that academic disciplines do not make use of God as a hypothesis within their study. We have grown so used to this fact in its application to science and even to the humanities that it no longer startles us; it fails to awaken us to the realization that we are no longer living in a religious age. But when religion becomes an academic discipline, and is also studied without the hypothesis of God, what then? The religious believer working in such a field will naturally be constantly tempted to invoke the hypothesis of God. But the moment he does so he is invoking "dogma." This matters, not because to do so is to infringe the legalities of a University Act, but because invoking dogma is not being scientific. Religion is not likely to prove an exception to the rule that progress in science has come about on the sole condition of refusing to be dogmatic, and of looking at everything with fresh and sceptical eyes. But if religion becomes a science, what has happened to its claim to give knowledge of a metaphysical world? For the scientific way of thinking, the metaphysical is inadmissible as such. Originally, of course, it is excluded simply on methodological grounds, but it is no long step from methodological exclusion to outright denial. Hence the success of the

crude and early form of logical positivism, which, it may be
suspected, still represents what large numbers of academic
people think, even though the philosophers have abandoned it.

Our academic world is radically empirical in its approach,
and religious studies will be no exception to this, once they
become fully at home in the university. It may be objected
that the humanities do not conform to this scientific model
which we have used to characterize the university's way of
thinking, and that the study of religion naturally belongs
with the humanities. The humanities may differ from science in being concerned with "values," and even with ethical and political commitment, at least occasionally. But no
supernatural sanction is invoked for the values here at work;
they are somehow supposed to arise out of the study itself,
just as the corporate values of the university arise from the
necessities of academic study in general—they are the values
without which academic work would be meaningless or impossible. In the humanities, as much as in the sciences,
"dogma" is excluded, from whatever source it comes. Perhaps this does not exclude the study of Christian dogmas,
considered simply as a historical phenomenon; it certainly
excludes the dogmatic proclamation of the Christian faith
through academic teaching and study. In practice, it will
probably exclude systematic theology, though a case could
be made out for its inclusion.

Long experience has made it perfectly clear that some
propositions are academic, and others are not. Academic
propositions are always public. They can never depend upon
some esoteric source of knowledge, even if that source be
the Christian revelation itself. They are established by evidence, not authority—by research, observation, experiment,
hypothesis, testing, the formulation of theories, and so on.
They must depend upon sources which anyone who will

take the trouble to qualify himself can consult, and thus verify, or, if need be, falsify, the conclusion for himself. Academic propositions may indeed include such things as literary and historical judgments, where the mind of the trained scholar admittedly enters in, and one man's opinion is not as good as another's. But in that case they carry no more authority than the man who makes them, and they can always be validly questioned. Indeed, a healthy academic community will constantly be questioning them, precisely to prevent them from becoming dogmas which would hinder the progress of scholarship. Religious studies must proceed in exactly the same way, or they will fail as scholarship.

On these assumptions, it is evident that the propositions of religion, in its own life, are not academic. This does not mean (though modern man will be tempted to say that it does) that religious propositions are less "true" than academic ones. Propositions derived from revelation, or expressing the faith or the worship of the believer in revelation, may perfectly well be true, and even certain. But they cannot be verified outside the system of religious faith, and to impose them within the university is to impose dogma, in the pejorative as well as in the proper sense. It is not wise for Christian apologists to blur this distinction by endeavoring to assimilate to each other religious and scientific propositions, or by attempting to give to the affirmations of faith the character of hypotheses. Moreover, if, in the manner of certain widely-read theologians, we take religion, or Christianity in particular, to be non-propositional, because it is based on "encounter," religious discourse is still inadmissible in the university, since it can be no part of a professor's task to promote such an "encounter."

The academic study of religion is thus a secular undertaking, no less than the study of science or history. It may be characterized as the formulation of improperly religious propositions about the subject matter of religion, and precisely to the extent that such propositions are religiously improper they are academically admissible. We need not argue a priori that such propositions are capable of being formulated, since so many have been formulated in fact, and we can point to them. Indeed, nowadays their formulation is the chief work even of those who are still called theologians, and those theologians who preserve the old meaning of their trade by formulating properly religious propositions do not expect to be able to carry on their work within the framework of the university. Likewise a man may have two capacities, in one of which he, for example, preaches or gives confirmation instruction, in this capacity uttering properly religious propositions, while in the other he is an academic, making secular utterances about the religion in which he nonetheless believes. So far, however, as the work of theologians has become assimilated to the work of other academic scholars, theology has changed its sense and come to signify what we here prefer to call the academic study of religion. Whether this is good or bad is not my present point. In any case it is a fact, and as such comparable to the revolution in all our studies brought about by the prestige of the physical sciences.

What, then, is the academic study of religion? Perhaps it is easier to begin by saying what it is not. It does not purport to settle the questions of ultimate truth that the religions themselves claim to settle. The aim of academic study is the more modest one of ascertaining what has been done, said, and thought by men in all those aspects of human behavior that we agree to call religious. Thus its place in the academic world is not dependent upon the truth or falsity of the claims of religion in general, or of any religion in particular. Our study would make sense even if all religions were illusory or if it were the case that only one were "true" and all the rest "false." Of course, our study may have some bearing upon claims for truth, especially where these are connected with supposed historical events, and we may be able to throw some light upon the psychological aspects of religion. But it is certainly not to be expected that any more far-reaching results could come of it; indeed, many would say that this is in principle impossible. Moreover, just as the understanding of the ultimate truth that the religions purport to offer demands a kind of submission to their claims, a commitment to their way of life, academic study demands detachment, the questioning, sceptical attitude, that tests everything that the ordinary man takes for granted. Such an attitude is not necessarily in the least incompatible with religious commitment, but it is certainly incompatible with the demand for commitment in advance of study. The academic student of religion cannot be committed in his study to the affirmation or the denial of any specific religious position. The "empathy" which participation brings may help the study of one's own religion, but it may also dull one's critical judgment of evidence. Detachment or hostility may make one critical but may also prevent one from understanding the phenomenon one studies. So subtle is the process of understanding religious positions, so personal the qualities required for it, that no one can say which of the possible attitudes to religion is academically profitable, and total freedom is the only practical attitude, even if it were not the only one allowable by academic ethics. The requirement that no religious test be applied to teacher or student is solidly based in the practical necessities of academic study. Clearly such a study cannot be confused with the preparation of students for a professional career in religion, for example as ministers of Christian churches. Such persons will certainly find some of our academic courses useful, but our aim is the study of our subject for its own sake. Religious studies belong within the sphere of a liberal education as far as the student is concerned, and within that of disinterested research for the faculty member.

It follows from all this that the secular university is a very suitable environment for the academic study of religion. It would be a very great mistake for the churches to try to change such universities in order to make them somehow more suitable homes for the study of religion. Certainly religion may encounter prejudice on the campus of such a university; but if it does, the protest should be made in the name of the very freedom for which such a university stands. It is very doubtful if a so-called Christian university will produce better scholarship in this field. Of course, in practice most of the best North American work in this field is done in theological seminaries, but the advantage of constant contact with colleagues in other disciplines is not to be overlooked, and the secular university abundantly provides it. Among such disciplines, religious studies can take a normal place. Once the discipline is properly understood, it may be seen that it is not "special" in any way; it differs from other disciplines no more than they differ among themselves. The department of religion is just one department among the rest. It needs neither special privileges nor special restrictions.

The field covered by a department of religion may vary in different circumstances. In fact, the meaning of the term "religion" is itself highly debatable. We do not know how to define religion in such a way that it applies equally well to all the phenomena we commonly call religious, and different scholars will give it a narrower or wider application. In the title of such a department, the word "religion" is simply a term of convenience. It does not profess to tell us anything significant about the material studied. Such departments, it seems to me, should study what their members seem able to teach and research into fruitfully and competently. It will not normally be difficult to reach agreement on what for practical and teaching purposes we mean by religion and the religions, and this, or such part of it as we can cover, is our field. If we find a danger of interdepartmental squabbles for a portion of the territory, we may take that, on the assumption that everyone is in good faith, as a signal that we have come upon a topic that might fruitfully be treated by an interdisciplinary approach. The nature of religion itself seems particularly a topic in regard to which the interdisciplinary approach might yield the best results.

I am much less inclined to be optimistic about the results to be attained by the methods of comparative religion. It needs to be said clearly that there is no ground for the rather common assumption that the comparative method will necessarily render the study of religion scientific or academic. Comparative religion seems to assume that it knows what religion is, and that all historic religions are cases of it, so that they are bound to be comparable, to exhibit a sort of family relationship. But as I have indicated, we do not really know what religion is. It may be multiform, so that different religions cannot be studied together without serious confusion; religions may differ radically among themselves and lack structural correspondences with each other, at some points or at many or all. In that case, it is better to approach each religion separately on its own terms, and try to discover what categories are appropriate for its description, without necessarily importing them from the study of other religions. In that case, too, it will be desirable to treat each religion as a world of its own, and not to attempt to judge one religion as higher or lower, or more essentially religious, than another. The comparative method, when employed by scholars who are themselves adherents of a particular religion, can hardly escape the danger that one's own religion supplies the normative categories, and implicitly appears as the highest. That this danger is not merely theoretical the history of scholarship clearly shows.

In the University of British Columbia, these considerations have led us to break altogether with the methods of comparative religion, though we are not engaged in a witchhunt to eliminate all trace of it. We think that more will be learned about a particular religion by a man who is willing to specialize in it than by one whose energy is taken up by comparing it with others. Of course, it may be helpful and illuminating to know enough about religions other than one's own speciality to be in a position to make a comparison or contrast, but this is incidental to the real aim. Likewise, we do not consider that insight into the nature of religion will necessarily come mainly from the pooling of knowledge of all particular religions; it may equally well or better come from the application of the insights of philosophy, anthropology, sociology, psychology, and other disciplines to the material provided by the specialists in the particular religions. The study of the nature of religion is in our view an advanced one, only to be attempted in a systematic way by graduate students, and we make little attempt to deal with it at the undergraduate level, even in an introductory course. In consequence we do not foresee a need to study every religion, even every "great" religion. In our geographical situation on the Pacific, we recognize a particular obligation to develop the study of Asian religions, especially Buddhism, as well as of the Christianity of our own culture. We see no need to compete with other Canadian centers whose interests lie elsewhere.

The mention, just made, of graduate work, raises a further question. In North America, Christian theology is usually studied in seminaries, at the graduate level, and we have made it clear that our own role does not include the training of ministers. Is there a place for graduate work in religion in secular universities? It seems to us not only that there is such a place, but that our role will lie increasingly in the more advanced parts of the field, which are covered by honors and graduate work. Our approach, which lays stress upon the specialized study of particular religions, is naturally at home in advanced work. It is not axiomatic that theological seminaries are the only places in which graduate work in religion may be done, and in any case even these have to call in the aid of universities where the award of the Ph.D. degree is in question. Moreover, a Christian seminary is perhaps not the ideal place to study Buddhism, for example. Graduate work presupposes a solid honors program, and for our purposes this ought to involve some acquaintance with original sources, and hence some knowledge of the languages in which these sources are written. It may be that relatively few students, even in a large university, will be prepared to specialize in studies whose only vocational outcome is likely to lie in the academic profession itself, but in this university the alternatives are not so simple as that, since the student has two majors and is accordingly committed to only a very low degree of specialization. We might expect that our honors students will mostly be going on to graduate work of some kind, whereas our majors will have some other profession in mind and will wish to learn about religion for its own intrinsic interest. Prospective theological students may also find something of value in our courses. This is especially the case with those whose intellectual abilities and interests may in the future incline them to the teaching of theology. For such a person, the more thorough his academic grounding the better, and he might well be encouraged to take honors in religion at the undergraduate level. But many pre-theological students, whose future lies in pastoral work, should perhaps delay their specialized studies in religion until they reach the seminary.

In conclusion, I turn to the consideration of the role of the department of religion in relation to the rest of the university, both from the academic and from the religious point of view. Earlier, I have remarked that the introduction of religious studies into a secular university may be attended with a degree of uneasiness on the part of many members of faculty and of the administration. Part of this uneasiness is undoubtedly due to the past misdeeds of religious people, and the consequent fear that academic courses might be misused for purposes of proselytism for one religious cause or another. The constant tendency of the churches to confuse the academic role of such a department with something called Christian education, or religious education, contributes to the maintenance of these fears. But from another point of view it is natural that there should be uneasiness. The study of religion, perhaps more than another academic subject, challenges us to a very difficult kind of objectivity, and in this case the difficulty is inherent in the subject as such. The accusations of grinding a religious ax, which may so easily be leveled at the professor of religion, are perhaps only the projection of an inner suspicion of one's own objectivity, especially in religious matters. Academic people often allow themselves quite a lot of bias in matters not immediately involved in their professional field, and it may be very easy to convey an impression, in a course in quite another subject, that religion is not worthy of an intelligent man's consideration. Such observations may be less easy to make if religion has its own highly qualified representatives on the campus. But the problem of objectivity faces all academic people, and the department of religion, which may seem to stand under a certain accusation, will be tempted to reply: "Which of you is without sin?"

However, it will certainly not be the aim of such a department to enter into a slanging match with exponents of other disciplines on the question of objectivity. On the contrary, it must aspire to take a normal place in the life of its university, and seek to gain the respect of colleagues in other disciplines by the scholarly excellence of its members. Its academic excellence is in fact of paramount importance. Members of the teaching staff must not be chosen for their church affiliation or their piety, but solely for their qualities as scholars and academic colleagues. Where members of a department of religion are able thus to command the respect of their colleagues in other disciplines, important and fruitful possibilities are opened up of cooperation and exchange, both in interdisciplinary studies and the mutual use of guest lecturers by allied departments. Nothing can be better for a department of religion than to be drawn out of its isolation into conversation with exponents of disciplines such as philosophy, anthropology, sociology, history, and so on. It has often been suspected that one ground for the distrust in which academic people hold theologians and the like is an impression that they are less academically competent than their colleagues in other fields. It is of the greatest importance that this impression should be without basis, and once it is dispelled, much may follow.

Finally, the obvious conclusion from all that has been said is that the academic study of religion has nothing to do with the mission of the church. Certainly, the professor of religion must renounce at the outset any ambition to make converts, either from among his students or his colleagues. Academically, he must be indifferent to the religious consequences of his work. He will in any case not find it easy to

predict what they will be. Students may as easily be shaken
in an existing religious faith by the critical nature of religious studies, as brought closer to faith by the realization
that religion is intellectually respectable. The professor is not
as such a preacher or a missionary, though, like any of his
colleagues in other departments, the member of a department of religion is free to concern himself with the religious
life of the university, and to support the work of the chap-
lains and of student religious clubs. In view of the fears of
proselytism found among the faculty, these are healthy as
well as necessary conclusions.

However, in a more profound sense, more closely connected with New Testament theology than with conven-
tional ideas, the Christian academic, including the professor
of religion who happens to be a Christian, is, like every
other Christian, a missionary. The very condition of his being
such is that he should renounce the wish to make converts by
his work, for without his academic integrity he will have lost
the ground of his missionary status. He is a missionary simply by his *presence*, as a believing, praying, and working
man, in a realm of which Christ is the Lord. He affirms the
lordship of Christ over the university and is thus a missionary, not by seeking to divert the secular university from the
purity of its search for truth into being a Christian and
therefore an apologetic, a *religious* institution (in the pejorative sense), but by being its servant in love. To affirm the
university, precisely in its secularity, and the values of the
university, and to be within it a loyal colleague and a diligent researcher and teacher, is to serve Christ and affirm
his lordship over the university. We do not "love" the university if we are always seeking to alter it, like a woman
who tries to reform the man she married, precisely because
she does not really love him.

Such a service, a mission through *diaconia,* is altogether

remote from the proselytizing activities feared by universities, and sometimes halfheartedly and unsuccessfully undertaken by Christian academics who mistakenly believe it their duty to engage in them. Only a corrupt administration could find a loyal colleague undesirable on the ground of his Christian faith. Such a colleague commends his love for the university, as Christ's university, by the quality of his service to it. In his participation in university life, propaganda for a Christian cause will have no legitimate place. Total silence about his faith, however, is not the right answer, in view of the growing desire of many younger professors to open up the rigid lines of academic neutrality and to introduce a free dialogue between various forms of commitment.

THEOLOGICAL STUDIES
IN COLLEGE AND SEMINARY

PAUL RAMSEY

In an address in connection with the inauguration of James I. McCord as the fourth president of Princeton Theological Seminary, President Robert F. Goheen of Princeton University directed attention to a point in Roland Bainton's *Yale and the Ministry*[1] on which there has been, so far as I know, no or insufficient comment heretofore.

"I am told," President Goheen said, "that, when theological seminaries were first introduced in this country, they took the place of the apprentice system for the training of ministers beyond their study in college. The practice had been for a young man upon graduation to attach himself to an older minister, living in his home to obtain further training in theology and to be brought along in preaching and pastoral care under the tutelage of an older, distinguished man. That system proved inadequate because of the growth of the population and the increasing need for ministers—possibly also because of the burden upon the parson's household, or at least upon his wife, who often had the care of several of these apprentices at once for more than a year's time.

"The establishment of seminaries and divinity schools seems, then, never to have been meant to remove theological education from among the primary tasks of the college. Rather the final stage of a minister's training was simply brought into closer affiliation with university instruction when these schools were located near colleges. Unfortunately, instruction in moral philosophy, theology, and Biblical languages was allowed to lapse in many colleges—though be it said that as late as 1876 the President of Princeton (James McCosh) was supposed to have the religious instruction of the whole undergraduate body directly under his own charge, while he also annually lectured in two courses (one on psychology, the other on the history of philosophy) and finally carried on the duties of the president as well. In any case, it came to be generally accepted, both in seminaries and in universities, that theological study was to be *begun* only after graduation. At most, college was a place where a small amount of pre-theological work might be done.

"Thus it would seem clear that an important reason in past years for any failure of theological education to unite solid learning in those who sustain the ministerial office—and a reason for any injury the Church may have suffered from failure to make possession of learning indispensable—has not been so much a lack of dedication to scholarship on the part of the faculty in our seminaries. Too often it has been because of what colleges and universities have left undone, so that it came to be supposed that all theological education from beginning to end could be crowded into the three years of a seminary curriculum.

"In this connection it is a matter of some pride that Princeton University, with the establishment of its Department of Religion 20 years ago and with the subsequent growth of that department in strength and stature, took a role of leadership in this country in restoring the study of religion (including Biblical and theological work) again to a proper place in the university curriculum. President Dodds said then, in introducing our first professor of religion to the university community, 'I believe that this occasion will in years to come be considered as an historical moment marking a long and significant step toward the accomplishment of a program of first importance to this university and to the nation which it serves.' That has proved true for undergraduate education, and it seems to be proving true also with the department's newer graduate program designed to prepare faculty members who will teach religion as an academic discipline and field of study in other colleges and universities. In any case, it does seem to me that the re-incorporation of the study of religion into the regular undergraduate and graduate work of the university is a step which may prove of first importance for theological education generally. For if the seminaries are able to build upon more and better college instruction, and to make again effective the assumption that it takes at least as long to produce a learned minister as to produce a well-trained historian, classicist, or scientist, then such developments within our colleges and universities can only be regarded as necessary and beneficial."[2]

The foregoing paragraphs have been quoted in full because by simply reflecting upon them we ought to be able to see at once the many things now being done in theological instruction, in both colleges and seminaries, that quite prevent the attainment of real strength in the logical education in this country. The colleges and seminaries are now in the middle of another year, and in the main they are continuing to operate as they always have. For all the supposed theological revival of recent decades, and despite the fact that certain practices current in college departments of religion and in seminaries can be demonstrated to be an unparalleled break with the basic educational assumptions that prevailed when theological studies constituted a discipline at least equal in importance to other fields of learning, no radical changes have been effected or even proposed. I shall undertake in this essay to air my views, asking only that the reader know *that I know* that the opinions expressed are from the particular parochial standpoint that my limited experience has given me, and are set forth as a small contribution to the discussion of some very important matters at stake in the future and for the increasing strength of theological education in this country.

I. College and University Departments of Religion

Few if any of the college departments of religion established in the last three decades were meant simply as "window dressing," or to please a sector of the alumni body or the parents of students with religious allegiances. They were a genuine effort to restore theological studies to a rightful place among the fields accessible for serious study. Nevertheless, it can certainly be said that the stress was too much upon only "enriching" the student's educational experience by providing him with the opportunity for "some" work in a field unquestionably adjacent, and only adjacent, to his main intellectual concerns. Religion was certain to be adjunct to the major concentration of future lawyers, doctors, or businessmen; it was also adjunct to the major concentration of future ministers and theologians, who while in college were supposed to learn literature or economics, etc., with a smattering of a beginning in the study of religion, while their fellow students, seriously aiming at becoming historians or scientists, were beginning already to concentrate on their life's work. Of course, the need for broader humanistic or liberal education has recently been stressed for all professions, but *along with,* not *instead of,* the student's acquiring a foundation of three or four undergraduate years of study in the subject matter he intends to pursue in graduate work. In contrast, students going on for graduate work in theology have been advised to aim at breadth in the very center of their future concerns as students, and to postpone obtaining a foundation or as yet seriously direct- ing themselves to a subject matter that (it must be pre- sumed) is believed to be so thin it can easily be covered in three graduate years while also taking practical profes- sional courses. I shall call this the "God and . . ." theory of undergraduate education in religion. Because God and a man's religion obviously are related to everything, they doubtless disappear into everything or at least are best got at by the study of one or more of those things. Thus, theol- ogy with its proper object and religion as an independent sphere of human experience and the literature of religion as a vast and complex field requiring all the powers of the mind to master are set to the side—this in the name of paying them our highest tribute, that religion or man's response to God should pervade all things and can by no means ever be separated from life and approached directly as such. The wonder is that college teachers of religion were not all called Adjunct Professors. (Far too many *are* exactly that: they are teacher-chaplains or teacher-ministers in a local church, and not teacher-scholars in their main vocation.)

The stress has been too little upon academic responsi- bility of the highest order to and for the entire range of theological studies as a university discipline. Thus, colleges that diversify and multiply teachers in other departments are content to have only one, two, or three teachers of reli- gion. It requires of course, it seems to be believed, more specialists to cover English literature or history. There will be one man for American history, another for modern Eu- ropean, etc., each responsible for three centuries, in colleges who appear to believe they have discharged their responsibility in their departments of religion by employing a teacher to cover twenty centuries of the history of Christianity alongside of one Bible man (this field itself including the life and literature of more than a millennium)! The result is that at this late date in the so-called restoration of religion to the college curriculum, it is a fact that almost the only numerically large departments of religion are those in colleges that have a *required* course.

I do not now question the educational value of such a course for the students; but it is important to query what is happening to the theological scholarship of men a main part of whose professional work is the repetition over and over again of the same elementary course. The absence of serious and diverse advanced work in religion, comparable to that of other departments of learning and elected by a number of students who are proposing themselves to become competent in the field by both the undergraduate and the graduate study of it, in most of the college departments of religion must be remembered when it is asked why —in view of the energetic life of the churches in this country and in view of the same vitality in our educational institutions—there is such a lack of theological scholars of first rank in the United States. The lack of a sufficient pool of theological scholars is revealed every time a vacancy occurs in some seminary faculty, and teachers begin to move around like Methodist preachers used to! On every such occasion we should ask what has happened to the doctors graduated every year for the last three decades. They simply had not the positions which in numbers and in the description of their duties sustained them as teacher-scholars. The theological revival has meant not much revival of theological scholarship and of serious theological work founded upon four, five, or six years of study with our undergraduate and graduate faculties but only the revival in some quarters of some interest in continental trends that formerly were ignored. This has been a chapter in the foreign influences in American life (for which God be praised from our gaps); it has not yet become much of a chapter in the history of American theology or of broadly based American theological scholarship.

Some years ago I had occasion to talk with a college teacher of religion who had been asked to accept a position at a large secular urban institution. He was the author of a number of books, and had considerable bargaining power at that moment, since the university in question evidently wanted very much to add him to its faculty and administration. I was dismayed to find that his main condition was that he be allowed to head the establishment of an interdenominational graduate "school of religion." The word "school" seemed mighty important, after the professional "school" of journalism in that place, even though the main advantage he as dean would receive from this concession would be the task of himself raising an enormous amount of money ever to hope to place such a school on a parity with other existing centers of theological study. I tried to tell him that the expression "department," graduate and undergraduate, had an even more respectable lineage and would better symbolize the rightful place of religion in a large university today and the acceptance of his faculty as scholarly teachers in their own right by their colleagues. I suggested that he should build upon and with the small group of undergraduate teachers that were there already, at the same time requiring that no teacher should be long regarded as fit to teach undergraduates or to be promoted in the ranks of the faculty unless by evident scholarly growth such a teacher was also fit to teach graduate students in theology. I was twice dismayed to hear him say, speaking of one of these men, that he belonged in college teaching because he "raised a lot of interesting questions among the students" and "stirred up concern."

Such an attitude which, perhaps only implicitly in our practices today is more widespread than I like to think, indicates that we have achieved only a token reintegration of religion to college and university courses of study. This also means a severe limitation upon our graduate schools where Ph.D. study in religion is presently pursued, which we are now beginning to feel acutely. The colleges have not taken the necessary steps beyond the establishment of departments of religion to strengthen and diversify them in scholarly specialization. This means that at the moment when we face a huge increase in college enrollments and when the need for an increasing number of competent teachers in all other fields is very great, the projected job openings for college teachers of religion in the next decade is down at the bottom of the fields, along with home economics.

This is not only because the biggest increase in college enrollment is taking place in state universities which, except in a few instances, have not gone in for religion departments. It is true not only because in a number of independent, liberal colleges the farther west you go—on the premise that the way to be objective in the teaching of religion is to be other-directed—courses in Buddhism may be offered but not courses in Bible or in Christianity. It is also because college and university administrators, faculties, and departments of religion have not paid theological studies the respect they give to other fields of learning as requiring the appointment of a *corps* of competent scholars, not just one or two who—if they were once on their way to contributing something significant to theological studies—will soon cease to be as intellectually alive as once they were in the eternal round of raising questions in a field nobody is supposed to begin studying seriously as an undergraduate.

It is clear that this next great step must be taken in the college teaching of religion, or else not only will college instruction fall short of its goal but centers of graduate instruction will have to limit rather than enlarge the number of students enrolled for study with the fine theological scholars on their faculties. This will be because the need for opening teaching positions has not been soundly thought through in terms of academic principle. As one of the orthodox said upon the rise of that pietism that still too much infects the role of religion in our colleges, if pietism prevails we may have to close our theological auditoria—or at least not use to the full the resources that are available for stimulating graduate theological study under the great scholars there assembled. In this way the replenishment of theological scholarship is thwarted, the colleges suffer, theology will never again become the disciplined intellectual task it was in every great religious age or in any era in which religion had any impact at all upon the cultural enterprises of mankind. Finally, the church suffers in that piety and enlightenment will continue to be separated in bed and board, while zealous and laborious seminary graduates are hastily produced who began the part-time study of theological subjects only three years ago, but not godly and learned ones to the enduring blessing of church and society.

The truth is that, on any sound academic analysis of the fields in religion, there should be *more* rather than fewer specialized scholar-teachers in college departments of religion than in many other departments of learning. A hundred years or more ago, students took degrees in "natural philosophy" instead of in physics or chemistry or biology. The vastness of man's knowledge of nature has required this field now to be broken down into separate departments. Religion as an academic discipline is today in about the same state as "natural philosophy" once was when teachers were strained beyond the possibility of competently encompassing their subject matter. This is not to suggest that the step of dividing the field into separate departments needs now to be taken; rather, that at the very least the vastness and diversity of the fields in religion, both in methodology and content, need to be taken into account by college departments and administration in analyzing their intrinsic responsibilities if religion is to be studied and taught well by their faculties.

One concluding comment upon the problems of an undergraduate department of religion in a university where also there is a divinity school and a doctoral program in religion. Here you have three different degree programs—the B.A., the B.D., and the Ph.D.—each a separate if sometimes overlapping community of learning with junior and senior members (i.e., students and faculty). Let it be well understood that I prize none of these learned and learning communities above the others, nor do I think that one sort of man will prove the most prized teacher in one but not in another of them. The vocation of seminary teacher is as much a scholarly vocation as any other, and no more. The qualities that make a good teacher of graduate students are needed to sustain in the long run the best undergraduate teaching, and vice versa.[3] My parochial experience fixes this as one of my most basic convictions concerning theological education at all so-called "levels." If I may refer to this plank in the platform upon which I teach, when in 1955 the Faculty of Princeton university moved to establish in its Department of Religion a program of graduate study leading to the Ph.D. degree the question to be decided was not whether the undergraduate department should now be allowed to admit and teach graduate students but whether we should be permitted to continue to teach religion to undergraduates unless we also engaged in graduate instruction like our colleagues in all other departments with the stimulus this gives to any teacher to keep alive his scholarly interests.

Nevertheless, it has often proved especially difficult to get an undergraduate program in religion off the ground in places where seminary and graduate theological education are also offered—for no intrinsic but for purely practical reasons. Human nature being what it is—so many people connected with it—the conditions for strong and diversified theological studies in the college often come off third best in struggles over the budget, in the reasons for calling a man to the faculty, and in the ranking of the different teaching roles in importance.

While the same competencies in a teacher-scholar are needed for college, seminary, or graduate teaching, it is practically impossible for an individual to combine all three teaching roles at once. He can teach in any combination of two of these "levels" at the same time, while participating fully in the student-faculty community in each case. He probably needs to be involved in more than just one of these, but he ought never attempt all three. The particular combination (whether B.D. with B.A., or B.D. with Ph.D., or B.A. with Ph.D. courses) need not be fixed forever. But a teacher who consents to teach religion to undergraduates, however distinguished a scholar he may be, should consent to do so for a period of time from three to five years. If he cannot do this, his services ought not to be invited for the sake of momentarily enriching the offerings and embellishing the department. Far better to employ a younger man who will make this a major part of his concern, and with whom a college faculty can be built.

Yet how often in seminary and graduate centers is the opposite decision made, and the undergraduate department of religion permanently immobilized from a proper assumption of responsibility for subject matters in the field of religion in the charge of relatively continuing members of the faculty? And how often in the subtle factors that determine hiring and promotion is the *same* weight given to a scholar's undergraduate teaching as to seminary or graduate teaching? How often does the need to augment the B.D. faculty prevail over these other considerations? There are still, even in the colleges of our great universities, too many Adjunct Professors of Religion; and the development and destiny of the undergraduate teaching of religion in universities that have divinity schools are a crucial test of whether, *in fact* today if not in history or in theory, seminaries are established to remove theological study from among the primary tasks of the college. At the same time, these seminaries and graduate schools are afforded a special opportunity to demonstrate that they were meant, and mean, to build firmly and directly upon the foundation of a full course in the study of religion, theology, Bible, philosophy of religion, church history, biblical languages, etc., at the college "level." The faculties of seminaries in university centers have a unique opportunity to support the strengthening of the undergraduate department in that place, in order that the day may come when graduates with majors in this department may be regarded as normative for admission to seminary, and the deficiency in the backgrounds of other admittees be measured accordingly.

II. The Theological Schools

How shall the theological seminaries—all of them—do this? Certainly not by any longer enforcing or recommending the statement about pre-theological education of the American Association of Theological Schools, usually reprinted or summarized by each seminary in its catalogue and circulated to hundreds of prospective "graduate" students while they are still in college. The AATS statement drawn up thirty-five years ago had the purpose of preventing candidates trained in agriculture, pharmacy, etc., from applying for immediate entrance to seminary. This recommendation concerning "Collegiate Preparation" by the AATS and "heartily endorsed by X Seminary" contains undeniably much that is sound. Concerning "Subjects in Pre-Seminary Study," under "Religion" in the catalogue I am using, however, the statement reads: "A thorough knowledge of the content of the Bible is indispensable, together with an introduction to the major religious traditions and theological problems in the context of the principal aspects of human culture outlined above," to which the notation is appended: "Three semester hours."

To this, on its face, the following objections have immediately to be made: (1) This statement asks too much in three semester hours; to wit, a "thorough" knowledge of the Bible and some disciplined knowledge, even "introductory," of the major religious traditions and of theological problems. In courses worth giving at all to decent undergraduates, that would require five or six semesters' work or more. It is as if the graduate schools of English literature directed their prospective applicants to plan their college courses so as to acquire a thorough knowledge of the major classics of Western literature together with an introduction to the major literary forms and the aesthetic-critical problems connected with the perceptive study of them; and having inserted the injunction that all this should be viewed in the context of the principal aspects of human culture generally, noted that such learning is expected to be acquired in a year and a half specifically devoted to it, while taking four other college courses at the same time.[4]

We shall have to ask whether in practice the seminaries act as if this has been done and give the student credit for it upon entrance. The fact is that he is exposed to additional general courses in Bible and courses introductory to the major religious traditions and to theological problems in their cultural context all over again, which the student is required to take. At least the presupposition is that he will take them, so that he would be venturesome indeed who would enroll in one of the advanced courses offered by the very professor who gives the introductory one, and even perhaps morally culpable who would try to avoid what he has to do now to *begin* his theological work upon sure foundations for the first time. The statement that he may already have made a beginning serves often only as an ideological formulation having no relation to the realities of seminary education.

The statement also (2) asks too little study of biblical literature, theology, philosophy and history of religion, Christian ethics, and history of Christianity in their own right. This is because of the stress placed upon "the context of the principal aspects of human culture" rather than upon religion as an independent object of knowledge—with integration of the student's knowledge of this with his other college subjects to come later, after he has gained a sufficient foundation in both religion and the other fields he chooses to study. That too little theological learning is supposed to be built upon by his seminary education is further stressed by the unqualified recommendation: "Of the various possible areas of concentration, where areas of concentration are required, English, philosophy, and history are regarded as the most desirable." A knowledge of other aspects of human culture is, of course and correctly, the aim of general education in the first two college years, and of minors in addition to majors in some colleges, and of elective courses in junior and senior years. But the seminaries still propose to continue to build upon the disestablishment of religious literature, history, and thought in the colleges, and its conscious removal from the center of a student's preparation for graduate work. Plainly, their conception of the college education of a learned minister is the "God and . . ." viewpoint.

We shall have to ask whether the seminaries act as if this has been accomplished in college, and give the student credit upon entrance for being prepared in theological studies "in the context of the principal aspects of human culture." Do they treat him as now ready to devote himself exclusively to graduate, disciplined work exclusively in theological subjects broadly understood in their depth and variety? Instead there suddenly takes place a curious shift of our angle of vision upon the college graduate going into the ministry. Because of his vocational decision, and in order to avoid the stuffiness of professionalism, he is, ironically enough, assumed to be already well versed in religion, and therefore gravely in need of not becoming too specialized and of relating his work to the context of a number of the principal aspects of human culture that remain unlearned.

So the "God and . . ." philosophy of theological education continues to prevail as the premise of many, if not most or all, seminary curricula. A breath of fresh air must be made to blow upon the student who—odd as this may seem when measured against the facts or by the AATS recommendations—can only be supposed to have already pored too long over his theological tomes or for too much of his voyage to have set his sails to the winds of doctrine. Psychology, sociology, politics, literature, drama, etc., must now be brought to his attention in "God and . . ." courses, lest he forget that religion and Providence are related to the whole of life, and lest indeed he know too little about other important aspects of life. Thus, theology, long ago dismissed from her queenly functions, serves too often as a lady-in-waiting to other sciences, as these are got up in seminary.

It is remarkable that during the recent decades of the so-called theological revival all sorts of ancillary programs doing the work that properly belongs to liberal arts colleges have continued to be multiplied in the seminaries. These are the things for which seminary administrators can most easily secure new funds from individual and corporate donors. The interests of the students may have meant their return in somewhat greater numbers to the classical fields of biblical, historical, theological, and philosophical subjects. But there is little observable influence upon the overall shape of the curriculum, simplifying it and providing for it a central aim and direction—to the end that students (who are supposed to be largely beginning their study of the immense fields of religion) will now take the time and concentration needed for this. Theirs seems a collection of studies, rather than a course of study.

Then there is "God and Field Work" to think of. H. Richard Niebuhr objects to the view that a student does church work while in seminary only because in the future he may have to teach Sunday school, etc. He criticizes "the theory that such participation in the church's work is self-loving preparation for the exercise of future other-loving action." He demands instead, as the premise of field work, requiring "the young man or young woman engaging in it to be a minister now, rather than to look forward merely to a future ministry." This would "put the intellectual love of God and neighbor into the rich context of the present moment."[5]

This suggestion is correct, of course, in that any adequate justification of field work, as presently conducted, would have to justify it constantly, or as an activity continuing for all three years of seminary education. As such, all that can be said in support of field work is that it supports the student. Surely Niebuhr is wrong in holding field work to be desirable in order to set the intellectual love of God and man-before-God in the rich context of the present moment. Is not concentrated theological study also done in the rich context of the present moment before God? To say that the student only comes into the full riches of the present moment by going out of the library seems an evidence of the general anti-intellectualism abroad today.

Moreover, this does violence to the Protestant doctrine of vocation. In our vocations we not only live before God in the special space or positions to which we are called. We also live before him in our special *times*. This means that the chief business of a theological student is, for the time being, to be a *student*. Of course, a seminary is not only "that place or occasion where the church exercises its intellectual love of God and neighbor" in a proper theoretic study of "God and man-before-God in their interrelation." It is also the place and occasion for "bringing reflection and criticism to bear on worship, preaching, teaching, and the care of souls."[6] How to keep these in balance may be a problem; and for the latter, experience in the action of a congregation may be necessary. (This experience the student may have as a layman and not as a professional.) But in everything it is the intellectual love of God and man, as Christians understand them, that is in exercise and undergoing training, looking to the day (perhaps after a year's internship at the end of the theological course of study) when the student graduates to become a minister who unites in the love of God no more of an effective love in practice than a skilled love of learning.

It is idle to suppose that most professional schools of theology presently aim at or achieve the levels of attainment in rigorous study and discipline of mind in their students and respect for the integrity and worth of their science as do certain other professional schools equally concerned—eventually—with practice. If anywhere they fail to do this, it would not be inappropriate to raise the question whether this may not be due in large part to the omnipresence of field work, and to its economic necessity in most cases. It is inexplicable that a seminary faculty should add on a fourth year, justified for one-half that time as an internship comparable to that which medical students take, without at the same time taking the step of withholding them up to that point from field work altogether. At the least, we should not allow the student's economic necessities to cause us to invent arguments that this is a good thing constantly. An adequate theological education cannot be obtained by minimum time on it in college and by part-time study in seminary. Yet this is what now is most often attempted. Those responsible for the training of men for any other profession today would be ashamed to admit this in public.

Of course, nothing college or seminary faculties can do will itself soon alter the fact that, in our culture, the most intelligent young men still do not, on the average, enter the ministry, but go into medicine, law, science, or business. The day when the church and theology called for the highest service of the most highly endowed of our youth may not come again. It certainly will not, unless we find a way to instill in them a real respect for theological learning and the exclusive commitment of their finest powers and many years to it. Ours not to say whom God gives to this calling. Ours only to make sure that we do not prove unfaithful to them by lack of single-minded devotion on our own parts to the cause that is between us or by failing to insist that it takes time and rigorous discipline of the mind to become a learned minister or teacher.

This can best begin to be done by explicitly formulating the graduate theological curriculum to presuppose a foundation already built in the college study of religion. Instead, we seem everywhere alert, in effect, to deny that theological subjects run as broadly or as deep as any other subject a student can take in college, or are as liberalizing and as well calculated to lead him on to a more profound understanding of any other of the enterprises of mankind. He who falls into a well while reading the works of some great theologian will find he can see the stars at noonday—and more of the horizon than if he is concentrating in any other area.

It is true that certain seminaries recognize the existence of college departments of religion, and the quality of the study of religion which the entering student may have already accomplished, by permitting him in select instances to omit one or two of the introductory courses normally prescribed for the first year. A student may accelerate in strength by going on to advanced courses in some areas. But this still takes as *standard* the beginning of theological or biblical studies only in seminary, while treating a man who may have done this earlier as an exception to the rule. The shift in our thinking and practice which can and should and must take place would define as standard the beginning of serious study of religion in undergraduate college, while treating as an exception a man who enters seminary without this background. The fact that he may not have had a solid and competent introduction to the fields in religion would be regarded as a deficiency to be made up; and, of course, for some time to come seminaries will have to continue to offer such introductory work. Men who begin their theological studies in seminaries would, of course, have to extend the time required for them to earn a B.D. degree, since they entered such a course of study with deficiencies in comparison with men who came with a background of several years of college work in the fields of religion. If this is not the case, the B.D. is scarcely a graduate degree. Until this is the case, the premise of our instruction is that, while it takes many years of training to make a good historian or scientist or doctor, one can become a theologically educated minister in no time at all.

Steps have been taken to move in this direction by the recent revision of the curriculum at Drew Theological Seminary. There the statement is made, under the division of the Bible, that, while Old and New Testament Introduction are prerequisite to all the advanced courses, "exemptions from either or both of these prerequisites may be granted, however, *on the basis of undergraduate work*" (italics added). Here again the standard seems to be that entering students take, for the first time, these introductory courses, even if "exemptions" may be granted. When we look at the *practice,* however, of the faculty at Drew with regard to the class that entered in 1960, the first year the new curriculum was in operation, it will be seen that theirs may be a significant step in revolutionizing the assumptions of American theological education. Of 83 B.D. and M.R.E. students entering Drew this year without advanced standing from any other theological school, 50.5 percent were exempted from the introductory courses in *both* Old and New Testament. An additional 2.5 percent were exempted from the beginning Old Testament course only, and 9.5 percent from the beginning New Testament course only. Only 37.5 percent were required to take both introductory courses before taking advanced Bible courses which the majority of the entering class were judged to have been prepared to enter by their college courses. Plainly, this practice is ahead of the faculty's statement of their new plan of study, since introductory courses taken at Drew are not, as stated, "prerequisite" to advanced work in Bible for 62.5 percent of the entering class. At most, these courses at Drew *or* solid work in a college department of religion are the actual prerequisites; or better, 62.5 percent of these students, by faculty decision, set the *standard* of introductory preparation in one or both Testaments, while the faculty at Drew continues to provide introductory courses for the remaining 37.5 percent who entered seminary with a *deficiency* in their preparation for graduate study. In subsequent years, the plan is to apply this same treatment to other fields and not only to Bible.

Another way may be indicated in which seminaries can lead the way to restoring theological instruction at the college level—by themselves presupposing it. It can be stated, without peradventure of successful dispute, that the revival of interest in Biblical Theology has made exegesis, based on the original languages, indispensable for the serious student of Scripture. Yet about the only faculties actively rethinking the question of a requirement in biblical languages are those who are thinking of dropping it, or requiring only Greek instead of both Greek and Hebrew. Certainly it is true that, in the more traditional seminaries which still maintain a requirement in two languages, too much of the time of the students is consumed by this. Too often they do not gain a mastery of these languages, so that these become real tools for theological studies; or they do not do so early enough. They do not have Hebrew. They only have to have had it. And by that time, they are graduated and the period in their lives of full-time theological study is over.

Years spent in the elementary study of biblical languages should not be a part of the graduate study of Bible and theology. They should rather be prerequisite to it. Gone past restoring are the days when theological students brought both

Hebrew and Greek with them from college. Yet we need not be content with this situation with regard to Greek. Seminaries that are thinking of dropping language requirements for graduation might well consider making Greek prerequisite to *admission*. And seminaries who long ago dropped both should consider restoring Greek as a requirement—for *admission*. Of course, I know that at present only a few men would meet this requirement. Others should be admitted as "qualifying" students, and elementary courses in Greek will still have to be offered in seminary—but to afford most students the chance to make up a *deficiency*.[7]

To define a *normal* expectation does not mean to define the average. One does not consult numbers or college records in stating the *standard* needed to put the student in a position to enter three years of graduate study which has the study of the Bible at its center. The result of this step taken by seminary faculties would be to put the colleges on their mettle in the "pre-theological" courses they offer to men intending this profession, and to encourage more undergraduates to build more solid foundations. It would also be to remove from the seminary the time spent in elementary preparation to be able to study the Bible—if only by extending the length of time students with this deficiency have to spend before they imagine they are educated minister-theologians, or yet in a position to begin to become such. This would be an adjustment to the widely acknowledged fact that three years is scarcely enough time for theological education, and far sounder than the announcement of four-year B.D. programs at a few places several years ago, which on closer inspection turned out to devote half of this additional year to supervised field work.

Whether or not I am correct that a greater integration between the study of languages in college with exegetical and theological studies in seminary would be desirable does not matter. This is only one illustration of the thesis of this essay,

namely, that seminaries should promptly move to get rid of
their introductory work (except to repair deficiencies) and
make standard the expectation that all of this will have been
done in college. By "introductory" is meant not generalities
about the subject but an understanding of the fields of religion up to a rather high level of comprehension. There is no
barrier to this being done in what the colleges can and should
provide. Of course, there will remain the objection that
the student needs to have each professor's viewpoint fully
laid out before him, or that he may have unsuspected gaps
in his training, or that we cannot be sure he is ready to go
on in strength unless the seminary has immediate control of
his progress and can insure that what the B.D. graduate
should know is begun, continued, and ended on their premises. Here we need not point again to the college departments, or call attention to ways of evaluating a student's
transcript or testing him, or discriminating among different
college backgrounds in measuring deficiencies or qualifications for really advanced work. It might better be claimed
that, if the purpose of graduate education is not to store
the head with information but to discipline the mind, it
does not much matter that in exegesis courses a student has
only done *Matthew* and not *John, Corinthians* and not *Romans,* in his entire course; or that he has mastered the
thought and life of the church in one period and not in
another; or has shaped his own theological reflection up
against a thorough knowledge of, say, Augustine, Aquinas,
Luther, Schleiermacher, and Barth, and knows scarcely anything at all about anybody else. Lacunae in his coverage
can be made up later, if he knows how to do this and has
experienced the rich rewards of having done so in areas he
selected in choosing his courses. You can produce a theological *student* without his being informed just a little bit on
everything in all the fields, classic and ancillary, that surround
him in seminary; and even without his having done every-

thing available in any one field, provided he has mastered the methodology and skills needed to make an understanding of anything about it an *event* in *his own* intellectual life and *his own* achievement by self-directed study and research.

Until fairly radical steps are taken in this direction, the seminaries spell "disestablishmentarianism" for religion in the college curriculum. What is more, they undercut themselves, and have not done all that might be done to make theological study graduate. Unless they stand for graduate theological work, they will continue to stand for the removal (except in service-courses) of the study of religion from liberal arts education.

(Reprinted from *Theology Today*, Vol. XVII, No. 4, January 1961.)

FOOTNOTES

1. New York: Harper and Bros., 1957
2. Robert F. Goheen, "The Seminary and the University," *Princeton Seminary Bulletin*, LIV, 1 (July, 1960), pp. 9-10.
3. If this statement is correct, the public announcement of the policies of the Rockefeller Doctoral Theological Program should be fundamentally reexamined and revised. This states the purpose of the Program "to strengthen Protestant theological education in the United States by aiding those students who evidence high promise as scholars, *and who have teaching at a theological school as a clear vocational goal*" (italics added). The purpose should rather be to enlarge the pool of theological scholars who have been enabled to give full time to their studies, whether they think they are going to teach in college or in seminary. This is especially the case when one remembers how nebulous in most cases is any such "clear vocational goal" and notices the constant recruitment of seminary faculties not only from one another but also from the colleges. The statement of this provision by the Doctoral Selection Committee, in their report to the Board of Directors of the Rockefeller Program, was considerably better. This required only "a genuine possibility for theological school teaching." Even that, however, does not recognize that theological school teaching is always a genuine possibility, except in rare instances, for any man who has become the sort of scholar-teacher needed in either college or seminary.
4. It is true that the reader is cautioned that "this is a statement in minimal terms"; but this means not that the student may build more soundly by taking more time to acquire this minimum, but only that it may be "possible to include many other elements in one's college courses, while still working in what the Association regards as the first essentials."
5. *The Purpose of the Church and Its Ministry* (New York: Harper & Bros., 1956), p. 132.
6. *Ibid.*, pp. 110, 113.
7. At present, students entering Princeton Theological Seminary are permitted, by examination in Greek, to go immediately into exegesis courses. In a new revision of the curriculum at Princeton Theological Seminary, Greek will be regarded as a prerequisite. While it may be too optimistic to hope that eventually the seminary will teach *no* beginning Greek, this may help to stem the decline of Greek in the colleges. In any case, it keeps clear the distinction between elementary liberal arts education and graduate professional studies, even when some of the former may have to be taken in seminary.

II. SEMINARY EDUCATION

Training
of
Theologians

INTEGRATION OF PRE-SEMINARY AND SEMINARY CURRICULA

ERNEST C. COLWELL

Theological education formally became a graduate education a generation ago. It became graduate education by separating the seminary sharply from the college. The adoption of the A.B. degree by the American Association of Theological Schools as a prerequisite for admission to a seminary was done with the laudable intention of "upgrading" seminary education—of grading it up to the level of graduate work. Prior to that time the line between college and seminary study was vaguely drawn. Weak junior colleges shared faculty strength (or weakness) with the seminary, whose graduates had seldom progressed beyond the bachelor's level.

Just as the North Central Association at the end of the 19th and the beginning of the 20th century dug a deep ditch between the secondary school and the college, the American Association of Theological Schools in the second quarter of this century has separated the theological school from the college, and incidentally has removed the college from theological education. Ironically this removal has blocked the achievement of graduate quality in theological education.

116

It is my contention that we now have the opportunity of correcting this error through the establishment of rational cooperation between the college and the seminary in the task of theological education.

I

At first, the A.A.T.S. acted as though just an A.B. degree as such would be adequate; therefore there was very little specification of the content-meaning of the A.B., and no serious effort was made to insure that the local seminary would insist on any of these specifications for pre-seminary work. But there was a strong insistence on admitting students with the A.B. degree or its equivalent, and on admitting them from accredited colleges.

The transition to a student body composed of college graduates did not take place at once. The first list of accredited schools (1938) included 46 institutions; more than one out of four of these had from 25% to 75% of its student body without college degrees. Constant pressure from both the A.A.T.S. and the major Protestant churches has reduced the percentage of non-A.B. students in accredited schools to insignificant proportions today.

The folly of insisting on the form without the substance became clear to me when I was Dean of the Divinity School of the University of Chicago and studied the college transcripts of an entering class.

At that time the "minimum list" as published by the Association included 15 or 16 subjects totalling 42-61 semester hours. The entering class (in 1939) of 47 students all came with A.B. or equivalent degrees from almost as many accredited colleges. They came also with 117 deficiencies, ranging from 1 to 7 per student—5 had no history, 18 no economics, 2 no English literature, 8 no sociology, 16 no biology, 1 no English composition, 6 no psychology, and 7 no philosophy. Evidently the requirement of an A.B. degree from an accredited college does not provide the "broad and comprehensive college education" which the A.A.T.S. regards as desirable.

II

Granted that other schools were better situated, had a more homogeneous student body, or had students drawn from a very few colleges, and so on, why would the Association be content with such a requirement? The answer lies in the one definite achievement of the requirement: *it postponed the study of religion to the beginning of the seminary's program.* The Association's attitude toward the study of religion in college has been one of hostility from its birth to the present day.

My own memories of its proceedings do not (mercifully) go all the way back to the beginning. But I vividly remember a meeting of the Association in 1940 at which a handful of us mavericks had to fight for more than two hours to get approval for the inclusion of biblical studies (for not more than two semesters) in the list of college courses suggested to pre-seminary students. The majority position was that the student should wait until he reached the seminary to study religion to avoid misinstruction or to make room for two more electives in Animal Husbandry (the work of the ministry requires an incredibly broad preparation, especially the Town and Country Ministry!).

Recently the Association has revised its list of prerequisites for the pre-seminarian (see Bulletin No. 24, June, 1960). The revision has improved details without making sense out of the list. The list has doubled in length since 1938; it suggests that the student take 30 semester courses or 90 semester hours or approximately three-fourths of his college work in specified areas. This is at once too much and too little specification: too much in detail to be seriously expected of many college graduates and too little because of escape-options that permit, for instance, no biology and the avoidance of all social sciences except psychology. The requirement in religion has been increased from two to three semesters. In these three courses the student is modestly required to achieve "a thorough knowledge of the content of the Bible . . . together with an introduction to the major religious traditions and theological problems in the context of the principal aspects of human culture." But the student is in effect urged not to major in religion, but rather in either English, philosophy, or history.

III

The arguments in support of the ban on religion as a collegiate study are superficial and unrealistic. Yet the reasons for their existence are worth examining.

(1) The minister of a Christian church in America today needs a broad education. (2) He needs education in the natural sciences, in the humanities, and in the behavioral sciences. He should know the language of his own nation so that he may read, write, and speak it with a modest competence. He should know two other languages: the mathematical language of science, and the language of another national culture. He should know some subject above the level of elementary introduction. (3) A "major" in any subject other than religion is obviously "broader" than one in religion, which he will be studying intensively and narrowly in the seminary. (4) If a "major" is taken at all, it should be a relatively small major.

Arguments 1 and 2 are sound, but 3 and 4 are false and unreasonable. Nine out of ten American colleges allow a *maximum* of two years' work for a broad liberal arts education. Until recently this program in breadth was restricted to the *first* two years; that it is now possible to spread it throughout the period of college residence has not increased its amount. It is not due to departmental repentance and self-denial. Quite the contrary, for the departmental specialized program to be able to carry its students to the level of educational achievement required by the graduate school for admission, extensive sequences of courses reaching through more than two years were required. Thus some parts of "broad liberal arts education" had to be pushed out of the first two years.

Nine out of ten American colleges live and move and have their being in programs of specialization controlled by departments whose *raison d'être* is in the Graduate School. These departments make up the power structure of the college. They insert their pre-specialization programs at the earliest possible point in the curriculum, baptizing them (if necessary) as General Education courses. They control the "distribution" requirements in such a way as to make them subservient to their own specialized programs.

As a result of this situation, it is futile to list the tremendous amount of distribution suggested by the most recent A.A.T.S. list. It is folly to describe the typical English or history or philosophy major as likely to contribute either breadth or depth for the future minister. In the first two he will be exceptionally fortunate if he escapes tedious and insignificant (i.e. thoughtless) pedantry. In the third, only an electronic computer could record the high degree of probability of his being limited to the doctrines of a single philosophical "school."

If the seminaries wish their students to have a broad liberal arts education, they must define and insist upon its minimum constituents, and they must thoughtfully consider whether or not a major in religion is desirable today.

IV

A broad liberal arts education does not ban collegiate study of religion. The most convincing evidence for this assertion is a specific list of pre-seminary studies. I take such a list from the faculty I know best, the School of Theology at Claremont. The student who enters this School in the future will be expected to have had the following courses in college, and he will be assessed a deficiency for each one he lacks—to be made up in noncredit courses.

Natural Science:	two semesters.
Humanities:	two semesters, plus a course in Literature, and a course in the History of Western Thought.
Language:	two semesters in German, or Russian, or French;[1] and two semesters in a biblical language.[2]
Behavioral Science:	two semesters, introducing the student to Sociology, Psychology, and Economics; plus a semester in Sociology, and a semester in Developmental Psychology, and a semester in either Political Science or International Relations.
History:	a semester in American History or American Government, and a semester in European History.

[1]Another modern language may be substituted by petition when the appropriateness of such language is supported by the student's academic or professional interest.
[2]A deficiency in this subject can be met by a special one-semester noncredit course at Claremont, offered regularly in the summer and in one other semester.

Beyond this, the School requires an undergraduate concentration of studies in religion, which I shall discuss later. (If it be argued that this is an "imposition" on the independence of the college, note that at least 90% of this fits college requirements, or is consonant with options or free elective systems. Certainly the requirement of the major cannot be objected to on principle by the faculty that has accepted this requirement from graduate departments of Anthropology, Biology, Botany, Chemistry, English, French, German, Education, Sociology, Economics, Government, and twice as many more.)

Let's compare these requirements with the current A.A.T.S. list. First, in quantity. It's a much shorter list. It will amount to between 50 and 55 semester hours. The A.A.T.S. list totals 90 semester hours. Second, in insistence. Each item in the shorter list is required; not one in the longer list is required —the very length of the list is made tolerable by this fact: it is a list of suggestions.

Should the list be a list of requirements? It should. As a requirement, it actually (not theoretically) recognizes the work of the college faculty as an essential part of theological education. But, more importantly for the seminary, it makes certain that elementary education in undergirding major areas of the theological curriculum will have been obtained before admission and in its secular setting. Thus the professor of Biblical Literature can count on some prior instruction in the interpretation of literature; the professor of Theology on some knowledge of the course of Western thought; the professor of Church History on some knowledge of European and American History; the professor of Counseling on more than an introduction to contemporary psychology, and the faculty as a whole on a similar study of contemporary society.

In other words, the specifics that are required for admission are of two kinds: first, those almost universally accepted elements of the liberal arts which have gone into "General Education" programs; second, courses which prepare a student for one of the major areas of theological study by carrying him beyond an introductory level of study in an area of that study. Where this second type of course is not re-

quired for admission, the seminary is driven to offer undergraduate courses in sociology, history, psychology, etc., and
the academic level of these courses is often still further reduced by bastardizing them by mixing into the basic college course a denatured professional course. Theological
education can become graduate level education only when
and if it relates its curriculum cooperatively and constructively to the curriculum of the college. To do this realistically
requires prescription.

These prescriptions must be made on a piecemeal basis—
seminary by seminary. The Association is the creature of the
seminaries; its standards reflect their standards. Thus the
Association's *Statement on Pre-Seminary Studies* legitimately
uses such language as "it is desirable," "students are urged,"
etc. This statement explicitly advises the student in college
to "seek counsel of the seminary of his choice." It is altogether fitting and proper for it to do this. The responsibility
for prescription is the seminary's. It alone has the power to
change the language of a statement on pre-seminary studies
from "it is desirable" to "it is required." And today this
change is not only desirable, it is required for the further
improvement of theological education.

<h1 style="text-align:center">V</h1>

The reasons that have led our faculty to require an undergraduate major in religion seemed overwhelming.

There has been a decided drop in a knowledge of religion
by entering classes in the last thirty years. The reasons for
this are complex, but the fact is inescapable. Today the professor who tries to point out the use of biblical symbols in
contemporary art must first patiently inform his seminary
students as to what the specific biblical symbols are. The
ignorance of non-Christian religions is often complete. Christian theology and the philosophy of religion are unknown

lands. Instruction in any of the major areas of the curriculum must begin at an elementary level. A study of seminary catalogues over the last decade will reveal the addition of undergraduate-level introductory courses in various areas; in fact, the seminaries have been adding sub-freshman courses.

One of the reasons is the decrease in the number of seminarians who come with college instruction in religion. Grant that the decrease in religious instruction in home and church is a major reason, yet another reason is certainly the failure of the seminaries to support collegiate departments of religion. New student after new student testifies that he was advised by his pastor (a seminary graduate) *not* to take any courses in religion in college. The same advice, derived from the same ultimate source, is given by the college adviser of pre-seminary students. The statement of the A.A.T.S. on majors in college strongly urges the pre-seminary student *not* to major in religion. Let it be granted that this hostile attitude toward the college department of religion was valid forty years ago when uneducated, incompetent teachers academically disgraced departments of religion. This cannot be charged today. The faculty in the college and university department has attended the same universities and taken the same degrees as the seminary faculty. Moreover, only seminarians who are blissfully ignorant of the collegiate world can utter such nonsense as implies that a major in religion is so narrow as to be an uncongenial part of a broad liberal arts education. Religion is a division rather than a department, and only the department of philosophy has in its own content anything approaching the breadth of the department of religion (and it is unfortunately often limited by philosophical sectarianism).

Anything less than the requirement of a concentration of studies in religion will be inadequate.

Some seminaries today have given recognition (often of a limited sort) to introductory college courses in one or two of the areas of religion. A student who has had a college course of Introduction to Biblical Literature is excused from the required seminary Introduction to Biblical Literature and is admitted to the intermediate level courses in Biblical Literature. But this limited recognition will not materially assist the college faculty in religion in its fierce interdepartmental struggle for survival. Unless the seminary's requirements encourage pre-seminary students to major in religion, the department of religion is deprived of needed and substantial support.

I have pointed out above the crucial importance of the department in the shaping of the life of the college. The very breadth of the subject we call religion demands a minimum faculty beyond what is required in some other fields. The size of the faculty that a college administration will hire depends upon two things: instructional load, which is heavy when there are required courses in the subject; and the number of students majoring in the department, which requires a diversity of advanced courses. Without the second, the work of the "department" is a general service function without prestige or stability in the curriculum. Nor will this service function attract and keep faculty members of high ability. Capable and ambitious teachers demand a chance for instruction at a level higher than this. They covet membership in a strong department. Without a program of concentration in the department, it cannot become strong.

The strong supporters of the departments are the graduate school departments. Listen to the recent boasts of some of our strong liberal arts colleges. Siwash had forty-two students given fellowships or assistantships at famous graduate schools; Utopia had a higher proportion of its senior class admitted to medical school than any other college in the country. The department of chemistry is distinguished and important because its graduates were accepted at eight of the Big Ten graduate schools. But none of the graduates of the department of religion were accepted by outstanding seminaries, because the seminaries had seen to it that students going their way avoided the department of religion as they would the plague.

If there is to be an adequate faculty of religion in the college, the seminary must be its strongest champion. This is true of all of the functions of the college department of religion. If it is to be adequate in educating laymen who will live and work outside the profession; if it is to be adequate in contributing to the general education of all students; if it is to serve effectively in its part of the theological education of future ministers—the seminary must require the major that will provide the core of students majoring in religion.

VI

The legislation of the individual college faculty will set the general pattern into which the major in religion must fit, but since one of the purposes of the Lilly Study is to find helpful suggestions for future development, the case may well be stated from the viewpoint of the seminary. From that viewpoint the program of studies of religion in college should make two contributions to the pre-seminarian.

In the first place, it should provide a general and elementary introduction to some of the major areas of religious study. Our own School will require of the college graduate that he have had an introduction to the study of Biblical Literature—Old and New Testaments, an introduction to the study of the major living non-Christian religions of the world, an introduction to the study of religious thought, either theological or philosophical, and an introduction to Christian social ethics.

This is not presented as a canonical list; it was made as all degree requirements are made, on other than purely rational grounds. But this list or one like it is defensible as an important part of theological education and one which could well be carried out in college. If it were so carried out, the survey-introductory courses of the seminary could be scrapped, and the seminary course could begin its instruction at the level at which college work ended and thus be more truly professional.

How far below these elementary introductions to four areas of religious study the major should descend must be a matter for each college to decide. If the seminary of tomorrow is once more to insist on the study of the Bible in the original languages (as now seems probable), then the first instruction in these languages should be assumed by the college. Our school at Claremont has added the requirement of one biblical language—an obvious compromise with the possible and with prejudice. Whether or not this pre-college level study of biblical language can legitimately be included in a "concentration" program is an open question which others must answer. So likewise is the question of the relation of any specifically religious content in a basic Humanities course, etc., to the concentration program.

But there can be no question about a second essential element of that program. The major in religion should provide advanced study, a vertical column, located in one of the major ways of learning that dominate the theological curriculum. These "ways of learning" include the study of history, of literature, of systematic thought, and of society. The major in religion should offer the student the opportunity to pursue his study beyond the elementary and general to the mastery of method and material in one of these disciplines.

If the faculty resources of the department of religion make

it possible and desirable, then this specialized program could be located within the department. But if, as is often the case, the limitations of faculty size make that pattern impossible, the specialization column should still be a part of the major in religion. In this latter case, strength can be drawn from the closely related departments: for Church History, from the department of History; for Christian Literature, from the department of English Literature; for Religious Thought, from the department of Philosophy; for Social Ethics, from the departments of Sociology, Cultural Anthropology, and so on. The further possibility of the development of special interdepartmental courses should not be overlooked.

A major of this sort, with studies based on the general and introductory but proceeding to advanced study of one of the major disciplines of the study of religion, would enable the college department of religion to serve nonministerial as well as ministerial students in the full panoply of academic respectability. Its service to the church would be valuable above rubies. It would return the serious study of religion to the American college. It would make specialization in this area a real possibility for many of our young people. It would help to hold for the ministry many a bright youth now lured elsewhere. It would make it possible for the seminary to take its place alongside other graduate-professional schools with integrity and comparable quality. The next great advance in the quality of seminary education waits upon the rapid establishment of these majors in religion in the American college.

In relation to this major, one additional opportunity needs to be pointed out to the seminaries. At the present time a student who comes to the seminary with a fair number of courses in religion in college is often disappointed with the level of his first course in seminary. When the major in religion is a common possession of the entering student, the seminary should exempt him from the first course in that area in which he specialized in his undergraduate major and move him on to the next-level course in that area. I hope it is clear that what is suggested here would operate one level above the present practice of exempting a student from an elementary introductory course.

VII

Since academicians are the timid rabbits of this world, the assertion that "this is all very well—but impossible" will be a common response. A realistic appraisal of the present situation will show that it is difficult but not impossible.

Let's look at the difficulties. Some colleges have inadequate departments of religion; some have none. What about the student in the tax-supported institution where religion is not taught? Where will the student be able to get the biblical languages? Many colleges today do not permit majors in religion.

Over against this, set some encouraging trends in the American college. More colleges each year are adding instruction in religion. This is true even of tax-supported institutions. Even in a state like California, justly famous for a hypersensitive fear of religious instruction in tax-supported schools, a large amount of instruction in religion is available. The offerings are most meager in the state universities (although even there any number of courses in non-Christian religions are available), and more plentiful in the state colleges and junior colleges.

Among the church-related and independent colleges the curriculum in religion is growing steadily. Even in the grim area of biblical languages there is growth (Stanford has added Hebrew to the offerings in classical languages, and Chapman has added biblical Greek). But in many of these schools, the size of the faculty would compel the use of related departments in establishing a satisfactory major in religion. Positive action by the seminaries in requiring a major would hasten the needed expansion of these departments.

We were pleasantly surprised by a study of the catalogues of the colleges which have been the major sources of our student body. The entire list of our requirements could have been met by these schools with no more than two deficiencies in the overwhelming majority of cases. Even where some of the requirements could not be met officially inside the college, qualified instruction was available off campus.

Finally, the prudent administration of the requirements would make it tolerable through the inevitable period of transition. Students with deficiencies should be admitted to the seminary with all the financial rights and privileges of students without deficiencies. The brilliant student who was a late-decider from an engineering college could be assessed the small economy size package of deficiencies. Seminaries would themselves offer, in pedagogically efficient packages, makeup opportunities in the one or two subjects most frequently assessed as deficiencies. Advisory explanations of the prerequisites should be provided to prospective students and to college advisers. By these devices, and at long last by action of the A.A.T.S., the program advocated here could be instituted without damaging stress and with tremendous benefit to the quality of theological education.

CULTURAL EDUCATION IS
PRE-THEOLOGICAL

MARTIN E. MARTY

Pre-theological education is and should remain *pre*-theological. That simple sentence of reminder is the thesis of this essay. It is written in the interest of defining some of the content and validity of education for cultural life as being *pre*-theological. At the same time the distinct precincts of the theological discipline are reserved and preserved. The thesis is designed to counter two main objections: one, that the ministry does not demand and need not presuppose training for life in culture; the other, that theological education must carry the burden for relating the student to secular culture. Pre-theological education is and should remain pre-theological both logically and chronologically.

Our first concern must be to preserve intact the theological enterprise. The complicated business of relating the Word of God to the world of men demands so much substance and knowledge, so much art and finesse, that it must be kept pure. Here, as so often, purity of heart is to will one thing. Theological education, too cluttered by concerns for relevance and relation (theology *of* culture, theology *of* square-dancing; theology *and* jazz; theology *and* modern lit-

131

erature), will be distracted from its demanding center. The modern ministry is haunted by lack of definition, a lack explainable by the diffuseness with which theology is regarded both by its practitioners and by the lay public.

A minister may be a preacher, a counselor, a pastoral director, a priest—but in every instance he is to be first of all a theologian. He has no other reason for separate vocational existence. He may lead an exposed life. Only the undertaker may see more death; the doctor, more disease; the executive, more administration; the psychiatrist, more counseling; the lawyer, more divorce—the minister is certainly but second to each in most communities in these exposures. But he *is* second. Society knows what to do with those who are "first best" at something; those who carry on the vocations can gather energy from a clear definition of their tasks. At what is the minister "first best"? Though neither he nor his public need use the term, they must grow in the understanding that he is to be trained to theologize. A technical society has no other way of regarding its servants, including the minister who must in many ways be a "general practitioner." Theology demands first attention during the students' optimum years of training and demands first place in their self-definition at the end of a course of study.

One need not try to define theology as a "pure" science, as some of its overzealous partisans do to take this position. Many doctrinaire students of Karl Barth, for example, misread his concern for the intactness of the theological discipline as a denial of the relational task. No denial of relation or correlation is involved or implied, either in Barth (who knows his Kant and may know his Mozart) or in this discussion. After all, the Word and the world are seen as polarities in constant relation to each other; the "logos" is rooted in the world of culture.

If theology is never "pure," it is better served, however,

if its students are free to pursue it unburdened by constant concern to make up for lost time in equipping themselves to know the Kants and the Mozarts to whom they are relating the Word of God and the words about God. Those seminaries which have chosen to be microcosms of whole universities (a host of new disciplines are born to satisfy this appetite) are justified *if* they think of the enterprise as being *post*-theological. *After* one is at home with the Bible, with the history of the church, with systematic theological thought, with "practical" theology, he had better begin to relate what he has learned to ethics, to arts, to the personality sciences. But to assume that enrollment in a seminary provides a charter to claim theological awareness and to possess theological substance does an injustice to the discipline.

If theology as a discipline is to be free to demand concentration, this is not to say for a moment that it can get along permanently without the cultural base. The nineteenth-century circuit rider could equip himself with horse, Testament, saddle bag, and the text "Behold the Lamb of God which taketh away the sin of the world." But that was the nineteenth century and that picture of cultural simplicity is an unrealistic and romantic model. "Not many wise" were chosen for preaching the Gospel, but the wisdom here referred to by St. Paul was that which was used to make a claim upon God and not to be "all things to all men." The Gospel, as the romantics insist, may be simple. But the world is not. Its myriad potentials demand complex connections. "Liberal studies," says Joseph Sittler, "constitute time's immemorial invitation to join the human race." He speaks out of an age-long Christian concern.

Even those who take refuge in Tertullian's radical and partly rhetorical question, "What has Athens to do with Jerusalem?" and vice versa must know that the questioner was a relatively sophisticated lawyer who, if he did not know his Athens, did know his Rome and was informed by it at every turn. Even where a particular theological bent places the church against the world and calls it to a denial of culture (à la Tolstoy), the culture to be rejected must be known and understood if theological decision is to be honest. The Protestant theologian faces a cloud of witnesses. "Those who are content with authority alone, and expend their efforts on good morals and holy desires, condemning the liberal arts or not being up to them, I do not see how they can be really happy among mortal men, though I believe with unshakable faith that they will be free and happy to the greatest extent in the next life who have lived best here" (Augustine, *De Ordine*). While Augustine may have used learning against learning, even in his concern for the City of God, there was a real knowledge of and love for Rome and *Romanitas*.

If Augustine set the terms for that aspect of the medieval millennium which has most informed Protestant thought, the Reformers set them for another half-millennium. Thus Luther's dictum that there will be no revival of theology unless there is a revival of letters. He, we must recall, was an editor of Aesop. John Calvin: "They are superstitious who dare not borrow anything from profane writers. For since all truth is from God, if anything has been aptly or truly said by those who have not piety, it ought not to be repudiated, for it came from God. Since then all things are of God, why is it not right to refer to his glory whatever can properly be applied to that?" *(Commentary on Titus, Opera III.)*

There is no point in walking down the long corridor of Christian history and inquiring in every nook and niche; the evidence would be unmistakable. Theology should presuppose a pre-theology of cultural bearing. Before theology is undertaken, culture (letters) should be studied technically; after, it should be digested or refined or seen relationally. So much for chronology. Logically, that very theology which demands awareness of Yeats and Keats, Goethe and Homer, General Motors and general literature is not to be cluttered during the optimum learning period.

I

What is the good of cultural education post-theologically; that is, chronologically and logically after the disciplines of the seminary? In subtle ways its good, its usefulness, is changing from the part it played in the Protestant past. Once the minister was *the* cultured man, often the only man in a community who was formally educated. He personified the tradition of culture and helped sustain civility. He towered over the unlearned or the barbarian of the community. He served as an occupational gatekeeper to the larger world and to the past of civilization. Today that role is, in most communities, changed. A technical society produces teachers, doctors, learned and trained men and women who are more familiar with segments of learning. The minister no longer towers. But he still has an amazing array of cultural responsibilities.

He is, first of all, head of a "voluntary" society. (Do not press an implied theology of the church into that adjective!) That is, he needs to summon all the arts of motivation and suasion to exert the leadership he can and to call for loyalty to the theological object in his community of the faithful. He may serve a limited association or subcommunity in the larger culture and may serve it in limited ways, but in his suasive arts there must be an awareness of what was once called rhetoric and a familiarity with the connections to men which the substance of culture provides.

The minister, after his theological education in its formal sense has transpired, must fuse liberal education with the theological art. Theodore M. Greene has divided the liberal curriculum along several lines of which the practitioner may not even remain aware. He must "communicate clearly," for which he needs mathematics, language, artistic idiom. He must "inquire accurately," and here his pre-theological education in natural and social sciences, in historical and literary methodologies must be resurrected and vivified. He must "evaluate wisely," and he cannot do so without the humanities. He must "understand synoptically," aided by history and philosophy. He must "reason validly," and for this logic and mathematics or grammar are his handmaidens. (Referred to by William H. K. Narum in *Christian Faith and the Liberal Arts.* Augsburg, 1960, p. 9.)

None of these tools precludes his belonging to the many who are to remain "unwise" or "childlike," and none will prevent him from preaching "the simple Gospel." But each is his ticket to a real world and not some docetic, pseudo-world of remote spirituality. He will summon the substance and suasion chartered in these disciplines whenever he enters the pulpit to preach even to the simplest flock. His administration will be informed by the history of ordering and organizing. He will be personally sustained by contact with the range of human experience. His counsel will acquire new depths by his awareness of the human experience.

Recently a new necessity has been placed upon the theologically-trained leader of people. In a time when "the best lack passion" and the worst alone have intensity to work their chaotic worst, a spirit of *anomia,* the lawlessness of the vacuum, has worked to disrupt the community. In the United States, for example, under the genteel and smooth surfaces of suburban graces, a violent undertone erupts from time to time. In the early 1960's the very communities where the churches were strong were the loci in which the "radical right" of anti-Communist suspicion made its way. The minister could best serve his people by serving as a voice of sanity and tradition, calling on the resources from "the long pull" of culture. This point deserves further development, as it will no doubt continue to play an important part in ministry in the cold war tenseness.

If we look into the future and ask what will be demanded of the minister of the Gospel beyond his proclamation of the Word, beyond his ministry in the Sacraments and in the care of souls, we can point to the ongoing necessity for ethical involvement. Both personally and corporately his people must be led to see the ethical concerns implied in Christian discipleship. This ethics has a social dimension which will also demand an awareness of human social patterns. *But* the ethico-social impulse will not appear in the dramatic form it did in the past.

Whether the minister wishes to address himself to the impossibly-scaled issue of peace, the somewhat localized issue of race, or the more diffuse and pervasive ethical questions of the business world and abundant society, his choices will not be made against the dramatic black-and-white contrasts that were open in a more individualistic society. The turn of the century saw a version of the Social Gospel which was occasioned by a black-and-white view of society. Walter Rauschenbusch, agonized by his personal vision of Hell's Kitchen in New York, soon learned what one Christian, one man, could do to light a candle to push back a bit of darkness. It was not difficult to pick out heroes and villains and name them, to point to exploiter and exploited. Many factors have accounted for the change.

Today the relative degree of welfare state life which is the common assumption in America has served to lessen awareness of the extremes. Today many social gains have been consolidated by law to remove some of the drama of personal concern. More recently most churches have been dislocated and mislocated away from areas of visible, physical, human need; the suburbs provide an island which screens vision of the rent-gouger or the loan shark, the gentlemanly-gloved racist. The ecological nooks and crannies have been crowded with other species of servants of man in need: voluntary agencies, public health services, social workers, theorists, teachers.

In such a world, where the immediate ethical drama is sometimes less intense, a parallel issue has arisen, and it is cultural. Culturally, what kind of person is needed (and can be produced) to give sanity and wholeness to such an illusory society? Today, when leisure becomes a dominant theme in the life of most men, or *Werkkrankheit*, the sickness of compulsive overwork, affects others, how will culture be regarded? Is the cultural root of business ethics perceived? Are the dynamics of political and economic decision apprehended? Can men think historically and learn from the intuitive or formal inherited wisdom of the people? What will today's man look like if he must face ultimate tests of survival and freedom and creativity?

The minister cannot begin to provide normative answers or solitary guidance in such matters. But his ministerial contacts all have their cultural aspect, and he is the better servant for forming as broad a base of bond as he can. Now, when he tries to help produce the "cultured man" who can meet the test, he does not do so only by "preaching the Gospel." The year A.D. 29 or 30 is certainly decisive, but it is not the only thing that has happened of a worthwhile character to the man in Christ. His, also, is the Hebrew world. He too belongs to the Greeks, and Rome is also his province. The medieval occurrence is not without meaning for him, and even the Enlightenment, the secularization of thought, the American experiment and experience have resources for him to use.

Not that culture is of itself redemptive and revelatory. From the Christian viewpoint culture serves as *ancilla,* as handmaiden to the redemptive word. It is itself judged and awaiting redemption. The trouble to which culture, unjudged by the divine Law, can bring a society is evident in the example of National Socialism in Germany. "Having" Goethe and Schiller, Beethoven and Brahms, Dürer and Lessing was no safeguard against that particular *anomia.* The German academic community, for the most part, had few resources with which to resist the Nazi intrusion. For all the weakness and paucity of Christian evidences in that dark decade, most observers agree that when an "ideological" resistance appeared among those who remained in Germany, it was usually of Protestant-Catholic origin and under religious auspices.

To argue for the sanity that can be produced by cultural understanding is not to argue for the self-sufficiency, the arrogation of autonomy to the secular realms. The American Way of Life, the American Business Creed, and the countless causes which find refuge in a free society are not themselves redemptive. But the Christian best serves the larger society if he does not shrink from cultural responsibility in it.

If sometimes the Christian is tempted to surrender all and leave the field to the cultural custodian and enlightened man, the opposite seduction is also a threat. He may, if he is not aware of the riches and texture of culture, engage in a form of theological imperialism. In its naiveté such an imperialism claims for religious disciplines what is not inherent in them. It calls for "the conversion of Khrushchev" as the means toward world peace. Such imperialism says, "If only" all businessmen would become Christian, the ethical questions of their realm would be solved. If only all American whites would be more Christian, the racial question would improve. Theological faithfulness is not a charter for cultural irresponsibility. The college choir that justifies its bad singing on the grounds that it represents a Christian campus and is singing Christian hymns and that piety can compensate for bad technique deserves the scorn of the critics. The sociologist who asserts that only the Christian who loves man as he does can be a good sociologist is intruding beyond the realms to which the promise of the Gospel carries him. The history of culture provides him little warrant for such assertions on empirical grounds. "It is necessary to let everything be what it is." Theology and culture are related but distinct, interconnected but not to be confused. There dare be no interest in social, ethical, or cultural monopolies in the name of the Christian faith.

The minister needs liberal education to be the suasive head of a subcommunity in a voluntary society. He needs the tools which a liberal education's disciplines provide to carry on his work. He must help draw on the resources of culture to help produce the kind of man needed for cultural choice today. There are more reasons for good pre-theological humane learning for the sake of post-theological fruitfulness. A fourth reason can relate to the mission and the strategy of the church.

An awareness of the complex of culture can help the minister-theologian better locate himself at the energy sources of the environment and near the cultural dynamisms. For all that must be said for the joy of ministerial faithfulness by that majority not located at cultural crossroads, yet the whole ministerium must be called to understand and support the minority that has other opportunities. It is pathetic to see the pastoral and theological talent of a man go to waste because he has a simplicistic definition of culture. "Build a better mousetrap and the world will beat a trail to your door" is not an honest cultural equivalent to the theological and moral "Seek first his kingdom and his righteousness, and all these things shall be yours as well." People today derive their notions of reality from too many other sources. Somehow the church must be aware of the cultural possibilities and the practical mechanisms of mass communication, politics, social work, and the arts, to be effective.

For this awareness a theological passion calls for a cultural base. Here the apathy of the pre-theological community might be faulted. With few exceptions, if one seeks intensity of concern for academic subject matter, he would not look to the typical seminary. An apathy if not an unbelief which permits low-keyed participation and drift is often established. I recall picking up a friend one day in a university physics lab. He was studying something about the self-diffusion of liquid sodium. (My pre-theological education in the sciences was too limited to permit me to speak with confidence or precision here.) As I walked into the laboratory I heard his friend exclaim, "That's a *damned* interesting substance." Does the substance of theology command such interest? If it does not, can it be because a misunderstanding of the cultural precariousness, the apparent social triviality, the thin thread by which the church hangs to life in the modern world are not perceived because of inadequate liberal education?

If the minister is to use such an education and if he is to help others equip the cultured man for Christian sanity in a confusing world, *when* will he get it?

II

After theological education the minister is to use the independently acquired and now fused disciplines of theology and the humanities. He cannot well acquire both well at the same optimum period. The distractions and competition are too demanding. The answer there must be: He receives pre-theological education *before* he undertakes the theological disciplines. This obvious and predestining term "pre" throws the whole burden on the liberal arts college where almost all seminarians will be prepared for their theological work.

Now we are ready for a negative assertion to parallel the contention that the seminary is not the place for cultural disciplines. Equally, the liberal arts college is not the place for theological education. It may well be for those who do not plan to go to seminary, and who will remain laymen or non-professional theologians. A good case can be made for the teaching, not of the religious impulse but of formal Christian theology in the liberal arts curriculum of certain schools but only if there is no intention further to pursue theology formally.

The distinction should not be pursued in doctrinaire fashion, nor be awkwardly rigid. It is true, one can begin to ask the theological question in the humanities curriculum. After all, "pre" is a leaning-forward term, it bends toward the word "theology." A liberal arts college should help poise the student. This is the time to begin to see to it that he is hooked by a theological question which will haunt him all his days. But in the liberal arts curriculum the question should be defined for the pre-theological student only as for other laymen: It should remain nascent, inchoate, partly non-formed and undisciplined or unprofessional. Insofar as a particular student becomes theologically precocious, it seems to me that he best be asked to forego articulation and be asked to "go underground" as it were.

Why? For one thing, to borrow a term from Diana Barrymore, "too much, too soon" can spoil him. The typical liberal arts college, while it may be well staffed in the religion department, cannot hope to be sufficiently comprehensive to encourage a wholesome approach to theology. For another, the student will reveal his readiness for the rigors of theology by his proof of restraint and self-discipline. On this scale, theological answers commensurate with an increasing depth of questions will more likely be forthcoming. Premature theological tantalization ordinarily leads to superficiality and—if my seminary professor friends are correct—unteachability when the prodigy reaches seminary.

It may be asked, Whom are you criticizing? Some years ago I shared in the task of scrutinizing a curriculum for a pre-theological school. Its program was laden with courses such as Christian Witness I, Christian Witness II, *before* there had been any courses in Bible, Christian thought, or Christian history. This type of course existed at the expense of history, philosophy, and science. As long as "Christian Witness" is conceived in laic terms as it might be in college *other* than in pre-theological education, well and good. But is it advisable to tantalize the pre-theologian into the expectation that he will have something to say merely by the fact that his piety or some inward yearning has placed him in a college where theologians are to be developed one day? Ripeness is all. Premature ripeness is fatal. It produces a narcissism, a dilettantism, or a fascination with religion at the expense of theological hard work. I am not here commenting on how many years the "American system" should expect of one in college and then in seminary; nor am I discussing the architecture and decor of seminary as opposed to college. Rather I am suggesting that wherever it happens, once theological education formally is undertaken, one violates liberal learning if pretense is made that it can be sustained in disciplined fashion or that theology can be done justice to if there are still assignments ahead in liberal learning.

A corollary of this position would be that the religion department of the liberal arts college would be unburdened from its theological task *for proto-theologians.* This is not in any way to join forces with those who would radically abolish religion departments in colleges, with a theologian's *hybris* that says that only the would-be professional has a right to study the subject. Not at all. No Operation Abolition, no Operation Disdain is called for. But definition is.

For the pre-theological student there is plenty for religion departments to do. They can teach the cultural context and the psychological roots of religion, the history of religions and comparative religion. I would even argue that for the non-professional student religion departments should move beyond these cultural approaches to religion and formally and specifically teach theological subjects.

The religion professor will ordinarily have many kinds of positive relation to the future minister. He is often the unacknowledged recruiter for the seminaries. (He may actually achieve this role by teaching theology to non-professionals who are moved to pursue the subject vocationally!) He will ordinarily work to nurture the theological underground on his campus. Bull sessions and quadrangle chats will help sustain the pre-theological student who too readily wants to move from cultural penultimates to ultimate questions. But the teacher is not a dean of a seminary *in nuce;* he, too, works chiefly on a pre-theological plane. He knows the perils of routine and repetition and boredom: he serves the student better by guiding him into the richness of a good liberal arts curriculum than by overripening him in the necessarily thinner resources of a religion department.

This self-restraint in religious student and teacher may be asking too much. But it is only asking what the stated purpose of a pre-theological college is. Ordinarily the signs on campus will define it as "liberal arts" college. It gathers endowments, builds buildings, organizes libraries, attracts faculties with all this in mind. Elsewhere others are doing the same for theological seminaries. A liberal arts college is not complete without making provision for the study of aspects of religion; it is overcomplete if it pretends to be a seminary.

III

Some of the argument that pre-theological education is to discipline and restrain itself along the lines of the liberal arts has been psychological or pedagogical. It seeks curricular sequences and optimum learning periods or divisions of labor. But underneath has been a theological assumption which removes some of the apparent blandness from the first sentence of this essay. Pre-theological education is and must remain pre-theological. It is not eventually subsumed, absorbed, conquered, displaced.

This assumption does not force the reader to make his choice between the two general options in seminaries today. (At this point we must bypass those forms of simplicism, fundamentalism, or pentecostalism which totally dismiss the need for human learning in theological training. They are not directly implied in this study and are not the temptation of the mainstream American denominations today.) One school of thought, which slightly misreads "neo-orthodoxy" and stresses the discontinuity between Word and world, between divine activity and human endeavor, minimizes or removes an *Anknüpfungspunkt,* a point of contact between Christ and culture. Even such advocates need the tools of liberal education; they live—even in a split-level education —as men in culture and ordinarily as extremely cultured men; they must know what it is that they are denying and rejecting. Actually the question of the point of contact is ordinarily raised chiefly *in loco justificationis,* in the doctrine or matter of God's justifying a claimless man. Only in that light are reason and works disparaged in a Christian lineage. In all other respects "neo-orthodoxy" does not remove motive or interests in contact.

The other option, equally misnamed, termed "post-liberal" or "chastened liberal," will stress the contact between Christ and culture, the contiguity between Word and world. If the former option needed the reminder to introduce pre-theological education with real seriousness at all, the latter needs the reminder that culture cannot do what Jesus Christ came to do; that the world is not redemptive apart from Word. Here again pre-theology must be pushed back into its place. But the *praeparatio evangelica* will be stressed theologically: in the Old Testament, in the religious impulse, in concrete spiritual realities apart from Jesus Christ.

For the "liberal" the reminder would no doubt have to come from another direction. Theologically (never "humanly") "when I became a man, I gave up childish ways." That is, *in loco justificationis* culture and humane learning are displaced, contradicted, corrected, or transformed. In the one theological strand Christ causes a breach in order to fulfill; in the other, he fulfills in order to transcend.

In either instance, liberal education provides a *natura* which is a potential in both the old and the new creation, to those elected to the City of God and those who are truly mobile in the City of Man. Art is long. Time is short. Four years of high school, four years of college—these are the "pre" years that will have to provide the raw material for a lifetime of more haphazard nurture and sustenance. Theology and humane learning may be fused in post-B.D. graduate theological education and will certainly be forced to mature in the university of life. But for the freedom of theology there must be a freedom of pre-theology, as a step toward producing the cultured man, the whole minister, the new servant of the servants of Jesus Christ.

TRAINING FOR A
FUNCTIONAL MINISTRY

ELWYN A. SMITH

The problem of the theological curriculum so much discussed these days is the product of Protestantism's failure to come clear about its ministry. At one point in particular the preparation of ministers in both college and seminary is affected: What should a minister know—and therefore what should theological education undertake to do—about the modern disciplines: sociology, psychology, educational theory, and all the others? Seminary and church alike have opened the interstices of the curriculum to these subjects but have not formulated a clear conception of their role either in the practice of the ministry or the education of the minister. Students are often left to decide simply whether they like or dislike elective courses in counseling, for example. Similarly in the pastorate it is left to the minister to determine whether he will give time to counseling people and, if so, on what level he will do it. Older thinking on the "cure of souls" seems unable to extend itself to the point of making solid contact with psychology and counseling so that neither the churches nor the seminaries nor the makers of pre-theological curriculums can address the young

147

in an authoritative way on the role of counseling in either ministerial practice or theological education. The case is similar with other modern subjects.

Our working formulas for handling the discrepancies of educational theory are superficial. For example, we advise the ministerial student in college to study the liberal arts, the social and natural sciences, and to stay generally away from the subject matter ordinarily found in the seminary curriculum: Bible, theology, church history. This posture is ordinarily defended as a means of avoiding impoverishment of the general education of the student and duplication with seminary work. But at the same time it conceals a failure to cope with the most difficult question that the 20th century poses to theological education: What is the ministry in these times? How does study of culture relate to the study of church tradition?

The division between a good liberal arts background and the theological curriculum is not just a question of preparation in two different but integrally related areas of learning, segregated at different educational levels. The fact is that the norms of liberal arts education worthy of a good college are cultural, and college work tends to prepare students for a social role that is itself governed by cultural norms, while the norms of theological education are heavily influenced by religio-traditional evaluations of man and society. A student moving from a sound college major in philosophy or history or sociology to seminary is not moving along a single, unbroken educational line of development oriented throughout to the ministry. For four years he is trained in values which are largely the product of the Enlightenment and the history of Western thought since 1650. These arose largely apart from the theological, liturgical, and ethical traditions of the church and were often at war with them. When a student enters seminary he finds himself suddenly plunged into a curriculum which is informed by presuppositions and values that arose in a different stream of history. He is enrolled in some classes where traditional values and concepts are presupposed but which his college work has not prepared him to understand or accept. In other classes the orientation is more in line with his undergraduate work, and often seminary teachers in the new subjects have themselves never really come to terms with church-traditional concepts and values. The seminary confronts the student with a conflict of values which he is unprepared to solve and which the curriculum itself may not discuss and hardly ever resolves.

When we inquire into the preparation of professional church personnel we need concepts that equip us to deal not with single elements of the tension defined here but with most of its principal elements. They must have meaning in two spheres and be capable of holding them together. What follows here is an effort to define one such concept. We do not think that it is sufficient in itself nor capable of comprehending, much less resolving, all the major tensions confronted by the theological educator. We dare not presume to resolve the church-culture tension in the modern period of history; but we must define conceptions that enable us to deal with it.

The concept of the *functional* has long been the property of technical education. It can and ought to be understood theologically as well. Even without the New Testament to remind us that action either flows from or in itself enunciates belief, we can see the inadequacy of limiting the idea of the functional to the technical. There was a time when a technician was a person who could operate a machine without understanding how it was built, the theory of its design, or the fundamental thought that led its inventors to conceive it in the first place. But increasingly the modern worker must understand theory if he is to perform technical operations effectively. This was once true of all professionals. Professional studies traditionally began with theory, often the whole Western heritage of philosophy, and moved gradually toward the technical, which was necessary to actual performance. The ignorance of the modern attorney of the history of Western thinking on the meaning of justice began when case law imposed its monopoly on the schools. This reform produced highly competent lawyers who, however, generally took an entirely conservative bent. Lawyers in the main lack the knowledge necessary to criticize their own materials and the society of which laws are an expression. In modern science the direction is different. Theoretical physics is prerequisite to technical performance in occupations which at an earlier stage of development could be satisfactorily pursued after technical training alone. The medical diagnostician is at a considerable advantage if he understands basic bodily function as well as how to read symptoms. Modern technical education, in short, is bringing a convergence of technical with fundamental studies— and they converge on the question of "function."

Ministerial education has gone through a similar evolution. Once composed entirely of theological, biblical, and historical studies, it swung heavily toward courses aimed to equip the seminary graduate to administer a church program, communicate skillfully, educate the young in ways consistent with up-to-date educational methods, counsel the disturbed in keeping with modern techniques, and otherwise perform well on the technical level. Successful preaching was long regarded as a problem of mastering the arts of communication. Little thought was given to the reason for its presence in Protestantism or ways of reinvigorating it through a fresh understanding of its function in the church.

Endless doctoring of the curriculum by altering the proportions of subject matter, lengthening or abbreviating the program, and adding or subtracting subjects, will never relieve the fundamental tension in which both church and seminary have been living and are going to live for some time to come. Such a release of tension can occur only if Western society itself arrives at general agreement on the values it considers durable and the rate of cultural evolution slows. If that happens, ministers will at least no longer have to shoot at a moving target. If churches disagree with the new cultural stabilization, they can at least define the differences and perhaps compete successfully for the loyalty of the majority of the people. Churches may, as with Unitarianism, simply modify their own history by massive ingestion of cultural values. But such a solution is embarrassed by rapid cultural change which produces conflicting cultural crosscurrents. Can a church in our time relate itself coherently and simultaneously to a number of major systems of value and competing social solutions? Even strongly conservative traditional churches feel this problem. Roman Catholicism until recently has depended largely on its structure of authority rather than the work of its theologians to express and sustain its unity. The tensions are manifold and complex. What is needed is a way of thinking about ministerial preparation that will bring some order into the way in which church traditions encounter each other and the swift changes that contemporary culture tirelessly produces.

The revival of theology has had at least two effects on the seminary curriculum: on the one hand, a resurgence of traditional subject matter at the expense of technical courses; on the other, an effort to understand the function of the clergyman theologically. Thus far there has been too little suggestion that theology needs to be understood technically —that is to say, that theology is not an inert body of data, a static sacred tradition existing apart from the tasks of those who study it, but a discipline necessary to a functional ministry. The study of theology is itself a function of the church and ought to be directly associated with technical training. But when technical training tends to create and express a fundamental theory of its own which is in competition with or even contradictory to traditional theology, the technical becomes a screen for a second set of theoretical presuppositions. A good seminary may teach a variety of theories, but this should be explicit. Differences of theory both recognized and taught are at bottom justified in a curriculum by a theory of education that makes a program fundamentally coherent. To have a second basic but concealed theory at work beneath the surface of a curriculum disorganizes it, confuses the students, and sets professors against one another. Technical training for the ministry, in short, needs to be understood and to understand itself in direct connection with the study of theology, while theology needs to understand that in its own way it is a function of the church and is designed to enable pastors to execute the pastoral function effectively.

The most substantive reason for a theologically oriented functionalism in ministerial education, however, is the New Testament view of the ministry itself. The apostles, prophets, and teachers of the New Testament church did not exhibit a new status but performed a new function. The classical statement is Paul's: "For as in one body we have many members, and all the members do not have the same function, so we, though many, are one body in Christ, and individually members one of another. Having gifts that differ according to the grace given to us, let us use them: if prophecy, in proportion to our faith; if service, in our serving; he who teaches, in his teaching; he who exhorts, in his exhortation; he who contributes, in liberality; he who gives aid, with zeal; he who does acts of mercy, with cheerfulness" (Romans 12:4-8). Pursuing the metaphor of the mutual service of the bodily members, he states further: "God has appointed in the church first apostles, second prophets, third teachers, then workers of miracles, then healers, helpers, administrators, speakers in various kinds of tongues." These functions display varieties of service, not degrees of spiritual excellence. "Now there are varieties of gifts, but the same Spirit; and there are varieties of service, but the same Lord; and there are varieties of working, but it is the same God who inspires them all in every one." Naming a familiar list of "workings," Paul concludes: "All these are inspired by one and the same Spirit, who apportions to each one individually as he wills" (1 Cor. 12:28, 4-6, 11). His point is precisely that while the same Spirit provides for all services, they differ functionally.

Paul expands on prophecy in 1 Cor. 14:3: ". . . he who prophesies speaks to men for their upbuilding and encouragement and consolation." Exalting the function of prophecy in the church, Paul says: ". . . since you are eager for manifestations of the Spirit, strive to excel in building up the church" (v. 12). Illustrations of the functional character of the varying ministries of the church could be multiplied. In New Testament times there was a vast work to be accomplished in obedience to the divine command. God had furnished his people with gifts to accomplish it, and a variety of offices meshed with one another in a grand design of ministry. Seeking superior position and claiming superior gifts had no place precisely because each office was furnished with fitting spiritual gifts. "To each is given the manifestation of the Spirit for the common good." Anyone who worked against the common good had not a spirit of apostleship or prophecy or teaching but a spirit of disorder.

The conception of the ministry here expounded looks in

two directions. Theologically, it is grounded in Paul's understanding of the Holy Spirit and the Spirit's peculiar relation to the church's function. The Holy Spirit was understood among other things as a functional manifestation of God in the church. The ministry is a task, or a complex of tasks, requiring technical competence in a number of functions. For the New Testament Christian this also was a gift of the Spirit.

The many functions of ministry are united by a comprehensive command: Witness. The overarching function of the church is to witness to the act of God in Christ and to spell out its implications for human life. Theologically considered, the witnessing function has at least two sides. The witness must know *what* happened and how to unfold its meaning; and he must understand the implications of what he is doing, of witness itself, as an act of the church. These demand theological reflection; neither question can be answered purely technically. On the other hand, the act of witness is technical. It requires intelligible speech, as Paul made unmistakably clear. ". . . in church I would rather speak five words with my mind, in order to instruct others, than ten thousand words in a tongue" (1 Cor. 14:19). It requires some grasp of the point at which another man's mind rests: Paul's introduction to the sermon at Athens displays his grasp of the religious preoccupations of the Greeks. But these illustrations raise theological questions also. In the first instance, Paul is not arguing for technical intelligibility against the spirituality of speaking in tongues, but for concrete witness to the Gospel in a form that can be apprehended and can therefore become an active power in the hearer, as against the fraudulent "Amen" of the outsider who "does not know what you are saying" (14-16). Paul's comment on the religion of the Greeks raises a theological question. He was not only starting to talk to them where they could understand him; he may also have believed that, in a dark and inverted way, the truth was known to the Greeks precisely as the "unknown God."

These observations on the New Testament simply illustrate what is increasingly evident to many: Communication is not a technical question alone but a highly complex problem that demands theoretical reflection as well. The ministry of the church demands both an understanding of the message to be communicated and a grasp of the processes of communication. The concept of a functional ministry, understood both theologically and technically, furnishes helpful guidance in organizing the theological and pre-theological curriculum.

The *theological* curriculum will probably always have to separate out types and areas of instruction, if only because professors continue to be trained in traditional specialties that leave them poorly prepared to teach inclusive subject matter-technique areas. Ideally, for example, instruction in communication should embrace and unify study of the theology of the Word at the one extreme with study of the modern processes of group dynamics at the other. Conflict and parallelism between the philosophical groundwork of the latter and the church's theological commitments should be spelled out and discussed until students are able to grasp the technical aspect of their instruction in the light of their study of theology. Few professors are equipped to handle this, but a reorganized curriculum can bring professors together in the classroom and force them into communication with one another. In the absence of a fully viable faculty life, students are thrown entirely on their own as they seek out the relationships between the men and ideas they encounter during their college and seminary education. A partial and deliberate obliterating of lines between practical courses and content courses is one way of forcing estranged systems of value (and professors), thriving in different branches of the curriculum, into communication with one another.

The *pre-theological* curriculum is more difficult precisely because the faculties of colleges and seminaries live permanently apart from one another. Some colleges are in position to promote discussion of the ministry and perhaps reorient a limited portion of the work they offer pre-theological students. But a very large proportion of students continue to come from colleges with neither motivation nor structure to conduct such discussion. The extent to which campus ministers are qualified to treat this question with pre-ministerial students varies widely. Here it is not a question of simply limiting or expanding the materials studied by the pre-ministerial student, but of making explicit the tension and conflict between the systems of value that are communicated in good liberal arts studies and the biblical perspective.

The adequate functioning of the ministry today undoubtedly requires a thorough grasp, not only of the content of liberal arts and theological studies but of the varying perspectives in which they are taught. We have not yet found a way to introduce explicitly into the education of the pre-theological student discussion of the problem which has always oriented the ministry and which is the norm of its function: the invitation of Jesus Christ to all men to receive him as the risen Lord, to live by the gifts of the Holy Spirit, and to accept the function of witness as a pervasive part of all human life, thought, and work.

THEOLOGICAL SCHOOLS: PARTNERS IN THE CONVERSATION

GIBSON WINTER

The Department of the Laity of the World Council of Churches set the question of the role of the ordained ministry in the context of the total ministry of Christ in the world.[1] The issue ultimately is whether ordained men can participate as partners in the conversation between the Christian message and the world. But so far as ordained men take the role of prima donna or treat a technical knowledge of religious matters as the equivalent of theological understanding, they are no longer partners in the conversation. The analysis set forth in the W.C.C. document, "Christ's Ministry and the Ministry of the Church," applies with equal force to the theological schools in the present situation. Religious educators are called to be partners in the conversation. They think of themselves as experts in the conversation, but those who experience the actual conversation wonder whether the theological schools have any contact with the real issues. The theological schools and the men whom they are training are called to join in the conversation in which both message and world are disclosed in their true meaning. The crisis in theological education has

157

arisen largely because the theological schools and the religious professionals find themselves more and more on the periphery of this fundamental conversation which is the mission and ministry of the church.

We can approach the nature of this crisis by considering the task of education for the ministry, or so-called B.D. Training. Education for the Christian ministry seems to be a fairly clearcut aim for a B.D. program. As in the training of a lawyer or a medical doctor, a certain body of knowledge is to be mastered as are certain techniques of manipulating the materials of that field in an orderly way. Several recent proposals for the reform of theological education start from this basic assumption about the situation of theological education. Some have suggested including the colleges in the task of imparting "knowledge" of the religious subject matter; others have offered patterns for closely graded integration of humanistic knowledge with the specialized knowledge of the religious field. Others, in a more continental manner, have emphasized an elaborate linguistic and philosophical study of religion as a pure science. In each case, the suggestions for renewal attempt to meet the crisis in theological education by treating religion as an objective science and devising tricks in order to make the American educational scheme fit into this notion of the place of religion. Since religion is of little concern to education in the United States, these attempts to recover the educational base which characterized the old Christendom only prove to be "gimmicks" inserted from the outside—"gimmicks" with little relevance and arising from a mental climate appropriate to a bygone age. In our day, the presuppositions of the traditional theological formulations are in question; the institutions in which the message was formerly embodied are no longer viable; the world to which the message is intended to be an ultimate answer finds itself asking questions which do not correlate with the responses that are being given. The religious world of the old Christendom has dissolved, but theological schools train men in the presuppositions, subject matters, and skills by which that old Christendom perpetuates itself. The crisis in theological education arises wherever one discerns this discontinuity between the theological enterprise and the religious actuality.

Theological schools have to ask fundamental questions today, even as all those concerned with the renewal and unity of the churches have found themselves driven to the most radical reconsideration of their grounds and task. The fundamental question in theological education is: Education for what? Or putting the same question in more concrete terms, one has to ask about the nature and scope of the ministry. A brief statement from the document published by the Department of the Laity presents at least the formal structure within which we can proceed with this questioning:

> We speak about Christ when we speak of the ministry, about what *he* does through his Church in and for the world. (I) He joins in baptism new members to himself, letting them share in his ministry. (II) He appointed the apostles to be the pioneers of his Church, and his continuing presence draws the whole Church into the apostolic ministry. (III) He gives grace to all the baptized, assigning to them their particular authority and function in his ministry. (IV) He lets the whole Church share in his suffering, calling each member to be spent in his ministry in love and obedience to God and in love and service to men.
>
> Only in the context of this total ministry of Christ through his Church in and for the world can the questions about the authority and function of ministers within the Church be answered.[2]

In a sum, one can speak of the ministry of Christians as participation in Christ's servanthood in and for the world. The church, as ministering body, is not something separate from the world but that segment of the world which is grasped by the promise and hope which belong to the world through Christ; consequently, it is that community which is committed to the disclosure and demonstration of that hope in its life.

Theological schools assume that they are preparing men for the ministry; by this they mean educating a specialized segment of the ministry which is concerned with the maintenance and operation of religious institutions. These professionals, or the "set-apart" ministry of special ordination, depend upon the viability of the institutional structures for the exercise of their particular ministry. So long as the religious institutions participate in the total servanthood of Christ's church in the world, deepening its reflection, nurturing its holiness, and participating in its sacrifices, as well as celebrating those sacrifices in its ritual life, the "set-apart" ministries of professionals continue to be part of the total ministry of Christ in the world.

The substance of the theological crisis can be traced to the institutional crisis which has shaken Christianity. Religious institutions are always ambiguous in Christianity, since they crystallize the dynamic of a life and faith that arise in historical decisions and remain open to a historical future. However, the institutional crisis of our day reflects a more fundamental ambiguity, since the religious institutions rest upon the assumptions of an old Christendom which no longer exists and embody a structure which was appropriate to a society that is rapidly disappearing. The dislocations of the "set-apart" ministries arise primarily from this dissolution of the ties which linked religious institutions with the world. The temporary success of American churches can be attributed largely to their service functions as community associations in rapidly changing, middle-class communities. Let us consider this disengagement of the religious institutions a little more closely.

The publication of J. A. T. Robinson's *Honest to God* and the stir which it has caused in England suggest the theological dimension of this institutional crisis. This book states in summary form much that has been thought in more developed theological reflection; indeed, it poses the problem of the nineteenth-century theologians in the post-Barthian context. The two world notions underlying the theological formulations of Christian orthodoxy have been collapsing for centuries, but their final demise has waited upon the emergence of radically different premises for truly human reflection. The scientific solutions of this crisis never proved very satisfactory because they were non-human and even inhuman in their intentional structure. The possibility of human reflection on a human world opens the way to an interpretation of the Gospel in history and marks the end of the two-world approach. In Ryle's cryptic phrase, the hypothesis of "the ghost in the machine" is no longer needed. This is not to suggest that the theological problem is even at the beginning of a solution but only to indicate that the older mythology is rapidly collapsing.

On the American scene, theology rests as a layer of piety on the top of the mind, while a totally different world view of scientific humanism operates on the deeper levels of consciousness. The only difference from the continental situation is that the layer of piety has practically dissolved in the old world. Such a layer of piety is not functional in a culture; it effects no changes in attitude, behavior, or social structure. Indeed, this is the false consciousness which perpetuates a traditional image through which a nation may see itself as pious, holy, pure, and noble in a wicked world. Every attempt to engage in serious reflection on the meaning of life as actually lived can then be rejected in the name of this pious image. Serious theological reflection is paralyzed so long as this false consciousness is taken for the functional consciousness of the American society. J. A. T. Robinson's book could gain a popular reading in England because that false consciousness had lost most of its credibility among English people. One can be quite sure that the American people will give it no such reading, because Americans are far from ready to face the actuality of their belief systems and attempt a reconstruction of their theological views. Bishop Robinson's book will probably be passed over by Americans until their plight becomes desperate enough to take seriously the Christian foundations which can make sense in the twentieth century.

The religious institutions have failed Christianity in the United States primarily because they are structurally irrelevant to contemporary society. Americans are religiously illiterate and happy in their blissful ignorance, since any confrontation at depth with their religious ideology would shake the whole success pattern on which America is built. However, the structural irrelevance of the parochial and congregational structures has paralyzed the professional ministries and made the churches peripheral to such major issues as poverty, racial struggle, and world peace. The churches have only been able to contribute to these fundamental problems through the National Council of Churches and the World Council. At every point where economic, social, and political decision-making is crucial to the formation of history, the ministry of Christ is blocked by its incarceration in irrelevant institutions. The ministry of the church in and for the world has thus been transmuted into a private preoccupation with the emotional problems of those whose social position warrants their being in the nice kind of neighborhood that can pay a professional friend. This institutional anomaly, the restriction of religious nurture to those of affluence and suitable skin color, has finally brought home to the "set-apart" ministry the hopelessness of their present institutional situation. These men know ever more clearly with each passing year that there can be no renewal of faith and ministry without a radical break in the institutional structures through which Christianity is imprisoned in our time. They feel that they can minister relevantly to selected individuals on a personal basis, and indeed this is true of anyone with a little extra time. They feel that their ministries and the churches are quite divorced from the world to which they are presumed to be ministering. Some dim sense of this situation may account for the recent finding that only one-third of the students in theological schools anticipate long-term work in a parish ministry.[3]

The theological and institutional collapse of the old Christendom, or as Martin Marty puts it for the United States, the "old Protestantdom," has important implications for theological schools. *Theological education can no longer be thought of as preparation of a "set-apart" ministry. Professional training has no relevance without institutions in which professionals may exercise their vocations.* Theological education will have to focus on the total ministry of Christ. If special gifts and situations call for institutional support, some men may receive special ordinations. So far as the actual work of theological schools is concerned, they will miss the point if they assume that they are training men for a professional role. This was expressed well in an unpublished paper on the ministry, when an author from Asia pointed out that the training of a "set-apart" ministry without a training of the people was equivalent to setting up schools of higher learning without a broad base in public education. This was, indeed, the pattern of Mandarin education; in some ways, our theological professionals are a kind of Mandarin class in the churches, cultivating a theological expertise which is quite irrelevant to the fundamental problems of life.

The first implication then would be that theological education can no longer direct itself to professional training, since there are no viable institutions to make a profession meaningful or even desirable at this point in Christian history. This is another way of saying that the churches, like department stores, are simply part of the world of contemporary society. Jobs in these religious institutions have nothing more and nothing less to do with the Christian faith than being lawyers, bookkeepers, or plumbers; each of these jobs provides occasions for Christian life and ministry, but none enjoys a peculiar privilege as a calling. Theological preparation is needed for all those who participate in Christ's servanthood, and theological schools have an opportunity and obligation to deepen the reflection of those engaged in these ministries.

In a peculiar way, the theological schools have become more and more aware of this general character of their education for the ministry. Some of the more traditional schools receive students who have some sense of vocation and desire training to work in religious institutions, but most of the theological schools find that their students are seeking basic answers to ultimate questions. These men are seekers in the Christian life, and a theological school should be a good place to carry on such reflections; unfortunately, the theological schools feel obliged to make professionals out of these seekers, clothing them with special language and odd manners which will prevent them from communicating with anyone about their deepest concerns. This professionalization misses the real search which brought the men and women to theological studies and instead eventuates in one more confused professional in the churches. What place, if any, the professional ministry has in the servanthood of God's people in the world today can only be discerned in the next generations of ministry and witness. When theological schools keep the professional straitjacket on the seekers who enter their classes, they postpone the discovery of the true place and character of "set-apart" ministries in the emerging society.

This first implication also makes it evident that college departments of religion, lay centers, and theological schools are all engaged in a single task at this point. Whether a ministry finds its expression through a political office or working in a church organization, these ministries in the world need to become reflective and open to the possibilities of servanthood. Whether a man commutes to an advertising office, shares a ride to the electronics plant, or tries to build some semblance of concern in a residential social fellowship—usually called a church—a ministry is a possibility and needs the nurture of theological reflection. If, when, and how a true "set-apart" ministry may emerge can then be only a matter of conjecture. Until Christ's ministry finds expression and consciousness, we cannot even know the social structures through which such an institutional form might crystallize. For the present, we have more than enough to do in theological work in attempting to discern the promise of Christ in our world.

The second major implication of our new situation is the interdisciplinary character of true theological reflection in our day. This problem can be stated in different ways. The theological schools often confront it in the challenge to isolated schools of theology—schools disengaged from dialogue in the university and concentrated on special subject matters. If the older two-world metaphysics is part of the past and theological interpretation of the message has to be recast in the language and symbols of the contemporary world, that task cannot be carried out in isolation from the cultural universe of our time. Every attempt to insulate theological reflection from the thought of our day only deepens the estrangement of the message from man's struggle to shape his new world. The Christian church owes a considerable debt to the neo-orthodox emphasis on the centrality of the events in which the Christian message became concrete, but to the extent that this movement encouraged a biblicist retreat from the contemporary world, it has retarded the task of theological reflection.

If the gap between the intentional structure of the message and its contemporary expressions is as great as we have suggested, biblical, historical, theological, and ethical reflections will have to be exercised in close correlation with the corresponding disciplines of literary, historical, philosophical, and social scientific study. To the extent that isolation of theological studies in special seminaries prevents such closely correlated study, these seminaries face some serious difficulties in the years ahead. On the other hand, a theological faculty on a university campus need not necessarily lead to the kind of dialogue in which this interpretative work can be fulfilled; physical proximity is not equivalent to dialogue.

Christianity is a historical faith, which is to say that its message of promise and hope is inextricably implicated in the events in which it became and becomes manifest. The appropriation of that message is inseparable from discerning it both within those crucial events and correspondingly understanding it within one's own situation. The message is not an abstract content or principle which can be applied from situation to situation but rather a meaning disclosed within varying situations. The correlation of contemporary engagement and historical interpretation poses the difficult problem of Christian reflection today. A disengaged study of the message or mere reflection on the universal aspects of experience fail to establish the kind of dialogue between event and contemporary experience in which the message can be grasped and expressed. The special task of theology is to take its own history and founding events seriously. University disciplines set the academic partners with whom the meaning of those events may be grasped and expressed in the life and language of our own time.

Hence, a theological faculty engages in the interpretative task with all of the ministry—with those objectively engaged in the decisions of history and with those who labor in other academic fields. This is not to suggest that the theological task is only an academic exercise, but it is a linguistic and cultural enterprise which must take its own cultural context seriously. Those seekers who enter theological schools receive theological training so far as they are introduced to this interpretative task.

One other aspect of this second implication needs to be recognized. Religious professionals today need a thorough retraining in theological work. There are, of course, exceptions, since some men have carried on constant reflection and research in their work, but most of the men in the professional life of the institution are at least one generation or more behind the contemporary struggle. We have an analogous situation in engineering, where students are told to expect at least two complete retraining experiences in the course of their careers. This applies as well to our religious professionals. Their contribution to the task of theological reflection is seriously limited by the need for reworking their basic disciplines. This should be the role of theological schools and special centers, but serious reflection is unfortunately avoided in the religious institutions.

The third major implication of our present situation is the need for research on the total ministry in the actual world of our time. This practical development of ministry cannot be separated from the interpretative task of theology any more than theological reflection can be carried forward apart from commitment and obedience. In most theological schools practical training is still on a professional basis so that men are taught to preach, hold babies, administer property, and counsel the disturbed. This is practical training for an institutional framework which no longer exists. The real research in ministry which is needed by the total ministry of God's people has little to do with such skills. Theological specialists should, indeed, become engaged in reflection with those who are objectively involved in labor, politics, education, and other fields. These are the men and women who are carrying on whatever ministry is available to our world. To be sure, some clergy are also engaged in ministry, especially of the personal and counseling type. However limited these ministries, they also deserve theological reflection.

Theological schools can only share in this research on the ministry by becoming objectively involved with groups in various walks of life who are attempting to develop the ministry of servanthood. The obvious way to carry out the research is through the practical field; students can explore the dimensions of ministry with those who serve in what used to be called secular or worldly vocations. What special ordination or institutional supports might be helpful to carry forward such ministries can only emerge from research and reflection on the appropriate structures of ministy in this new world. This major field of research is missed if practical training becomes preparation in pastoral counseling or introduction to curricula on religious education. The pastoral ministries of our new world are exercised by shop stewards, foremen, office supervisors, and hundreds of other specialized roles. These are the ministries in which we need theological understanding and preparation.

The question arises whether theological schools designed for another age and presupposing another institutional world can possibly have anything to do with our present tasks. Any serious consideration leads to the admission that these institutions may have served their time and be ready for the ash heap of history. However, if this be so, one cannot make such a judgment until the theological schools have had opportunity to confront the tasks of our time. Research indicates thus far that most theological professors are unconcerned with what is actually happening in the churches and the world. If this proves to be true, then the theological schools are actually on the way to becoming museums.

Another serious difficulty arises from this view of theological work, for many theologians consider that their work needs to be free of the practical concerns of faith and life. What can be said for the theological professor who works on manuscripts, keeps himself aloof from the world's struggles, and educates the professional ministry in his spare time? One can only say what has already been said of the professional ministry and the churches! Theological schools, like other religious institutions, are worldly enterprises; teaching theology is like running a gas station or digging a ditch. Some of the real theological reflection which touches church and ministry is done totally outside the environment of religious institutions. On the other hand, here and there one meets a theological professor who is participating in the servanthood of Christ's ministry. However, theological faculties are like plumbers who solder pipes or salesmen who market soap. They do another worldly piece of work well or poorly, and that work may be the occasion for disclosing the promise of Christ and embodying his sacrificial life, or it may be only an occasion for self-centered preoccupation. In all of the various occupations and structures, including churches and theological faculties, one hopes to see the depth of reflection and reality of commitment through which the servanthood of the church is disclosed.

Nevertheless, the ministry can benefit from studies and labors in all fields, for the disclosure of depth is to be found throughout this created world. The task of theological reflection depends, therefore, upon discerning the depth and the truth in every field and encouraging every ministry, while waiting upon the disclosure of those ministries through which our new society can be hallowed and lifted up. This hallowing of life through concern and sacrifice is the true mark of that servanthood which our world thought to find in its professional and religious institutions but now knows to be given wherever men give declaration and demonstration of the faith that is in them.

In this broader context, the problem confronting theological schools is whether they can and will participate in the conversation of message and world through which Christ's mission is going forward. The church bureaucracies certainly press the theological schools to develop a professional ministry no matter how empty of meaning the religious institutions may be. To this extent university theological faculties may prove much better placed for training if not recruitment in the years to come. The most serious difficulties lie within the theological faculties themselves, however, for they are out of touch with the spiritual emptiness which marks all religious institutions today, and they seek protection from the struggles which seem to interrupt their theological work. Amidst this worldly business of theological science, men and women may be found who are concerned enough with the servanthood of Christ to engage in serious reflection and participate with their students in research on the authentic ministries of Christ in the world. These teachers and students may be able to avoid the neat professional boxes and irrelevant practical courses, and thus keep the theological schools in the fundamental conversation.

ACKNOWLEDGMENTS

The author is indebted to many people for the ideas developed in this essay and particularly to the members of the faculty of the Divinity School of the University of Chicago with whom these problems have been discussed. The particular ideas and the break which they create with the way in which the problem of theological education has been posed are not necessarily shared by any of these colleagues, but they follow as implications from premises which are widely shared. Several books have been particularly helpful; notably Hendrik Kraemer's *Theology of the Laity,* Francis O. Ayre's *The Ministry of the Laity,* and the document developed by the Department of the Laity of the World Council of Churches under the title "Christ's Ministry and the Ministry of the Church."

FOOTNOTES

1. *Laity,* No. 15, May 1963.

2. *Ibid.,* p. 14.

3. K. R. Bridston and D. W. Culver, "The Lilly Endowment Study of Pre-Seminary Education," Part II, mimeographed A.A.T.S. Bulletin, March, 1963.

III. CHURCH EDIFICATION

Maturation of Ministers

THE SCHOLARLY EQUIPMENT
OF THE PASTOR

CHARLES L. TAYLOR

He enrolled in the arts course at Trinity,
But failing repeatedly in it he
    Exclaimed with vexation,
    "Confound education,"
And took his degree in divinity.

Thus this unfortunate's superstructure was built upon insecure foundation. His technical training was unsupported by a general education.

The case against four years of college prior to theological studies may be summarized briefly in some such argument as this:

The B.A. degree is unnecessary. What the minister needs is a warm heart, not a clever head. The Lord Jesus never went to college.

The B.A. degree is dangerous. As statistics indicate, it may unsettle the faith of the freshman. It may make even the faithful man proud, proud both of piety and learning in a combination that does not attract, but repels.

The B.A. degree is costly, in time, effort, and money. The time might be spent usefully in some other way more di-

174

rectly connected with the Christian ministry, and there would be more immediate returns. The courses prescribed for the B.A. candidate, especially in the physical sciences, are not sufficiently relevant to the needs of the pastor.

The B.A. degree may be disastrous to the family. For a married man to embark on a period of seven years prior to his acceptance into the ministry may impose too heavy strains upon wife and children. Not all women covet the degree of P.H.T. (Putting Hubby Through).

And some husbands will say, "Even though general education is important for some, I shall never be an intellectual leader; my forte is befriending people, and for this a college course might unfit me rather than prepare me. I'll read my Bible, say my prayers, and get out among the folks."

Over against this argument, we may think of the importance of scholarly equipment for the pastor in terms of what he is to be, what he is to know, and what he is to do.

What He Is to Be

He is to be an educated man because he must live in an increasingly educated world, in which no amiability takes the place of mature intelligence. A century ago a minister might not have seen a college hall, but he could still be a "parson," a leading person in his community, called "reverend" because he deserved respect and a "cleric" because he could write and read. Now, in a land where more people go to college than went to high school then, he can scarcely be a revered parson and cleric if he has been offered an opportunity to receive the equivalent education of those around him and has failed to avail himself of it. Bungling amateurs, with all the goodwill in the world, simply do not fare well in the company of experts.

Nowhere is this truth more strikingly illustrated than among Negroes. Except for Martin Luther King and a few more, to the young Negro his ministers do not seem to have the equipment for life that shines out above or even matches that of men in science, in politics, or in business. The Negro turns elsewhere for leadership and for persons to emulate, and the ministry languishes.

To illustrate this need for educated competence rather graphically, the Episcopal Bishop of Missouri soon after his consecration had occasion to visit the towns of Rolla and Sikeston. In the first, in a beautiful church with a large, cosmopolitan, and very intelligent-appearing congregation, he was introduced after the service to more than a score of men called doctor. Somebody had to remind him that Rolla was a world center of mining engineering. At Sikeston a woman played ethereally beautiful music upon the harp. "What's this?" asked the Bishop with his looks if not his voice. The woman, a harpist in the New York Philharmonic Orchestra, makes this music part of her contribution to her church when she happens to be at home. Will an ill-prepared ministry be adequate for congregations such as these? Will those doctors of mining engineering, will that harpist, and will thousands of people like them all over rural and urban America, people who are accustomed to high standards in their various callings, be content with an uneducated ministry?

It is true that education may lead to pride, but let there be no inverted pride like that of the monk who insisted that his order excelled in humility! Under the conditions of our world, no man is to boast of his ignorance; the church that does not value trained intelligence is unlikely to endure. Further, even if a particular congregation contains no mining engineers, no harpists, and even if no men and women of comparable equipment are present, it is a fallacy to declare that the minister in an out-of-the-way spot needs no education or only inferior education. The truth is that he frequently needs a better education than his brother in suburbia, for he needs more imagination, more courage, more tact, more devotion, and more godly wisdom if he is to cope with his more difficult problems.

Sometimes, as mentioned above, the denial of the necessity for education takes the form of an excuse, "I'm no theologian. I must leave theology to others. My part is to do the church's work." While it is true that he that does the will of God, learns the doctrine, the work of the church is not unquestionably God's will, and some theological presuppositions underlie all of it, so that the contrast is not between theology and no theology, but between better and worse theologies. No effort should be spared to insure that the church's work rests upon the right theological foundations. It is easier to organize one thousand people than to save one; activity may be only the cover for emptiness; the minister who disclaims interests in theology may be only "idly busy." A true theology, moreover, is not spun like a spider's web in some attic corner. Thought and action must interpenetrate. The "worker" must think and the "theologian" must learn from life. Neither can properly abdicate to the other.

Amid all the specialization of our time, there are grave dangers lest ministers, and laity also, slough off responsibility on the ground that only the expert knows the right answer. The expert is fortunate if he knows the answer even in a very limited field. We have recently been reminded that the first nuclear bomb was tested and used without the knowledge of Congress, still less without that of the people. Even the accounts of the Treasury Department were falsified in the interests of secrecy. Can we afford to trust mankind's very existence to the few, no matter what their skill in any field? As in the case of the moral problems created by nuclear physics, so in theology, does not the common welfare depend on widely diffused knowledge, hard thought, the realization of consequences, and responsible action? All of us must be contributing to a great treasury of educated wisdom if the church's word on the life-and-death issues of our time is to be more than adolescent sentimentality of doctrinaire miscalculation. Even in what may seem to be strictly church affairs, in particular the relationship between the denominations and the coming great church, nothing less than the most mature understanding on the part of the most people will suffice. Can the minister say, as not a few do, "I'm not a theologian," and then proceed to control the church's official position from a wrong theological perspective of which he may not even be conscious? Rather, how vital it is that every minister be fully aware and competent to deal with the theological issues.

Aware! Mr. Douglas Dillon has written that "the history of man is a struggle toward freedom and awareness." Because freedom depends upon awareness, the tragedy of our time is that it produces so many people, even ministers, who go through the motions of life, sometimes in a kind of animal existence, sometimes in confused bewilderment, sometimes as "faceless technicians," sometimes as Mark Twain's "best people of the worst sort," without knowing life's heights or its depths, its joys or its sorrows, its possibilities and its glories. If the minister is to follow him who came to bring life abundantly, the minister must be educated to awareness.

What He Is to Know

Sometimes the objection to a general college arts education comes from the side opposite to that of the man who abdicates his responsibility to be a theologian. One may say, "Why not spend all my time in specialized theological studies rather than 'secular' history or physical science?" In other words, why not leap over arts and sciences to the seminary, and if the seminary objects, to the Bible school? Why not be a theological expert by giving entire attention to this subject?

The answer, which is by no means unconnected with what a minister is to be, may properly start from two biblical texts, "You shall love the Lord your God . . . with all your mind," and "But we have the mind of Christ." The first of these warns us against withholding any part of our intellectual endeavor from the Lord's allegiance; indeed we are to love him with all our interests, and with more than our minds also. There is to be no separation of subject matter into sacred and secular. The dominical command forbids us the luxury of loving God, as it were, in our pursuit of Christian doctrine but forgetting him as we turn to sociology. As he rules all life and reveals himself in all, mathematics cannot be consigned to the devil nor biology to "dangerous heretics."

The other text, "But we have the mind of Christ," humbles us when we reflect how little our brethren see in us what they saw in him. For they see in us members of a clerical order, cogs in ecclesiastical machinery, men jealous for our prerogatives in a select group; they saw in him the Lord of life, who in a narrow corner of the Roman Empire, obscure and despised, uttered words such as no other man ever spoke concerning the deepest and highest dimensions of life itself. His illustrations were taken, not from ecclesiastical circles, but from cooking, plowing, the use of money, and the various businesses of his time. Only twice in the parables he referred to church worthies, and on both occasions to expose their error. Wherever the mind of Christ is, there is a breath of fresh air, a broadness of vision, an acceptance of the stuff of life, a discovery of the eternal in the commonplace, that forever rebukes any narrow confinement of our attention to things sacred while we hand over all else to "the world."

It is vital, therefore, to distinguish education from training. The preparation of the minister is to make him, in his entirety, a fit person. It will equip him with knowledge that ranges widely over the range of human interests, and, as we shall see, it will enable him to act, not in a corner, but as one who works usefully and helpfully in the midst of man's most important efforts. Whether we think of the minister's being, or knowing, or doing, his equipment must be such as to cope with the demands of a rapidly changing culture, in which specialized training might leave him in a role as vanishing as that of the blacksmith or railroad telegrapher.

Training for the moment is often more efficient than education. Indeed the churches are constantly faulting higher education on the ground that what it teaches has so inadequately prepared students to mimeograph the weekly bulletin or manage the wild Indians in the Boy Scout troop. College and seminary professors on their part must not maintain a cold indifference and disdain to the legitimate needs of the churches. But it is possible also for the churches to put illegitimate pressure upon their educational institutions, and to be so greedy for "results" that they miss the ultimate significance of what is resulting. When men and women choose their church allegiance on the basis of the minister's personal charm, or the cheerful atmosphere of the Sunday school as a place to provide a kind of baby sitting service on a Sunday morning, or the proximity of the building, or the music, what does all the fuss and fury add up to? Why? Is this the Gospel or the mind of Christ? In the churches' efforts to "produce," to show more and more members on the rolls and larger and larger contributions, have they forgotten the one thing needful, congratulated themselves that they were not as other men are, and so passed by on the other side?

In a world so different today from what it was yesterday, and certain to be vastly changed tomorrow, training is not enough. There is no possibility of teaching the future minister all of the skills he will need. The bag of tricks that might enable him to "produce" today will alienate the people of tomorrow. Only if he has become an educated man, only if he knows how to select from a treasury of knowledge what is pertinent, will he be equal to the new occasion and the new duties.

What, then, must he know? It is scarcely necessary to reproduce here the statement on pre-seminary studies that has been so widely used by the members of the American Association of Theological Schools and the students whom these schools can influence. But let us not forget the assumptions on which it is based. In brief, these are that a college course should provide a student with tools of scholarship, with a broad understanding of his world, and with a sense of achievement in academic pursuits. The tools are the ability to write correctly, to think clearly, and to use a language not one's own. Understanding comprehends the world of men and ideas, the world of nature, and the world of human affairs. In this period of his life the student will be grasping what has been thought, said, and done in the world; he will be learning to discriminate between the important and the unessential; he will be fitting the parts of his knowledge into a cohesive synthesis; and he will cultivate the ability both to adapt what he has learned to new problems and to communicate clearly that which he has discovered. The specific subjects are of less importance than these goals. If agencies other than colleges or universities can equip a man with those tools and that type of understanding, one can only thank God and pray for his blessing upon them. If colleges fail to achieve these ends, one can only try to correct the distortion of their purpose. If the individual student is confused as to why colleges exist, one can only hopefully enlighten him.

As for the actual courses to be taken, there is room for wide choice. Those who urge limitation of range at an early point in a minister's development are right in their assertion that nobody can master all the fields of learning. Trying to "get it all in," to graze lightly—and superficially—over a wide pasture, is a common fault of the academic sheep and their shepherds too. The sheepskin at graduation always covers considerable intellectual nakedness. Moreover, during his college course the man of God should not leave his religion at the gate, or fail to develop his knowledge of theology, the Bible, and other fundamentals of his discipleship. But surely, given the importance of awareness, it is essential that the student should not restrict his range prematurely, nor close the doors to what subsequently might prove to be the brightest lights by which God shines into his understanding.

Christ is the Lord of all life. Who, then, will follow those devoted ascetics of our day, the scientists, into their monasteries, the laboratories, to work out with them the perennial problem of the relation between scientific knowledge and faith? Must it always be the other fellow? Or must this sphere of life be relinquished? Who will enter understandingly into the forces and passions that account for the rising nationalisms and the emancipation of the nonwhite races? Who will study the exploding population, the urbanization, the results of automation, the feeding of the new multitudes, gerontology, or the uses of leisure? Are these the business only of laymen? Granted that they all will require technical experts, how can ministers deal creatively with these and many other problems with which they will be confronted? Only if their education has given these ministers such awareness and insight that they are on the way to become lifelong students of the Word of God in these difficult places where men live. Are these Christ's business? Clearly so, and if his, then his ministers'!

What must the minister know? It is assumed, and correctly assumed, that he will be well versed in the Scriptures. The undergraduate years are not too early for the reading and study of these; indeed the best equipped man will be one who has known the Bible all his life, at each stage progressing in understanding as he becomes more capable of hearing it. Yet the Gospel in isolation is no Gospel; it needs to be presented in the context of nineteen hundred years of history of its life in the church, of the society which receives or rebuffs or reformulates it, and of the nature of the individual man to whom it comes. With increasing certainty, the theological school must work with history, social ethics, anthropology, and psychology. But in the division of labor it is well for the college to emphasize history, the social sciences, and the discoveries of this century about human behavior, while the theological school, building upon these, specializes in the study of the Christian faith itself. Let the professor of literature ask, as Richard Hoggart does, questions for the theologian to answer: How can the springs of assent that have nearly dried up be renewed? Where is freedom to be found? Why do we grope anxiously for something deeper than the passing show, fearful at the same time that illusions will be punctured? Why does education fail to educate and entertainment fail to entertain? At every level of instruction there might well be, indeed should be, dialogue that insures interpenetration of faith with other disciplines. Nor must the representatives of these other disciplines be tamed to do the bidding of lazy men of faith. They too must be given freedom to pursue truth according to their best lights in their own way, and theology, queen of the sciences, find its royalty as the handmaid of the Lord. Nothing can take the place of an apprenticeship served in the midst of the scornful, nor can critical faculties be left undeveloped, nor is it well for any man not to be cut down to proper size by those who are his intellectual equals and superiors.

Behind church history, in particular the record of only one branch of Christendom, lies the story of men and multitudes who also are God's people in God's world; behind theology rests the whole effort of man to understand truth, e.g., in the philosophy of Plato or in the wisdom of the Orient; behind the minister's work of telling people who they are stands the development of the twentieth-century understanding of man; behind all preaching with words is the presentation of the meaning of life through the arts; and behind all communication, mastery of forms of expression.

If a minister is to avoid the sin of excessive contemporaneity or its twin sin of provincialism, is there any doubt as to his need for the perspectives that historical studies can provide? If he is not to be negligent as he contends for the truth, must he not have disciplined his mind through philosophy and literature; if he is to avoid misunderstanding the very person he seeks to help, should he omit psychology; and if he is to convince, persuade, rebuke, encourage, and in the end win men to Christ, what studies of language are superfluous? How else may the man of God be complete, equipped for every good work?

What He Is to Do

We may approach this question of what equipment a minister needs from another side of the mountain by recalling some of his functions. He is preacher, teacher, pastor, counselor, leader of worship, organizer, and administrator. (He is much else, also, but at least these.) If what we have said above is valid, even in his administrative and organizing tasks, he requires more than technical skill; a big business demands intelligent direction and puts a high value on ideas. But "we are not, like so many, peddlers of God's word." We are not hawkers of the Gospel, measuring our success by the increased count of heads in the pews or dollars in the bank. "Nothing fails like success when it substitutes triumph for trust and pride for discipleship." A great feverish round of activity may merely cover up the emptiness of the enterprise, the lack of loving meaning without which the whole structure will collapse as surely as a rotten tree is doomed to fall. The business of the minister is to explain the meaning, not only of the work of the church, but of life itself.

Traditionally the minister has been preacher, pastor, and the leader of worship. "New occasions teach new duties"; it is possible that in the plan of God there will be other roles for him to fill which will properly modify the tradition. For example, there seems to be a far-reaching change in the character of twentieth-century preaching, less reliance upon oratory, less telling of people what they ought to do, less emotional fervor, while greater attention is given to teaching, to the word of the congregation to the preacher, and to a mutual, quiet search for the will of God for his people. Pastoral work may take the form of more and more counseling. But the traditional roles, for all that, may supply modern life with ingredients it sorely needs and are not to be surrendered lightly. And all of them demand scholarly equipment in the person of the minister.

The preacher, as he ascends the pulpit steps, does well to pray, "O God, day by day lead us deeper into the mystery of life, and make us interpreters of life to our fellows." This is his function, to interpret, to reflect, to see beneath the surface of the passing show. The community sets aside this man to think in the presence of God. Woe to him if his busyness interferes with this! The minister is called to do what no other calling, not even that of the news analyst, equips a person to do—to evaluate the occurrences of the present moment in the light of God's eternal purpose as revealed in the Scriptures and particularly in his Son Jesus Christ. "In the sight of

God we speak in Christ." To the young man considering his call to the ministry, the prospect of fifty or one hundred different sermons a year is frightening. He knows, as everyone else knows, that he is unlikely to hit upon that many bright ideas. But his fear is misplaced. He is not called upon to be clever, but to be faithful in interpretation. His task is to understand thoroughly the work of God and the predicament of man in order to bring the one to the other. How can he if he be careless in his attempt to master either?

The pastor, whoever else he is, is the minister of reconciliation, the man who moves among his fellows with sympathy, appreciation, and insight. He can counsel because in some true sense he has stood in God's counsel; he can forgive because he knows his own need for forgiveness. He has himself been brought close to the great reconciling Shepherd and learned from him how to break down the wall worse than any Berlin wall, that divides man from man. But is the love of God and neighbor learned out of books? Isn't this work of reconciliation an art learned in life that frequently is forgotten in colleges and universities, and even in theological schools? To these questions those connected with educational enterprises can only penitently confess their sins. But those outside can see even here the value of books, and of the training of the critical faculty that makes one constantly ask whether church activity does actually promote the fellowship of man with God and with his fellowman, and of skills that assist the reconciler.

The leader of worship knows how to celebrate because he knows what is worth praising. What does our world need more than a right sense of values, of proportion, of the truth about life? How despicably shallow is the prevalent cult of sincerity, as if being sincere were enough to make a man right with God! A man of miserably low standards and goals may be perfectly "sincere" in his fidelity to them. But there is one greater than man who judges; man's end is to know him and in knowing to enjoy him forever. Otherwise man is a piece of driftwood floating on the tides of public opinion, weeping and cheering because it is the fashion of the moment rather than because of honest response to truth. The business of the minister is never to manipulate emotion, which is a most contemptible kind of peddling and hawking. He is never to be a cog whirled by ecclesiastical machinery. Rather he is to say, "Holy, holy, holy, Lord God of Sabaoth; heaven and earth are full of the majesty of thy glory," in such a way, not only in words but in life, that the holy church throughout the world may acknowledge God. Here again we recognize, in Evelyn Underhill's words, that intellectual concepts are "paper currency which permits the circulation of spiritual wealth, but must never be mistaken for gold." But how impoverished life would be without this currency, without the word of St. Augustine, "God is the only reality; and we are only real insofar as we are in his order and he in us," or the declaration of the Psalmist: "Lord, thou hast been our dwelling place in all generations," or other figures of modern saints which bring home to us the truth about ourselves and our world.

"Our so-called civilization gets more and more complicated, more and more noisy. It is like one of those mills where the noise of the looms makes it impossible for the workers to hear each other speak. And if we go on at it long enough without a break we begin to think the looms are all that matter, and we are merely there to keep them going and must not bother about anything else. . . . There is a real danger that Christian spirituality in its deepest and loveliest reaches will be killed out by the pressure and demands of the social machine, and even of the ecclesiastical machines. Man will get ever more utilitarian and this-world, and will wholly forget his true relation to God."[1]

Does something like this need to be said in various ways again and again, and said in the most convincing and persuasive "currency" that education can provide?

The Prospective Minister in College

If the man of God is to be complete, equipped for every good work, what in brief does the church wish for him in his college years? Beyond the desire of the church, which may settle for less, do we hear the voice of God's call to our situation?

1. At stake is not intellectual growth alone, but the development to full stature of the Christian man. God's service is for everyone at his appropriate age; only a child of eight can render the fealty of an eight-year-old; only an octogenarian knows the particular obedience of one who is eighty. There can be no hiatus in the discipleship of the man who is eighteen. Ideally his participation in the company of faithful people, the church, will be no less real, his arcane or secret personal discipline will be as stringent at this period as at any other time of his life.

2. There will, however, be a marked difference, as we have already noted, in the emphases of his exposure. He will not be seeking security, but be ready for dangerous adventure. Like Samuel Rutherford he is "persuaded that although some say, 'Down crosses and up umbrellas,' we must take heaven with the wind and rain in our face." He knows that true faith cannot be fearful or protective, evasive or careless. He will explore truth, as from God, wherever it may lead.

3. Because his Lord came into the world where it is rough, and left it where it is roughest, the disciple will not shrink into a nice or pretty corner but be with the Master in the midst of the smells of the stable and the cruelty of the cross.

We cannot be too emphatic about this. The world that surrounds the church constantly ignores Christians because the latter seem to live in a dream world, or a protected world, or an irresponsible world. The Christian too easily can be contemptuous of those who make hard decisions in the midst of contending powers because to engage in the battle is almost inevitably to get dirty. "Knock down," says Evelyn Underhill, "the partition between living-room and oratory, even if it does mean that tobacco smoke and incense get a bit mixed up." Or, as George MacLeod described it, the cross was set up, not on an altar between two candles but at a place between two bandits where soldiers gamble and talk smut and curse and kill. Or, as Dietrich Bonhoeffer so cogently urged, ours must be a worldly discipleship, not removed from but in the midst of the world for the sake of the world —not to save our own tender skins—if it is to be Christian at all.

4. In the face of all that he does not know, the Christian will strive to maintain a quiet, not noisy, humility. As one who worships, he will be conscious of the majesty and the mystery of God. As one who seeks to help rather than to hurt, he will strive to discover the truth in the other man's point of view. He will be objective rather than blatantly partisan; he will be aware of his weaknesses and eager to welcome truth he has not grasped before. And he will be constantly asking questions that delve deeper than the ordinary: not "How can I succeed?" or "How can I get what I want?" or "How can I crack open the world, my oyster?" but "What is God's purpose for the world and my part in it?" "How can the basic reconciliations come to pass that will enable all men to live as citizens of the kingdom?" and "What do we do now in our eternal pilgrimage?"

5. These are some of the ways by which men and women are "equipped for every good work," although not yet com-

plete, put into the way of lifelong maturation toward the measure of the stature of the fullness of Christ. There is another vitally important consideration. No man can say, "Go to, now; I'll equip myself to be a well-educated minister." This is not a matter of human attainment. Notice in the New Testament the frequency of the passive voice. Obedient man finds that God does for him that which no man could do. Prison doors are opened, the waves of the stormy sea are stilled, men are called and filled with the Spirit, the eyes of the blind are opened, the sick are healed, and the dead are raised up. Who is able to be a worthy minister of Christ? Nobody, no, not one. But the Lord's command does not return to him empty. It accomplishes that which he purposes, and prospers in the thing for which he issued it. He equips those whom he calls, who become aware of their emptiness and the fullness which he alone can supply. The part of the creature is to wait upon the Creator, of the sinner to seek forgiveness at the feet of the Holy One, and of transitory man to open his heart and mind to the knowledge and love of the eternal God.

FOOTNOTE

1. Evelyn Underhill, *Light of Christ* (New York: Longmans, Green & Company, 1944. Courtesy David McKay Company), p. 103.

THEOLOGY FOR THE PARISH MINISTRY

C. UMHAU WOLF

Many have tried in recent years to indicate what is wrong with the ministry. Some of these critics are men who have left the vocation of the parish ministry completely, often with some bitterness. Others are those who have left the vocation of the parish ministry in order to become executives, administrators, researchers, or even seminary professors. Still others were never in the parish ministry and are lay professors or self-engendered, self-perpetuating student-teachers come to be full professors. Perhaps it is neither far-fetched nor outrageous for someone who has experience both in the seminary and in the parish ministry to speak on the subject of the parish ministry and theological education.[1]

I. The Dilemma of the Ministry and the Ambiguities of Theological Education

There is a dilemma about the parish ministry. Is this a particular vocation? If so, is the vocation to the parish ministry to be evaluated as higher, lower, or equal to the voca-

191

tion to seminary teaching, college instruction, or church administration? Is the parish ministry primarily a trade like plumbing, or a job like refuse collection? Even the word "trade" has ambiguities and "job" has lower-class connotations to many. If it is either of the last two, there is a different relationship to the seminary, the graduate school, and the denominational headquarters than if it is yet a vocation at least equal before God and the world to that of professors and administrators. Is the parish ministry a learned profession, and if so, how is it distinct from or equal to others?

The parish ministry is not only a skilled trade, as those who would have the seminary become merely a "trade school" and train in "practical" subjects affirm, but it is also, and will remain such, in spite of the trade-school advocates, a learned profession. The trade and the learned profession must be combined in the parish ministry if it is to maintain itself as a truly Christian vocation.

Many parish ministers are confused over their roles, and their confusion is not clarified by seminary professors' attacking the parish ministry without experience in a congregation and failing to call on the parish minister himself to help the seminary. Much of the maceration of the ministry is not the fault of the congregation or even of the world in which we live, but of the mixed-up pseudo-psychiatrist teaching counseling, and the "practical" teacher who has never served a simple parish. So we find some young ministers acting like young doctors (with pseudo-professionalism), who feel that parish calls, even on the hospitalized and the aged, are not so important as are lengthy counseling sessions. Professionalism shows itself in this so-called efficiency which undercuts the vocation. The doctor is too busy to make house calls; the lawyer is too busy to write a simple will or take over a small real-estate transaction. The parish pastor is too busy to make hospital calls and much too busy to call on chronic shut-ins. Since pseudo-psychiatrists are teaching pastoral theology without any theology (and with an eclectic anthropology), we should not be surprised to discover that it is considered more impressive and glamorous to report a saved marriage, a rehabilitated alcoholic, or even a prevented suicide through the open midnight telephone, than it is to report that faith has been kept alive through the help of the Holy Spirit in ten or fifteen patients in rest homes. Miller writes succinctly, "To succumb either to popular sentimentality or institutional professionalism is to betray not only our own calling but the world's need as well."[2]

Protestantism has traditionally a strong feeling against the hierarchical system, and yet part of the maceration of the pastor is the pressure for prestige in a new type of hierarchy. Is there a Protestant hierarchy from parish minister, to college teacher, to seminary professor, to denominational administrator, to ecumenical executive? It might be true in the New Testament and in the "good old days" that it was a good thing for a man to desire the office of a bishop. Now, however, it appears that many ministers (and seminary students) as well as laymen and seminary professors think the word "bishop" should be modernized to "top banana." So the translation would be: "It is a good thing for a man to desire to be a seminary professor." This kind of thinking almost implies: "Don't settle for a parish, even a challenging one: If you must compromise, it is better to be only a college religion teacher."

A recent survey sponsored by the NABI and the AATS through the help of the Lilly Foundation suggested that seventy percent of present seminarians plan to leave the parish ministry shortly after their training.[3] It is patent, then, that the complaints that congregations are chasing men out of the ministry and that parish pressures are too much for the average pastor are false. Perhaps the college teachers and seminary professors by emphasizing the new hierarchy are as much at fault as any pressures from society, urban, suburban, or exurban! With all the attacks on the parish ministry, both secular and religious, but especially those by nonparish ministers and seminary professors, what chance does he have?

In the statistics noted by Keith Bridston, thirty-three percent of the students plan to leave the ministry immediately and never enter the parish. The appeal of intellectual respectability in the college chair, in the administrative field, and on the seminary faculty is part of the problem. This will be noted later in some suggestions on the type of faculty demanded by seminaries.

II. The Need for Unity: Integration of Theological Education and the Ministry

Basic to our problem is the fact that neither the ministry nor the seminary has any integrating basis.[4] If there is not unity, the seminary will be a multi-headed hydra. The maceration of the ministry begins in the seminary and is as much the fault of the paranoid schizophrenia of overly departmentalized seminary faculties and disjointed curricula as it is of the parish pressures. Reuel Howe has noted[5] that many young ministers are confused because they are unable to distinguish the image from reality: in the seminary, in the congregation, in the laity, in the world, and most of all in their own self-image.

Seeking an adequate unity means for Christians the seeking in the Bible or more broadly in fundamental theology. Miller notes clearly that pastoral theology must be "theological at heart."[6] Lewis notes that the integrating principle of seminary education must be a proper theological orientation.[7] To seek a central focus through organizational unification or managerial efficiency is an impossible and frustrating task. Unless seminary education has theological unity and the parish minister absorbs this as his integrating factor, both have failed. Unless the ministry of all is to open for men God's saving and holy purpose that they may be drawn into the kingdom of God, all will have failed. The parish ministry will have failed most of all, regardless of the statistical success of parochial reports or of recognized theological acumen which will eventuate in a seminary professorship. Unless theological orientation and integration are begun in the seminary, the parish minister is lost, and the outside world will be permeating him instead of his word penetrating the lost world.

III. The Problem of Communication

One of the pressing problems of the parish ministry is that of communication from the pulpit to the pew, from the chancel to the assembly line. Theological jargon or specialized language, often in the one-day stand of the visiting seminary professor, may impress and overawe, but it seldom communicates or inspires to daily Christian commitment. Again Reuel Howe notes that ninety-nine percent of the ministers coming to his Institute are almost traumatic in their concern for communication. For this, a course in the communication arts in the seminary or summer school, taught by a man with no parish experience, can hardly be helpful. Too many of the laymen report, "He talks just like his professors." There can be no dialogue between the pulpit and the pew. There can only be little professors with some learning, using big words in the large setting of the parish. Bridston underscores this failure in reporting that seminarians themselves criticize their home pastors primarily because of this failure in communication.

There are many intellectually astute individuals who might

make good college professors of religion, but who are unable to communicate with the laymen. One must recognize that the sermon is not a performance, but to use Reuel Howe's image, it is the first stage of a rocket and it must go into orbit in the lives of the laity. Lewis writes, "No satisfactory answer is found to the question of the proper relationship between the *what* and the *how*. I have known men whose heads were stuffed with Kierkegaard and Niebuhr, who have had one course in homiletics. Such men may have the root of the matter in them, but they can't say it or preach it. . . . The hungry sheep look up and are not fed."[8] The parish minister's task really is not to be seen and heard himself, but let the living God be seen and heard. "The minister has the dialectic task of so speaking that men hear not him but the voice of the living God."[9]

Protestants have sometimes smiled at the recent debate between Roman Catholic biblical scholars and more conservative Latin theologians. But the same debate with less publicity is carried on in every seminary, where the biblical department cannot understand the jargon of the theological department, and neither can make sense to the so-called homiletical and practical department which ignores them. Many seminary professors are teaching brilliantly but irrelevantly. This may be permissible in a graduate school environment, but it is not acceptable if the purpose is to prepare men to deal with the lives of others in relationship to God and their fellows. Too many of the younger ministers were trained in homiletics by men who never had been in the parish, and so they continue to prepare their sermons as if the seminary faculty and the students, not humble laymen, were the congregation. What is vitally missing in many seminaries that makes it most difficult, if not impossible, for the seminary to be the church, is the total dimension and context of the church in the world of laymen.

IV. Theological Education and the Parish Ministry

Obviously there is a close connection between theological education and the parish. Studies of theological education are chronic.[10] The most recent series on graduate theological education are primarily oriented toward professional teaching of religion and give only an occasional nod toward the effective parish ministry.

Those who emphasize the so-called "graduate school" education and better (or more prestigious) degrees to indicate it as graduate education are not necessarily offering the ultimate panacea. Many students enter seminary with ideals, with a sense of mission and vocation, but are graduated with only a degree. Regardless of how high-sounding or prestigious this degree, they are no better or more effective in the parish. Surely there should be just as much intellectual integrity in the training and in the school doing the training of men entering the parish ministry, as there is for the man who plans to go on beyond seminary in further preparation for teaching religion in college, seminary, or graduate school.

Those who emphasize the fact that the seminary must be a graduate school debate the issue as if there were only one alternative to good professional graduate training, namely a "mere" trade school. If this were really true and not a straw-man, and if the only alternative were an exaggerated emphasis on skills and practical trades, then the seminary would be destroyed and the ministry emasculated. Such purely vocational training is "training for unemployment." This is not quite true, of course, of the ministry where so-called shortages appear, and where most of the crocodile tears come from professors and executives (who are not in the parish themselves) whenever anybody leaves, even if the church of Christ would be the better for it. A trade school seminary with only practical emphasis would be training in obsolescence, since communication techniques, and many others including counseling methods, change. This year's fad in liturgical goose-stepping may seem as funny (and as outdated) as Mack Sennett, after the young minister has spent five years in the parish. But this is a false antithesis.

Many parish ministers have reported a basic discontent with their seminary training.[11] Yet, very few seminaries do anything about it. The ministers indicate a greater need for Bible study and for understanding the social sciences. But in the curriculum, social science as an intellectual discipline is replaced by "practical" courses, and requirements in Bible become more and more minimal.

The seminary, its faculty and administration, never seems to decide what it really is. Outside pressures often make it what it is. So if it is in a university setting, it may try to become a graduate professional school, an equal of the law school or the medical school down the street. If, however, it is a school set in a rural scene, whose students come from the farms and villages, and whose pastors go out into the bush, it may be a farm trade-school in religion.

The pastor who is trained in a graduate school of religion, a seminary, a professional school, a trade school, or a preacher factory, has the same right to expect academic excellence, theological integrity, and biblical understanding as the aspiring college teacher of religion.[12] But the standard is not simply raised by requiring an undergraduate major in religion. A graduate school does not become a graduate school through the statistical study of the type of majors presented by its matriculating students, but by the standards of excellence and depth realized in the end product, after they have been tried and tested in parish, college teaching, or seminary.

V. Experiments in Theological Education

Although the majority of seminarians come from rural or open country homes, the church is, nevertheless, in its totality becoming more and more urban. Therefore the educational emphasis must show the primacy of the Word in the urban world. Many have discovered that much of the practical (trade-school) training can be learned out in the parish through a good internship, or even after graduation as an assistant. The place to learn about the world is through the world of the parish, not just in a sociology survey course. No suburban church is quite like Park Forest and no single church in Detroit is identical with another. But the man of average intelligence can learn by doing. More than one-third of the parish ministers expressed need for more supervised field work outside of the seminary.[13] More and more schools and even denominations are requiring field work and various types of internships.

The field work supervisor should be a man who knows the parish and knows theology. Then he can really supervise the field work and not merely be a human data-processing machine. It seems preferable to have the internship before the theoretical "practical" courses are taken. Because many of the courses in pastoral theology are taught by men who have never been parish pastors, the private experience of many parishes is to prefer interns from foreign countries who come to learn with an open mind and are not already brain-washed into thinking they know all the theoretical answers to the parish in direct confrontation with the world. They are not theoreticians in homiletics, nor faddists in liturgy, nor devotees of a particular school of psychology, religious education, or administration.

Another suggested cure (the darling of the NABI) for the ministry and the seminary is to demand of all entering seminary students a college major in religion or at least to recommend a strong minor.[14] Unfortunately this is not going to solve the problem. As noted above, graduate-level education and effective parish ministry are not correlated with undergraduate majors. There are many effective parish pastors, and probably a good many seminary professors, who had undergraduate majors in another subject and perhaps even had no religion courses in college. The mere fact of a religion major does not necessarily produce greater intellectual respectability or parish success.

Similarly the suggestion for changing the degree, perhaps granting the graduate a Ph.D. or Th.D. at the end of 3 or 4 years, will not help either unless the problem of religious integration is solved first. Someone has said that a universal college education will become a monument to procrastination: everyone getting ready to live but never really living. This could be true if we have universal Ph.D.'s or Th.D.'s for every seminary graduate, with or without an undergraduate religion major. A universal Ph.D. for all seminary graduates would become nothing more than a monument to mediocrity, regardless of all the good intentions of comprehensive exams and idealistic core curricula. In fact, the universal doctorate would only encourage the non-churched cynic who sincerely believes that the major motivation for entering the ministry is the desire for prestige. Since the greatest source of students is rural, the security of the ministry with some academic respectability is in many ways a matter of increased prestige.

There is also the possibility of again having at least two types of programs in the seminary, or two or more types of seminaries. There could be specialized schools for specialized ministries (or students). This could be effected readily where there are denominations such as the American Lutheran Church having one Board of Regents with three or four campuses under the same Board. Even within one seminary there could be several acceptable programs of study.

It would be better to have two or more schools. This may be too idealistic. The competition of statistics may prevent such a plan's becoming a reality. It could only happen if the ALC Board, for example, could convince its seminary faculties to operate different programs on the separate campuses. Subsidy, with honesty and humility, would be requisite.

Then it could be possible that on one campus Greek, Hebrew, Latin, French, and German were all required for entrance, and the graduates could continue into professional graduate work without the internship. Those who entered such a school and still sought the parish ministry could have the internship immediately before or after the final year.

A second type could accept only college graduates with no undergraduate religion. It would matriculate nonreligion majors only and require only one foreign language for entrance. The third campus probably would be the smallest, and would take only older professional and businessmen who were called to the ministry past the age of 35. Perhaps this could also include all students married before entrance into the seminary. There is an obvious maceration of the seminary student through marriage, childbirths, and attendant financial pressures. These are just as strong as any pressures of the parish later.

A fourth campus perhaps could be large enough to have a dual program and cater to the first two types of students. Those who enter with a creditable religion major could receive the B.D. or S.T.M. at the end of the first year of seminary, and the doctorate at the end of the fourth year. Those

without an undergraduate religion major would receive only
one degree (what it should be is debatable) at the end of
four years.[15]

There could be an easy exchange of faculties between
these various schools, especially if under one board. The
exchange could even be arranged with related colleges, so
that occasionally a college professor of sociology or communication arts would serve on the seminary faculty, and
the seminary professor of theology or Bible would teach a
year in the college. This would prevent one denominational
seminary from having all the brains, so-called, or all the
prestige names.

VI. Additional Suggestion Concerning Seminary Professorships

The problem of theological education is not simply in the
location of the school or in its curriculum. There is also
some concern about the seminary professor. Many have
suggested that "more successful (sic!) pastors be included
in seminary faculties."[16] This in itself poses a problem in
the determination of criteria. Is a good or "successful" minister one who has reported counseling successes? What about
the cases with which he was less "successful" in gaining
results? Is it largest membership? Greatest attendances? Most
appearances on radio and TV? Or any other statistic of
nonvital information?

Perhaps it should simply be stated that there should be
more experienced pastors included on the seminary faculty.
It has been suggested that a fruitful exchange could be
made between the faculties of our colleges and theological
schools.[17] Such an exchange of parish pastors and professors
makes just as good sense. Harvard, for financial reasons,
has been able to have a full-time department of the church
consisting of only two men, but this is supplemented with

parish pastors. This emergency measure may offer a solution to the practical department quite in contrast to the proliferation of courses and specialized professors in many other schools.

This exchange could be accomplished by having the seminary professor, especially if he is from the pastoral theology department, spend half of his sabbatical in parish work. A board member of Hamma Divinity School of the LCA recently wrote to the newly elected lay president, "I suggest that every professor in the seminary be given six months or a year, every five years, in order that he might serve a congregation. The professor would learn firsthand the parish problems and the thinking of our laymen." With the prestige of fellowships, overseas study, and additional work or degrees with great and famous scholars, it might be asking too much to suggest that half of a sabbatical be devoted to the parish.

Therefore the same results can be accomplished in another way. The NABI has been pushing for a stronger religion prerequisite for seminary. The results would be more striking if there were prerequisites for seminary instructorships and professorships. Too many men have drifted into the seminary teaching profession by reason of some substitute or emergency senior or graduate instructorship or teaching fellowship. These in themselves are fine, but many recipients never depart, except for additional graduate study, and fling themselves headlong up the hierarchy to full professor.

Could it be possible that the seminary student and future parish pastor is as important to the church as the man in uniform in our Armed Forces? The usual requirement is two or three years of parish experience before denominational certification for the military chaplaincy. Roman Catholics emphasize an even stronger parish experience and therefore often have a stronger chaplaincy. Surely there are minimum standards for all seminary students of any type institution mentioned above. There should be minimum standards for the professors, including experience somewhere other than in the hallowed halls of learning. For the professors of practical or pastoral theology there should be a higher minimum: a prerequisite of from three to five years of parish experience.

The second suggestion to accomplish the same results may have more doctrinal complications. Seminary appointments or calls could be limited. This would be most appropriate and vital in the pastoral theology department and for all professors involved in the communication arts. Methodist district superintendents are frequently appointed in this way: They serve for a certain period of time and then return to the parish. Members of the seminary pastoral department, or department of the church, could be called for seven or ten years and then return to the parish either for a full year sabbatical, as suggested above, or return to the parish fully committed, without keeping one eye on the call back to a seminary. This would serve quite well to take care of the problem of communication and isolation reported by pastors. It is impossible, even for the best, to remember, after ten or twenty years out of the parish, what the parish or even the layman is like. Worse, many of the "practical" professors have never served in the parish at all, so they have nothing to remember! My four-year-old, after listening to the babbling of a four-month-old child, came home rather frustrated. "I wish," she said, "I could remember what I used to think about, then I could understand what Susan is saying."

Conclusion

In all honesty, we must recognize that to blame anyone is no way to solve the problem of the parish and theological education. Berger may blame the community and the congregation: Sittler may blame the congregation and administrative headquarters and in a way put the blame directly with Berger, on the minister's psychological problems. Colleges blame the seminaries and seminaries blame the colleges, just as the liberal arts colleges frequently blame the high schools and the high schools blame the elementary schools and the elementary schools "pass the buck" to the parents. Pastors frequently blame both the seminary and the college, while college and seminary professors look down their noses as if the average parish pastor is a useless, ineffectual, nonintellectual cog.

A proper biblical and theological integration as noted above should recognize that all are to blame and all need to accept the criticism and the guilt about reshaping the ministry. Perhaps it is too late after ordination. Maybe we need to do some reshaping of theological education, of seminary faculties, of college religion departments, if we insist the ministry needs reshaping. After all, they worked together in much of the shaping of the parish minister in the first place.

The dilemma of the pastor or the maceration of the minister is not solved by hiring business managers, reducing mail from headquarters, developing home study courses for well-read parochial theologians—not even by coming back for summer courses in communication arts. There is rather need for self-discipline and self-criticism, both in seminary and in the parish. If we find a theological orientation and have prerequisites for professorships, we will be well on the way toward reshaping the ministry.

FOOTNOTES

1. My interest in this subject dates back more than 25 years. While in seminary I published several surveys of Lutheran seminary curricula in the *Lutheran Church Quarterly, Augustana Quarterly,* and *Journal of the American Lutheran Conference.* Three

years of parish experience in a rural setting and three years in Army chaplaincy were completed before I spent some nine years in seminary teaching. That was interrupted by a leave of absence to serve a metropolitan parish—the same one in which I have now served ten years. In the parish I have continued my "professional" learned society contacts and my writing. For 1963 I was program chairman for Mid West NABI and President of Middle Western SBLE. I have continued teaching at university and summer schools. The "practical" field is not neglected in full accredited membership in American Association of Marriage Counselors, and in pioneering programs in the parish.

2. Samuel H. Miller, "But Find the Point Again," a convocation address at Harvard Divinity School, September 30, 1959, p. 5.

3. Oral report to Mid West NABI at Garrett Biblical Institute, Evanston, Illinois, of the Lilly Study by Keith Bridston.

4. Cf. the Harvard Report: *General Education in a Free Society*, 1950, pp. 43 f.

5. Oral report, "Images of the Ministry," to a midwestern gathering of pastors, college teachers, seminary professors or presidents, at Divinity School, University of Chicago, called by Lilly Pre-Seminary Study 1962.

6. Samuel H. Miller, "The Focus of Theological Training," *Harvard Divinity School Bulletin*, April 1960, p. 5.

7. Harland Lewis, "The Parish Ministry and Theological Education," *Hartford Seminary Bulletin*, July 1960, p. 16.

8. *Ibid.*, p. 19.

9. Daniel Jenkins, *Tradition, Freedom and Spirit*, 1950, p. 186.

10. Walter Williams, "Theological Education in Retrospect and Prospect," *JBR* xxviii, 2 (April, 1960, pp. 167 ff.), reviews the Kelly study of 1924, Brown and May of 1934, Niebuhr, Williams, and Gustafson 1954-1957. *JBR* in 1961-1962 had a series on new experiments in graduate theological Education. A serious proposal was made in 1955 by Merrimon Cuninggim "Changing Emphases in the Seminary Curriculum," *JBR* xxiii, 2 (April 1955), pp. 110 ff. The two-year Lilly Endowment Study indicates there is still a long way to go.

11. Samuel W. Blizzard, "The Urban Parish Minister and His Training Needs," confidential report May 1, 1956, to participants, pp. 66 ff.

12. Ernest C. Colwell, "Closing the Gap Between College and Seminary," *JBR* xxvi 2 (April 1958), pp. 107 ff.

13. Blizzard, *ibid.*, cf. 71. Cf. Miller, Samuel, *HDSB* 1960, p. 7. "It is precisely in so-called field work that theological training stands in need of a revolution."

14. J. Allen Easley, "The Statement on Pre-Theological Studies," *JBR* xxv, 3 (July 1957), pp. 211 ff. It was this debate that laid the groundwork for the Lilly Study.

15. The National Science Foundation program encourages a dual program with a Ph. in Physics or a Ph.D. in Education with a major in Physics. However, there is even a hierarchy developing on this small ladder. Is the teacher of natural sciences more effective and more important with a straight Ph.D. in Physics than with the NSF educational doctorate?

16. Blizzard, *op. cit.*, p. 70.

17. Williams, *op. cit.*, p. 170.

THEOLOGICAL EDUCATION
AND THE IMAGE OF THE MINISTRY

REUEL L. HOWE

I. Introduction

During the last seven years as Director of the Institute for Advanced Pastoral Studies I have had opportunity to discuss concepts of the ministry with sixteen hundred ministers, representing thirty-eight denominations, ranging in age from the very young seminary graduate to men who have been in the ministry for twenty-five years or more.

I have been struck by the contrast between the certainty of the theological student's preconceptions of the ministry and the veteran minister's confusion about it. Some are frank to say that if they had known what it would be like, they would not have accepted ordination. There are indications that many more ministers think these thoughts but are unable to admit them. Some of the confusion, frustration, and despair experienced by ministers today is due to the expectations of the ministry produced by their training for it, complicated by conditions met in the ministry itself. Much of their instruction, for example, assumes an eighteenth- and nineteenth-century conception of the parish and local con-

gregation in which the minister is the shepherd of his people and of the community. In most places the church is no
longer a center of life but lives on the periphery of men's
interests. The lives of men are no longer centered where
their families live, and the modern minister is dismayed to
find that he is pastor mainly to women and children. Again,
the language of his education carries the assumption that
it is an effective means of communication to contemporary
man. After graduation the new minister soon discovers that
the biblical and theological language in which he was trained
and on which he based his hopes is not understood by
most of his people. Or again, many seminary communities
are so biblically and theologically centered that students
begin to think that the seminary world is the real world.
When they are ejected from this womb of theological cozi-
ness they discover that the world does not operate on the
same presuppositions or that it is not motivated by the same
orientations. Often they do not receive help to make the transition. As one man put it: "On formal occasions, as in preaching and teaching, I speak out of what I learned at the seminary. For work with people I am faced with the necessity
of building my own theology, which is drawn from all kinds
of sources and accepted because it works. The contrast between my two 'theologies' confuses both me and my people." This is the educational background that feeds the confusion and images from which the modern minister suffers.

II. Sources of Current Images of the Ministry

Every person, and therefore every minister, is, first of all,
what he is although he may not know what he is. Second,
he is influenced by what he thinks he is; and third,
he is influenced by what he thinks other people think he is.
First, many ministers have received no help in the acquisition of insight as to what and who they are. The most neg-

lected area in theological education is the person of the student himself, a surprising neglect in view of the nature of Christianity and its concern for persons; and in view also of the necessary correlation between person and function for the carrying out of any responsibility, and especially the ministry.

Second, they have not received help to understand the source, nature, and effect of their concepts of themselves. Many of them are not even aware of the distinction between psychic reality and reality, between what they think is true and what is true. Consequently the creative possibilities of many ministers are locked up in their misconceptions about themselves as persons.

Third, they are influenced and frustrated by other people's conception of them. *New Yorker* clergy cartoons represent much of the world's image of ministers and of their concerns and purposes. So influential are these images that some are reluctant to be known as ministers because they do not want to be identified with these caricatures. Other images have their source in the church's conception of ministers, many of which grow out of the clericalized condition of the ministry. On them, for example, is placed responsibility for the whole of the church's ministry. Again, ministers are expected to be more ethical and moral than laymen and are thus put on a pedestal. Their lives, this image says, should be better than other men's. Finally, as has already been indicated, some of the images of the ministry come from the preparation men have received for their work. Because much of their study is rooted in the past, the concepts of the past have a decisive influence over the images men have of themselves as ministers today.

A lack of knowledge and understanding of the world also contributes to the formation of images of the ministry. The world is regarded as alien and hostile, to which the term "secular" is applied. An oversimple distinction between church and world is made in which the church has the answer to the world if the world would only listen. This causes ministers to make oversimplified interpretations about the world and the church that thoughtful men living in the world cannot accept and which make it difficult for them to accept what is said about the church. Because ministers fail to help them accept and understand the world as the arena of self-actualization, or the place for commitment and responsibility rather than as an embarrassment and complication for Christian belief and practice, they imagize ministers as "Cloud Nine Boys" who are not to be taken seriously except in their formal and ritual functions.

We turn now to a consideration of some of the images present-day ministers have of themselves.

III. Some Images of the Ministry

These images concern the major functions of the minister's work such as communication, preaching, teaching, pastoral care, administration, and the priestly function.

A. The Images of Communication

Communication is a fundamental function, and a misconception of it would be disastrous for the whole work of the ministry, since its primary task is to make the Good News known. The prevailing image of communication is the monological one, the "tell 'em and leave 'em" approach. Of the sixteen hundred men referred to earlier, easily ninety-five percent have identified communication with the world today as their major concern. And when they speak of their frustrations, their difficulties of communication show up most frequently. They discover that the language in which they have been trained is not used by contemporary man, either to receive or to convey meaning. Preachers are overwhelmed by the observation that while they preach "grace," their people live by the "law." Many ministers are unaware that communication requires the use of ears as well as tongues; that what they might hear from laymen has human significance and often is the means of God's speaking to them as well.

In contrast to the monological misconception, they do not understand that by its very nature communication is dialogue, and that unless dialogue takes place either consciously or unconsciously, no communication occurs. Once in a while they recognize that they have been participants in a meeting of meaning between themselves and their people, but they know no more why it happened than why it did not occur on other occasions. This misconception of communication correlates with their clericalized conception of the ministry. It is easy for them to believe that God speaks through them to the laymen but difficult for them to believe that he speaks through laymen to them, and that it takes the whole church, speaking in dialogue, to proclaim the Gospel.

Where does this misconception of communication come from? Certainly not from Jesus the Teacher who embodied in himself the dialogue between God and man, and who in his own communication addressed himself to the meanings that people brought to him. Ministers pick up this concept of communication from the churches in which they were raised and from the example of their own teachers. Many of them complain that their thinking was done for them by their teachers and that they were led to believe that if they would repeat what they had heard in seminary, they would be heard in their parishes. They do not know how to use what they "learned" because they did not learn it in terms of their own meanings and words. Now their own people suffer from the same condition, and although they have "heard" the Good News, they cannot witness to it because they have not been helped to make it their own. The dumbness of the church member's witness is not due to a lack of subjection to the ideas of the Gospel but to the employment of an inadequate method of communication.

B. THE IMAGE OF PREACHING

Consistent with the monological misconception of communication, the prevailing image on the part of both ministers and laity of the preacher is that of a performer, of the sermon as the performance, and of the congregation as the audience. Contrary to the doctrine held by most churches, that the functions of the ministry, including preaching, are the responsibility of the whole church, this image of preaching puts the entire burden on the clergy and renders the congregation passive. It also means that the sermon is identified with what the preacher says to people gathered in the church building rather than with the message delivered by the people through their words and lives in the world where they live and work. The burden this image imposes produces two extreme reactions. First, the "performer" image of the preacher calls forth exhibitionistic tendencies so that preaching becomes an occasion when a man is tempted to exploit his congregation in the development of himself as a performer. A second reaction is paralysis. Many men are made so anxious by the lonely burden of preaching that they can never get down to the job. Paralysis keeps them from adequately preparing themselves for their part in the preaching function, causing them to preach hastily prepared, inadequately assimilated, and unconvincingly presented messages. This reaction takes a terrific toll on the health of the minister and on his relations with his family and others.

His monological conception of communication keeps the preacher from trying to find out as accurately and completely as possible what is being heard, and, therefore, robs him of the benefit he could receive from the response and thinking of his people. The consequent loneliness of the role of preacher has become intolerable to many.

C. The Image of Teaching

The prevailing image of the teacher is that of a lecturer, one who exercises his authority directly. He conceives of himself as one who is supposed to have the answers and is responsible for giving them. This concept of the teacher causes ministers to be concerned primarily with answers, forgetting that answers are for questions. They find themselves giving answers to questions that have not been asked, and they do not realize that a part of their responsibility is to help people formulate their conscious and unconscious questions. They do not seem to realize that the asking of questions prepares people for the answers and that learning is accomplished through a dialogue between question and answer.

The image of teacher held by many ministers does not prepare them to understand that a person has not learned the truth until he is able to think and present it out of his own meanings and his own terms. Many of them have not had this experience themselves. They may know their theological formulations and could pass an examination in systematic theology, but they do not as easily think theologically about life. They are slow to see the theological significance of a human situation. They are often blind to the incipient truth in people's lives. Unless they can be explicitly and obviously theological, they do not feel that theological significance is present. The need to be obviously theological makes them insensitive to the meanings that are to be found in people's lives which, when recognized, give them opportunity to teach dialogically and relevantly.

Another aspect of this image of the teacher is seen in ministers' concept of their authority. When a question or matter is put to them as authorities they often answer what is being asked instead of using their knowledge, understanding, and skill to help their inquirers move in the direction of answers to their own questions. This image of themselves as authorities seems to require that they exercise it in primitive and naive ways rather than in more creative and educative ways. Many of them have not discovered the greater excitement and satisfaction of having learners experience for themselves, with the guidance of the authority, of course, the joy of acquiring insight and knowledge. Because teachers of various kinds rush to give their own answers and opinions to questions instead of using their resources to help others learn, much that passes for education weakens rather than strengthens persons and makes them more dependent rather than more resourceful. Here again we see the effects of some theological education on the training of ministers. As was mentioned earlier, many of them complain that their teachers thought and spoke for them, and now that they have the responsibility of leadership they cannot exercise a true authority because they have been made dependent upon the authority of others, and they feel uncomfortable and guilty in relation to the authority that goes with their office. When they are forced to assume authority they have no alternative but to practice the same version of it as is demonstrated by their teachers.

D. THE IMAGE OF THE PASTOR

Confusion about the pastoral image is due in part to the contributions of the psychiatric and social sciences to pastoral care and the emergence of the psychiatric and psycho-analytic images of the pastor's role. The contributions that have come from these disciplines to the understanding of people and of human relations have been invaluable, but the correlation and assimilation of them have often presented some problems. Many pastors, for instance, have been intimidated by the impression they have of psychiatric insight and care in dealing with human difficulties and the greater complexity of which has been revealed. They have been made unclear about their own responsibilities and uncertain as to their qualifications to meet them.

Some tensions exist which unfortunately have not been resolved creatively. The first is the tension between counseling and pastoral care. In the minds of many, counseling has usurped the whole field of pastoral care instead of being but one aspect of it. The principles of counseling have become the principles of pastoral care, so that the perspective of the field has become much narrower than it should be.

Another tension about which there is great confusion is the tension between sickness and guilt. Because of the medical and psychiatric orientation recently acquired, pastors tend to think of human problems in terms of sickness, and they minimize the reality of guilt. In some ways psychologists take guilt more seriously than do ministers. While many pastors are caring for their parishioners as if they were sick, psychologists are taking seriously their patients' sense of guilt and are beginning to think in terms of sin.

Another tension that confuses pastoral images is that between adjustment and forgiveness. It is only natural that pastors who think of human behavior mainly in terms of illness would also think in terms of adjustments that would either cure or relieve the illness; whereas pastors who accept the reality of guilt and see its significance in the process of redemption would think in terms of forgiveness as the source of healing that releases men from the bondage of their alienation from themselves, one another, and God.

Three other tensions need to be noted. One is paternalism versus guidance. There is the kind of pastor who sees himself as a father. He may be motivated by sentiment or by severity. The sentimental pastor weakens his parishioner; the severe pastor who bases his ministry on the administration of discipline often alienates people. In contrast there is guidance: the recognition that the pastor's role is to be a resource to the parishioner, to help him think through his situation, to recognize his resources, to check his decisions; and encouraging and strengthening his actions in order that he may become a more responsible person.

Another tension exists between the non-directive and the participating concept of the pastor. For some pastors non-direction means allowing people to think through their problems at their own pace while the pastor merely reflects what they say in order that they may see themselves in his reflection. This has become a new doctrine of pastoral care that gives disappointing results when adhered to rigidly. Such pastors feel guilty whenever they slip into the role of advisor, exhorter, persuader, instructor, guide, or friend. In contrast to this is the concept of the pastor who participates in the living of his people. He meets them in all their living, seriously engages their meanings with his own, and seeks to bring their common human meanings into dialogue with the meanings of the Gospel.

A final and related tension is between the role of condescension and representation. The image produced by attitudes of condescension is that of the pastor who helps his people, through whom God acts in their behalf, and to whom he administers the grace of God. This image is one of the symptoms of a clericalized ministry. A corollary to this, although many would not admit it in so many words, is that the clergy are first-class citizens of the church and the laity are an inferior order. While these ministers would not subscribe to this doctrine formally, it is implicit in their way of carrying out their duties. In sharp contrast stands the concept of representation which is common to Protestant doctrine of the church and its ministry. The functions of the ministry are thought to reside in the church as a whole for which every member has responsibility. The clergy exist as delegated representatives for the carrying out of some of these functions for the sake of convenience and order, but without any abdication of responsibility by the body of believers.

We have, then, one image of the pastor as a "psychiatric" counselor concerned with sickness, working for adjustment, operating sometimes paternalistically, frequently nondirectively, and often in a spirit of condescension. Over against that image is one that is rooted in the broad concept of pastoral care, concerned with the guilt of men as well as their sickness, recognizing a need for forgiveness, helping people exercise their own powers of responsible decision and action, participating in their lives, and acting as representative both of God's action and of the church's ministry.

E. The Image of the Minister as Administrator and Director

Considerable resistance is to be found among ministers to the administrative work involved in maintaining the organizational life of the church. They feel that they are unprepared for it, that it is not what they entered the ministry to do, and that it takes too large a portion of their time. The situation is made worse by their inability to recognize the ministry in administration. When ministers are able to accept the inevitable tensions between the church as institution and the church as mission and look for its creative possibilities, parish administration can become ministry just as surely as is teaching or preaching or counseling. Rather than being a block, it can be an opportunity.

Another concept that ministers have of themselves is that of a director: one who directs the program and activities of the church. They regard themselves as responsible for the church but do not feel that they are a part of it. It is appalling to discover how really unchurched many clergy are. This in part accounts for their experiences of loneliness, for the spirit of competitiveness that anguishes their spirit, and for the sense of hopelessness in having to be the problem solvers for the organization. When their churches have a problem they feel that they must assume responsibility for it instead of sharing it with their people to whom the problem also belongs. Many of them are afraid to accept the honest concern and ministry of their people and feel that it is wrong for them to be ministered unto. Instead, they believe that they must present to their people the picture of a man who has no problems, with a family that lives in perfect accord, and who is charged with a ministry that requires him to be equal to every question, problem, and situation. That they do not fulfill these conditions only increases their sense of frustration and guilt.

F. The Priestly Image

Another image has to do with the priestly office. This image is weak among Protestant churches except those with a liturgical orientation. Many in the latter group look to the past, even to the Middle Ages, for both inspiration and pattern. A liturgical revival is bringing this area of ministry into focus again, but it is too new to have produced any decisive changes in the thinking of ministers of local congregations. Some concept of the minister as priest and of the Sacraments as a means of grace is needed if there is to be any synthesis of the Protestant and Catholic principle upon which depends reunion of Christian faith and practice.

G. Image of the Church

A widely prevailing image of the church and its ministry is parochial. Both clergy and laity think of the church in terms of the local congregation and its internal concerns. When asked to identify where their church is, they commonly specify the place where the church building is located, and inquiry reveals that they are thinking of services, meetings, and in-church activities of various kinds. The relation to the world of politics, law, and custom is either not thought of at all or done so ambiguously. Neither is there awareness among many people of the meanings being expressed by the plastic and performing arts, by science and industry, and the significance they have for the meanings of the Gospel. The parochialism of this image of the church often reduces the church's faith and practice to the dimensions of a cult.

No doctrine of the church and the ministry of any denomination supports the images just described. And all are in contradiction to the theological views of most of the men who hold them. It seems obvious that the theory about the church and the ministry does not have much effect on the practice of the average minister.

IV. Conclusion

I have been asked to conclude this description of the images held by ministers with a statement of a concept of ministry that might be relevant for our own time. No one of us can presume to formulate such a concept, but any of us may hope to identify some aspect of it and even contribute to its formulation.

The form of the ordained ministry may change if the church is equally responsive to the Spirit and to the vitality and need of each generation. We should not discard what we have received, but neither should we hold the form of what we have received so rigidly that it is no longer available to God to make it what he wills.

But how shall we live in this kind of tension, treasuring what we have and yet expecting what we are to become? The answer is: By keeping the ministry, whatever its present form, focused on its most true and relevant purpose for the time. The present time is one in which men are looking for meaning. Many people doubt that there is any over-all ultimate meaning, and so grab at any little meaning they can find. Others, believing that there is an enduring meaning, seize upon and settle for partial meanings to which they give their devotion and thus serve idols such as religion, politics, fame, efficiency, success, etc. And still other men are searching for the pearl of great price, the meaning that connects and completes all meaning. The purpose of the ministry in a generation that is searching for meaning is to meet that search with understanding and response. The meanings of the Gospel cannot be imposed on the meanings of each generation like a veneer. As we saw earlier, the relationship between him who was the Good News and his generation was one of dialogue in which the meanings of man and those of God met. I would say, then, that the function of the church is to be in dialogue with the world, and the function of the pastoral, homiletical, educational, and priestly ministry is to promote and maintain the dialogue between the Word of God and the word of man in order that men may know their own need and possibility, and know and accept what God has given them.

One purpose of theological education, at least, is to train ministers for that dialogical task. Both clergy and laity need training that will prepare them to become persons with dialogical understanding and abilities. For a majority of them this would mean a revolution in their present understandings and approaches because of the prevalence of the monological attitude and method which have been ingrained in them by their life in the church and the training given them for their ministry.

One of the frustrations experienced by many ministers is that they find themselves separated from their lay people and able to talk with them only about religion and the church at the level of program and organization. And laymen speak of the same separation and discussion limitations. Most clergy seem not to have been trained to ask their people about their interests, their work, what it means to them, their questions, beliefs, and thoughts. There is limited conversation between clergy and laity because the clergy are not aware that the laity have anything to say that has meaning in itself and is necessary to what they would say. Their expectation based on their training is quite the opposite: that their task is to tell people monologically what they should know and believe. Ministers' education should increase rather than decrease their capacity to communicate with the people to whom they are sent, remembering that communication requires the use of ears as well as mouths. Resources used to be developed that would keep students for the ministry in dialogue with the world from which they came, to which they belong, and to which they will be sent.

Clinical training and supervised field work programs are a step in that direction, but they need further development and other resources need to be found. Practice preaching in seminary, for example, could be done not only to fellow students and instructors, which is the usual custom, but to representative lay people who would be invited to the class for the occasion, if it were held in the evening. Lay people are interested in assisting in the training of clergy and will make all kinds of adjustments and sacrifices to do so. The benefits of lay participation in this kind of training should be obvious. The comments of the teachers and fellow students are valuable, of course, but of equal, if not greater, importance are the comments of the kinds of people to whom the future minister will be preaching. The comments of the laity could be as valuable to the instructor and the students not preaching as to the student preacher; and the whole experience, including the comments of instructor and students, would be edifying to the lay discussants.

Other resources need to be developed to acquaint the future minister with the world in which he is to serve in order that he may have eyes that see and ears that hear the life that goes on behind the masks that men wear, the questions behind the questions that men ask, and the meanings that they bring out of their life and work to every kind of encounter.

It would seem, therefore, that we should change the purpose of our teaching from that of transmitting knowledge about the faith to training men for action in the faith. People should know the Gospel, not for the sake of possessing that knowledge, but in order that they may *live* it. The Gospel is a saving event that occurs in human relations, and not a body of knowledge for mere verbal transmission. There is a place for knowledge, of course. There is nothing more deplorable and ineffectual than an ignorant minister, whether ordained or unordained, but also there is nothing more sterile than the transmission of information without its incarnation in the power of the personal. Our Lord did not add much to our knowledge of God. He embodied God for us so that we could know him, instead of knowing about him.

Yet, one of the most incapacitating anxieties of both clergy and laity is the "agenda anxiety" to which I referred earlier.

They are so concerned with transmission of content of the Christian faith that they are blind and deaf to its relation to the people themselves, to their meanings, and their questions about human life. They make idols out of the propositions about the faith and worship them.

Many clergy are victims of what we call the "content" illusion. This will continue to be the case as long as centers of learning continue to teach subject matter exclusively, and in so doing overlook their responsibility for the student and his relation to the world in which he lives and to which he is to be sent. And clergy transmit this preoccupation with content to their people. A man filled with subject matter does not make an adequate minister. An adequate minister is one in whom the meaning of life and the meaning of the Gospel are correlated. The "didactic and dogmatic stance" referred to by Richard Niebuhr in *The Advancement of Theological Education* produces a ministry that is unequal to proclaiming the Gospel in our day. When profound questions are being asked in every aspect of life, ministers trained in this way come to resent the indignity of having been turned into subject-matter peddlers instead of ambassadors for Christ.

The principle of dialogue needs to be employed in the reforming of the teacher's role. The dialogical teacher is alert to the meanings that his students bring to the moment of learning; he helps them formulate their questions and meanings as preparation for learning; he accepts himself and his relationship with his students as a primary resource in education; he is free to be versatile in his choice and use of methods; and he has faith in the student and the future of the word spoken in dialogue.

The application of the principle of dialogue to theological education would produce a different kind of graduate. In the first place, he would be one who would feel as at home in the world as he did in the classroom; he would be able to communicate, at least to some degree, with the people to whom he is sent to minister; he would be more interested in life than in religion as an end in itself; and he would be better able also to resist the insidious clericalizing influences within the church which today eliminate the potential power of laity from the witness of the church in the world.

Dialogical education would help the future minister know deeply what it means to be a person living the human life with other persons. This cannot be taken for granted. It does not follow that because a man has lived for twenty or forty years he knows what it means to be a person, and that he brings the insight of what it means to his theological training. It is a part of the responsibility of the seminary to provide a means whereby the student may come to know himself as a person living in relation to others, and to do this through programs such as clinical training, field work, and intern programs of one kind or another, as well as through the employment of psychotherapy. The direction of his study and worship-life as a part of the educational community would be to this end. For many ministers one of the chief obstacles to the exercise of an effective ministry is a deficiency of preparation, which partially goes back to the inadequacy of their education. Of course, if a man enters the ministry as a way of evading the real questions and problems of human existence, he can never be a true minister.

Second, dialogical education would help students recognize themselves as members of the *laos,* the people of God. Too many ministers forget this identity and, instead, search for the meaning of their calling in their role as priest or ordained minister. And too few laymen are aware of having any real status in the church. Unless the priesthood or ministry is grounded in this concept, and unless there are people who know themselves as such, clericalism and hierarchical conceptions of the ministry will inevitably develop. These are inimical to the truth of the fellowship of the Holy Spirit.

Third, dialogical education for the ministry would help men to recognize and accept their dependence upon the Holy Spirit for carrying on the work of the ministry. Again it must be affirmed that the church is the incarnation of the Holy Spirit; and all the people of God, ordained or not, are the instruments of the Spirit, rather than the Spirit being the instrument of their work. The ministry becomes, then, a participation in what God is doing in the world. Right orientation and faith at this point would be decisive for radical change in the conception of the minister's task and that of the laity. Furthermore, there would be a basis for accepting the tension between vitality and form, between the Spirit and the various forms that often threaten to strangle the life of the church. And the leaders of the church would be much more creative if they could be freed from slavery to obsolete form and open to the Spirit's guidance in the creation of new ones.

Fourth, dialogical education would help ministers recognize that the church's mission is to the world and not to the church. There is too much preoccupation with the church as an institution, and not enough with its responsibilities to the world in which it is set. Along with and even as a part of the study of the Bible, the history of the church, theology, pastoral care, and denominational lore, should go the study of the world in which the church now lives and in which its ministry will have to be carried on. More needs to be done to familiarize men with the cultural influences that are dynamically opposed to the working of the Spirit. They need help in distinguishing that part of the secular life which can be affirmed from that part which needs to be brought unto judgment. They need help in recognizing the meaning to men of their work, and help in showing men how their work may be their service to the world which they may offer to God as a part of their worship. When ministers do not know how to enter into a meaningful dialogue with the world, they are not able to teach people to know what they are accepting when they accept the Christian faith, or what they are rejecting when they reject it. This is the case, not because ministers do not know their theology, but because they do not understand the meaning of the life into which they are sent. Many of them, therefore, are bitter because they feel they are dealing with the trivia of life, both in the world and in the church, rather than with the depth of meaning of the meeting between the church and the world.

Finally, dialogical education would help students see the unity that binds the different functions of the ministry. It is ridiculous for ministers to choose between being priests and being preachers or pastors, or to choose being pastors rather than being teachers and administrators, as if such a division of the dynamically interrelated Christian ministry were possible. There is too much equating of the work and fruits of the Spirit with the human talents of men. God may use a man's talents, or he may seem to ignore them and call him to a work for which he does not have a natural talent. Here again the applied doctrine of the Holy Spirit is essential. We do not enter the ministry on the basis of our talents alone. We enter because we are called by him who is doing his work in the world and who will use those who surrender themselves to him. But because he is the worker, there is a unity in the different functions that we perform. When we teach, we are also caring for souls, and our pastoral care gives opportunity also to teach. The principles of teaching are equally relevant to counseling and preaching.

The interrelationships of the different functions of the ministry derive from the unity of God's working, and from the basic principles of relationship upon which all functions of persons and, therefore, of ministers, must depend. A sense of this unity of the ministry is needed by ministers, not only for the sake of their work, but also for the sake of their health as workmen. A reflection of this unity in the very educational process would restore to the whole church a sense of unity between the parts of the ministry.

If the church is to speak to the present generation, its ministry must be able to listen as well as speak. A listening ministry, in contrast to a monological one, will always be renewed and need not be afraid of change. Instead of being defensive in response to the new insights and discoveries of man, it will courageously enter into dialogue with them in the confidence that out of it a living and relevant concept of the ministry will appear.

PROPHETS *AND* PROMOTERS?

MALCOLM BOYD

The question of how ministers can be educated in such a way that they will really be able to communicate the Gospel to contemporary culture is, of course, second to none in importance in the present-day Christian church.

Often one feels that a seminary education somehow retards rather than encourages a proclamation of the Gospel. A danger of seminary training is that the polishing process may transform a man into a church conformist. Christianly radical though he may consider himself and be considered by others, henceforth his radicalism may tend to be confined within a context. Therefore, he may not be Christianly radical even when appearing to be so.

There is a gulf between training and experience which must always be bridged. For example, one may have studied about prophets without being able to identify a prophet sitting in one's livingroom; or one may have studied the lives of saints without being able to determine, really, and on the basis of modern industrial and technological life, what constitutes a saintly life.

Any answers couched in old sentimentalisms, overt piety worn on sleeves, the mere casting of eyes heavenward or heretical irrelevancy masked by self-righteousness, will have little or no meaning for contemporary persons.

I feel that seminary has probably succeeded best when it has enabled a man to start asking at least some of the right questions. Until these questions can be asked—by any man —surely no answers of relevance can be distributed, as one might hand out so many sheets of paper in a classroom. A major problem of our culture is that so many answers are being handed out to questions that have never been raised and that right questions often seem not to be articulated at all. Such a tragedy as this bars all possibility that the right questions will ever be answered correctly. Most answers have to be hammered out by a man in the experience of living his life. A man should be commencing rather than ending his learning process when he graduates from a theological seminary.

He is, for example, supposed to learn the Bible. But how can he do this unless his Bible study is existential and related to life in such a way that a man *experiences* God's Word?

A man is to learn theology, but theology dare not be separated from life if it is to possess dynamic. Theology lacking dynamic is a self-contradiction.

A man is to learn church history, but church history continues to be written today, and one must see the relationship of the history of this moment to past history.

A man is to learn Christian education, but it remains an empty phrase until correlated with the life, education problems, and learning potential of people: quite specific men, women, and children, in quite specific situations.

A man is to learn to preach, but the power of preaching grows out of a pastoral relationship with men, women, and children; a knowledge of their lives and needs, drawn from individual counseling and relationship; and a sharing of day-by-day life with them.

A man is to learn the liturgy, but he cannot do this unless he can relate liturgy to life—otherwise he will only have retreated farther toward that ingrown, unrelated caricature of church life which has frequently and tragically managed to separate liturgy from life.

In endeavoring to go forward with its essential vocation of Christian evangelism, the church is immediately faced by the crisis in communication brought about by the loss of meaning of traditional words. Changing concepts within culture have produced caricatures of such words as "love" and "man" and "sin."

Too, the church is caught in a web of grotesque, inexplicable images: the images and words it desires to be understood become hopelessly distorted in the process of communicating. We have observed the seeming impotency of the church on numerous occasions to communicate except by clear, hard action (as, for example, on occasion in South Africa), yet the church seems never before to have been so involved with words!

Is not our task to make Jesus Christ identifiable in word and image for contemporary man in mass culture? Is not our task to achieve points of contact for the Gospel with contemporary man in mass culture by creating new images which possess meaning for him?

Images within mass culture are rampant; a number of them must be made identifiable with Christianity. This is difficult to do, for the culture is post-Christian and has rejected explicit Christian words and images. One cannot, therefore, approach the culture in a traditional way, trying to make use of old words and images in order to establish dialogue.

I recall sitting one night in a club which was, I felt, a Christian image of hell, yet I was surrounded by persons who did not believe in hell. Therefore, they would have summarily rejected the present statement of their condition had I attempted to offer it to them. They were isolated from one another, though seated tightly alongside each other at the bar and at tables jammed closely together, in the illusory security and denseness of the overly-crowded room. Music was played without a break, at a peak level of screaming sound; the musicians themselves appeared ready to drop from exhaustion and the boredom of the sameness of the music without end. There was a beat, a rhythm, so insistent that it carried with it body, mind, and soul: but it led nowhere; it was only a respite, a filling-in and obliterating of time which was unendurable.

Another Christian image of hell can be found at the heart of a modern city, a dozen blocks from the smart center of hotels and stores: here is the slum, the "underprivileged area," where life continues as an existence away from the vision of the great city. Here, in a lost pocket of the city, in a touch of wilderness within the teeming jungle of the city, people need to eat, to love, to sleep, but they are out-of-step with progress and glamor and bigness and success, and they know it and feel dead. They could reach out to one another, but instead they play a frozen charade and remain alone. They inhabit a Christian image of hell, but they have ceased to believe in hell. How may one make identifiable to them the condition of their very life, its consequences, indeed the possibilities and hopes stemming from it?

W. H. Auden, in *The Enchafed Flood*,[1] discusses the image of the city in *Moby Dick*: a city in which Ishmael still remains an individual who can identify an image of hell and exercises his freedom of will in turning his back upon it. "Urban society is, like the desert, a place without limits. The city walls of tradition, mythos, and cultus have crumbled. There is no direction in which Ishmael is forbidden or forcibly prevented from moving. The only outside 'necessities' are

the random winds of fashion or the lifeless chains of a meaningless job, which so long as he remains an individual, he
can and will reject. At the same time, however, he fails to
find a necessity within himself to take their place. So he
must take drastic measures and go down to the waters. . . . "

The images rampant in our culture are directly related to
the church's task of mission. In being missionary, in relating
to the culture in which it has its life, the church shall have
to be able to relate to the images of the culture in order to
establish fundamental point of contact for a meaningful dialogue. Presumably the church has learned that it cannot simply stand back, or up, and "preach" to the culture. It must
interpenetrate the culture. In order to do this, it must com-
prehend the culture, its mores, its words, and its images.

A few key personalities emerge from mass culture in an
intriguingly forceful way to stimulate, challenge, and influence men. Their very emergence out of anonymity into
spheres of spiritual power is directly related to their images.
One of the most arresting personalities of our time was Al-
bert Camus. He deeply influenced the culture in which he
lived, and his death was felt as a personal loss in many widely
separated parts of the world.

Men's images of Camus tended to identify his struggle
for meaning with their own struggle. Images of his books—
*The Rebel, The Stranger, The Plague, The Fall, The Myth
of Sisyphus*—became most powerful as other men related
these images to their own images of themselves. Robert M.
Adams, writing about Camus in *The Nation,* caught the
spirit of the vitality and depth of the meaning of his image
to other men sharing culture and time with him: "And
Camus himself is an admirable subject; for he is evidently
one of those spiritual lightning rods around whom our age
concentrates its darkest clouds, its most outrageous fires.
. . . The intense and sensitive face which looks out of his

portraits is insatiable in its attraction to the great questions of life—the ones to which we must have answers in order to get on with it. And the residual restlessness we sense in his character, as in his art, is the best guarantee that he will not fob us off with easy answers."[2]

The images of the culture are directly related to the church's task of mission in a yet more profound way. There are images of the church itself which are perpetuated in the culture. Mission cannot seriously be undertaken until the church has determined what are the images of itself in the culture—and, most particularly, what are the images of its mission.

How many persons, one wonders, have rejected the Christian faith for the wrong reasons—for reasons related to false images which have distorted the faith instead of showing forth its fundamental nature? (Of course, one wonders, too, how many persons have accepted the Christian faith for the wrong reasons—equally related to false images.) Many thinking, conscientious, troubled, searching men and women have felt that they had to reject the Christian faith on the basis of its images which had come to their attention. When one becomes aware of some of these false or distorted images, one quite comprehends why they have acted in the way they have.

In his book *Act One*,[3] Moss Hart shared a very important image with his readers—an image of "worthy institutions" and "good causes" which many, many persons hold in common with him. It is, of course, an image directly related to the churches and church work. "Once more I looked up the address in the telephone book to make sure and then I hurried out. The Clara De Hirsch Home for Working Girls was an estimable charity run by good people to provide unattached and homeless girls with decent food and shelter in a city not much interested in their welfare. Yet as I hurried toward the building at the corner of Third Avenue, I wondered if any edifice need actually look so cheerless and desolate. Why do worthy institutions or good causes always lack any single element of gaiety or joy?"

I discovered something of one man's images of the church while I was discussing Christianity with him as he seriously struggled with the question of whether or not to become a member of the church. "I can't believe the Creed—oh, maybe the first line, that one about I believe in God," he said. "I can probably believe that. But when it comes, say, to Communion because I feel a part of the ritual that thousands and millions of people have taken part in—good, honest people—but it means absolutely nothing more than that to me."

This immediately brings us back to basic Christian images in the culture.

> The church is the body of Christ: Who is Christ, what is the image of Christ?
> The church is the instrument of salvation: What does that mean, what is the image of salvation?
> The church mediates grace: What is that, what is the image of grace?
> The church pronounces absolution for sins: What is sin, what is the image of sin, the image of absolution for sin?
> The church strives to prepare persons for eternal life with God in heaven: what is eternal life, what is heaven, what are the images of these?
> The church glorifies and adores God. Who is God, what is the image of God?
> The church is indwelt by the Holy Spirit: Who is the Holy Spirit, what is the image of the Holy Spirit?
> The church proclaims the Gospel to man in the world: What is the Gospel, who is man, what is the world, what are the images of these?

If the church does not discover these basic images of itself and its work in mass culture, it pursues its mission at the terrible risk of perpetuating false, useless, or quite dangerous images by means of its very missionary endeavor.

The church needs to find out the basic images in mass culture of the church and the fundamental tenets of the Christian faith.

Where it finds that such images are in correlation with the Christian faith, the church may utilize existing images in its work of mission.

On the other hand, where it finds that such images are not in correlation with the Christian faith—are, in fact, contradictory to it—the church must reshape or discard these images and set about the task of creating some new Christian images of basic Christian tenets.

The Christian clergyman will be dealing, at a crucial level of involvement, with the question of the relation of church to culture. It is an unavoidable question. It need not, in fact, be raised; it asks itself. It is of paramount importance that the tension between evangelism and exploitation be understood, particularly amidst an affluent society which states constantly—and frequently through church channels—its own terms of secular salvation.

Every Christian, simply by virtue of being a Christian, is called to be an evangelist. The mass culture image of an evangelist is made up of such component parts as a crowd, the "hero" as "evangelist," mammoth size and scope, and expert publicity machinery. Actually, this image, oversimplified and distorted as it is, may be related somewhat to a revivalist. It is a false image of an evangelist. *Every Christian is an evangelist.*

Living in the world, the church lives also in what has been called the contemporary "Age of Publicity." Naturally, methods and techniques of modern communication are employed by the church. This results in a tension which is sharply experienced by the contemporary Christian who is identified with the organization of the machinery of evangelistic enterprise. Where is the line to be drawn between discipleship and huckstering? Or, in other words, where is the line to be drawn between evangelization and exploitation?

Always the person of Jesus Christ and the Christian Gospel stand in judgment upon any and all methods utilized by men to communicate the meaning of "life with Christ." It is entirely possible that a church or an evangelist might experience success in the *how* of his communication (by a system of organizing groups, arranging for mass publicity media, and in consequence of men's already tried responses to various techniques). At the same time, it is entirely possible that a church or an evangelist, engaged in this activity, might experience failure in the non-computable area of the *what* of communication. If the *how* of such communication itself, standing under the judgment of Jesus Christ, were sharply antithetical to the whole spirit of Jesus' life and Gospel, then the failure to communicate the *what* could be the more clearly discernible within the successful *how* of mere human propaganda.

Carlo Coccioli, in his novel *Heaven and Earth*,[4] has one of his characters speak bluntly and memorably about the quality of self-contradiction contained in many channels of Christian communication which have been emptied of their dynamic

"Monsignor," he said, "I say that there is no flame, no Christ. This so-called Christian society of ours is a decayed corpse. People are married in church after they have been to the town hall. They bring their children to be baptized and call a priest when they are at death's door, but these things do not make for a Christian society—God is something like the major or the police sergeant, only kindlier; He came down from heaven (if He was ever really there) to earth and if He hasn't put on earthly dress it is only a matter of

time before He does so. Tepidity is everywhere. Even God
has become tepid. The earth turns, the seasons follow one
another, night comes after day and when a man is about to
die, good God, please take his soul to heaven (if there is
such a place and he has a soul to be taken)!"

When we attempt to communicate the Christian Gospel
—by actions, words, or images—God, who is not bound by
our categories, measures the quality of our love and service
in his own ways which are different from our ways. We always have the duty of relying upon God's grace rather than
upon our tactics and techniques. In this way, when we
utilize tactics and techniques, we seek to achieve the quality of abandonment, love, and service which he wills for
us, and we sacrifice being primarily motivated by worldly
standards.

Christian evangelism takes place in an environment wherein it is pursued in a spirit of abandonment to God, love of
God and brother man (which means an awareness of the
sanctity of personal meaning which God, by creation and redemption, has bestowed upon one's brother man), and service
to God's kingdom. Non-Christian exploitation, on the other
hand, takes place in an environment marked by a singular
lack of concern for the sanctity of personal meaning which
God has given to each human life; manipulation accordingly
plays a vital role in exploitation.

The Christian evangelist is automatically caught-up in
the world of culture. *How* he is to communicate his message, however, is second always to the Gospel he exists as an
evangelist to communicate. Why? Because the Gospel he
exists as an evangelist to communicate always stands in
judgment upon the means used to communicate it.

An interesting example of how improper exploitation may
boomerang is given us by William Albig in his study *Modern
Public Opinion*,[5] "Major cultural symbols, such as those of a

religion or nation, may be purposely depreciated or defiled, as in the sacrilege of the Black Mass, the defacement of the flag or other national emblems. However, more often, significant symbols are cheapened by overuse or commercial exploitation. The cross is such a venerated symbol. Yet, recently, fashion has decreed the wearing by young women of 'streamlined crosses.' Crosses as religious symbols and crosses as simple designs for the adornment of young women have quite a different functional significance."

A major question confronting the Christian church is that of proper use of the media of mass communication. Such media—TV, films, radio, mass-circulation newspapers and magazines—have caused a revolution in the dissemination of ideas to mass publics. Oversimplification, overemphasis on entertainment, loss of depth in dealing with essential issues: these and other equally grave criticisms are leveled at the mass media. "Exactly what kind of insight and care are needed to avoid misuse of the mass media of communication?" This question is asked insistently and validly. An answer must include the following elements.

The insight needed to avoid misuse of the media of mass communication is an insight into one's own motivations—both as an individual and as an individual standing within his societies (including his church). To place technique ahead of motivation is, for truly effective Christian communication, absolutely contradictory. The care needed to avoid such misuse must incorporate technical excellence (offered to the glory of God) with the intention of purity of heart (also offered to the glory of God).

Manipulation almost invariably marks opinion-formation, public relations, and image-conception, Irwin Ross declares in his book *The Image Merchants.*[6] This is true at least in the sense of being indirect, subtle, and ingenious. "The intent of such manipulation may well be innocuous; its by-products may also be a positive boon to the community; but manipulation it remains, nonetheless." Deliberate manipulation is the mark of exploitation.

I am shocked by the callousness of much so-called evangelism which is mere exploitation. I am particularly shocked when a spade is not called a spade, and added to the sin of deceit is the worse sin of self-righteousness. The name of Jesus Christ is added, almost as a gimmick for self-induced holiness, to projects which bear little or no resemblance to serious Christian evangelism. There is a smoggy climate of self-righteousness which does not effectively cover a multitude of sins identifiable as religious-financial or religious-prestige gimmicks in our mass culture. The wheat and the tares grow together, as they always have.

"Exactly what kind of insight and care are needed to avoid misuse of the media of mass communication?" Insight and care to accept moral ambiguities but to remember that God transcends even these (and rationalizations about them!). Insight and care to present the unattractiveness of the Gospel attractively. Insight and care to present the person of the crucified and risen Lord as over against the celebrity cult to which he does not belong. Insight and care to present the demands of the Gospel in a demanding way, its hope in a hopeful way, its joy in a joyful way. Insight and care to accept our always mixed motives honestly and without morbidity and to confess these to the Lord simply and in repentance (avoiding the pitfall of labeling motives in "religious" work as being "good"), and joyfully receiving the Lord's forgiveness of our individual and social sins in our very possession of mixed motives; then, going on with our work for the Lord, trusting in his real guidance, being concerned more for his love and power and service than for our own salvation, and having sufficient faith in him to do with our mixed motives as he might wish!

Insight and care to respect the media of mass communication as parts of God's good creation and to avoid using them in deliberate exploitation of other human beings. Insight and care to respect other persons created by God with dignity and free will instead of looking at them as objects to be used to serve one's own ends. Insight and care to discard the "old" that has been retained only because it was a symbol of status quo and to retain the "old" that might be tossed out in favor of mere passing taste. Insight and care to discard the "new" if it represents false religion (for example, if it is an exploitation gimmick which has no respect for the dignity of human beings and their bodily, mental, and spiritual needs), and to retain the "new," even at the cost of being condemned for being radical, if it is an honest, indigenous, striking expression which rightly demythologizes more cultural accretions and points to Jesus Christ.

"If only Christ were preached and practiced in all his simplicity to the world, how fast Christianity would spread." We have heard this statement uttered many times.

The English theologian P. T. Forsyth offered a rather devastating answer to this statement, and one which contributes excellently to our discussion, in his book *The Work of Christ.*[7] Forsyth commented: "Would it? Do you really find that the deeper you get into Christ and the meaning of His demands Christianity spreads faster in your heart? Is it not very much the other way? When it comes to close quarters you have actually to be got down and broken, that the old man may be pulverized and the new man created from the dust. Therefore when we hear people abusing the Church and its history the first thing we have to say is, Yes, there is a great deal too much truth in what you say, but there is also a greater truth which you are not allowing for, and it is this. One reason why the Church has been so slow in its progress in mankind and its effect on human history is because it has been so faithful to Christ, so faithful to His Cross. You have to subdue the most intractable, difficult, and slow thing in the world—man's self-will. You cannot expect rapid successes if you truly preach the Cross whereon Christ died, and which He surmounted not simply by leaving it behind but by rising again and converting the very Cross into a power and glory."

In our use of the media of mass communication in the vocation of Christian communication we seem to need less self-conscious witnessing of men and a greater disposition to witnessing of God the Holy Spirit, acting through faithful and willing men who live unselfconsciously "in Christ"; perhaps fewer gimmicks and more devout prayer; less measurement of our success by worldly standards and more acceptance of the Lord's standards. Christian hope is manifested too strongly in the world's methods and timetables and not in waiting upon the Lord. Man is seen as a machine and not as a person uniquely created in the image of God.

Always it is necessary to bear in mind that the "means" towards any "end" may implicitly refute the "end" itself. For example, there is a tendency in using mass media, for the church as well as for a product, to rely upon size and scope and to minimize the value of the individual person. The individual is dehumanized by much of modern society.

It is self-contradictory for the church to pronounce the Gospel message by means of the mass media if, by the very process, it reduces the individual listener or viewer or reader to the status of an object, a statistic, or a digit. This need not, certainly, be the result of use of the mass media. There is a considerable use of the mass media by Christians which is deserving of commendation. However, insight and care must be exerted if misuse of the mass media is to be avoided. Does one "save" a statistic? If so, how? And does one "love" a statistic, especially if one's motivations are geared to exploitation?

The temptation to use a "means to an end" is pointed up sharply by the potential correct use or misuse of a new, powerful technique known as Motivation Research. It is concerned with subsurface motivating factors in buying and selling.

The church is an institution which has its being in *this* world, one of advertising, public relations, "hard" and "soft" sell and Motivation Research. The church is not only called on to speak prophetically about such new techniques but has the difficult chore of deciding what makes for proper use, and what makes for misuse. This is true, not only in regard to its members, and its own public relations approach to the world, but also to its prophetic task to speak to the whole of culture.

The magnitude of the church's prophetic task is clearly evidenced by the manipulative forces that work around us ceaselessly. John Kenneth Galbraith, in *The Affluent Society*,[8] takes note of such an incredible change in our society "that many of the desires of the individual are no longer even evident to him. They become so only as they are synthesized, elaborated, and nurtured by advertising and salesmanship, and these, in turn, have become among our most important and talented professions. Few people at the beginning of the nineteenth century needed an adman to tell them what they wanted."

Pierre Martineau, in his book *Motivation in Advertising*,[9] states that "Modern advertising can and does reach into the emotional structure, the unconscious, the deepest sources of motivation in the individual. This is what the creative people are trying to create—a message which will incorporate this power to move human beings just because it *can* get at their primitive, fundamental, prelogical motives and impulses."

In Motivation Research, *the person becomes the center of dominant interest.* He is seen as being changeable, suggestible, highly nonrational, motivated far more by emotion and habit and unconscious causes than by reason and logic. Individual behavior is seen, too, as being shaped by ideals and pressures of one's particular society. "Even such a factor as religion bends a personality. There are very few Episcopalian farmers, Presbyterian farmers, or Jewish farmers." Motivation Research—which is generally known in the trade as M.R.—offers techniques and bodies of theory from the various humanistic sciences, particularly sociology, social anthropology, psychology, psychoanalysis, psychiatry, and social psychology. Semantics and the various disciplines grouped under communication are also extremely relevant.

There is a desire, in the use of M.R., to reach the real person "behind all the masks that he has to wear" and to penetrate underneath "his conforming conduct" and "the parts of his personality also concerned with the psychological meanings which play such a considerable role in the life history of institutions and products."

Any buying process is an interaction between the personality of the individual and the so-called "personality" of the product or institution, writes Mr. Martineau. He usefully reminds his admen colleagues—and it is good advice for all other communicators, too—that there is a tremendous gap between what we *think* we are saying and what we are *really* saying. In this vein, he says that it is important to ascertain whether one's creative symbols are meaningful and whether the audience might possibly be reading in a different set of broad meanings from the symbols than was intended.

"Product image"—what is it? It consists of "the total set of attitudes, the halo of psychological meanings, the associations of feeling, the indelibly written esthetic messages over and above the bare physical qualities." One wonders what is the popular image, say of the Methodist Church or the Episcopal Church or the Roman Catholic Church, or the Presbyterian Church. One wonders what is the popular image of "a Christian" or a particular local church or clergyman, in a specific neighborhood.

The discrepancies between a church's own ideas of its various images, on the one hand, and the actual images held about it by outside persons, may be pronounced. The churches, along with political forces, giant industries, labor, brand products, and the arts, are searching for an image: their own.

A church dare not succumb to the temptation to exploit Motivation Research or any other technique in order to exploit persons. What about proper use of a technique like M.R.? We have seen how it can help to disclose what is essentially real human behavior and motivation. It seems always a good thing to bring such hidden and vital factors to the surface, into the light of inquiry and examination. But even considering the good that can come of such research, it cannot—in the opinion of this writer—be done without the consent of free will. I am suggesting that in any way it makes use of such a technique as M.R., a church must guarantee at least two things: (1) It must receive permission to engage in psychological depth research on a given person or group of persons by the same person or persons involved, and (2) following such research, it must disclose to the person or persons involved the nature of subconscious images which have been disclosed.

It then follows that a church, using a technique such as M.R., must allow the person who is the subject of psychological depth research to decide if he wishes to have an image which he possesses changed or not. A church, armed with psychological depth research about someone's subconscious image of something, must never fail to disclose the nature of that image to the person himself, or proceed to try, without first having received explicit permission, to change the image by other techniques. As a matter of fact, if a person's image of a Methodist, a Roman Catholic, a Presbyterian, or an Episcopalian church, for example, were derogatory to the church and a decisive factor in church nonmembership, it might well be that, instead of trying to change the person's image, it would be mandatory to change the element in the church (economic snobbery, racial discrimination, dictatorial church government, excessive parochialism) which the person found derogatory! I submit that uncovering images that people have of churches might be a profitable way for the churches to see themselves (through other people's eyes) and to correct some bad elements in the churches which stand seriously in need of correction and amendment. Of course, it might be necessary to take a courageous stand *not* to change some elements which culture might find "bad" but which were indicative of fidelity to Jesus Christ.

Churches must remember their vocation to respect individual free will and integrity more than institutional prestige and success. As Christians, we should try to bring the hidden persuaders out in the open, and then to work with them (as open persuaders) when they labor for the betterment of society rather than simply for selfish motives. We must discourage all "hucksters for Jesus" and "hidden persuaders for Jesus," and thereby shape these very damaging Christian images in mass culture which tragically exist when Christian evangelism is perverted and twisted into exploitation. Our Lord calls us to be honest evangelists of his Gospel and to follow in his own way. It is a way which respects man's free will so much that Jesus Christ died upon the cross and revealed himself to men, not as the expected Messiah but as the Suffering Servant and the Son of God.

Our task is to preach the Gospel of Jesus Christ and to live so faithfully in his way of life that others may be drawn to his way. We cannot ever be "hucksters for Jesus" or "hidden persuaders for Jesus," zealously exploiting persons for God in Christ, making point of contact with secret psychological depth research or by "selling Jesus like soap." We ought not even to call ourselves persuaders, for we know that God's persuasion is by the Holy Spirit. We will be content to be known as evangelists—as disciples—preaching Jesus Christ and him crucified, relying on his resurrection power and glory.

FOOTNOTES

1. New York: Random House, 1959, p. 37.
2. "Adventurer in Morality," *Nation, 188* (May 2, 1959), pp. 412-13.
3. New York: Random House, 1959, pp. 50-51.
4. *Le Ciel et la Terre* (Paris, 1958).
5. New York: McGraw Hill Book Company, 1956.
6. Garden City, N. Y.: Doubleday, 1959, p. 183.
7. New York: Hodder and Stoughton, 1910, pp. 20-21.
8. Boston: Houghton Mifflin Company, 1958, p. 2.
9. New York: McGraw Hill Book Company, 1957.

A Concluding Warning

EVERYTHING HAS A
THEOLOGICAL ANGLE

ARNOLD S. NASH

The specific terms of the assignment, in the light of which this essay was to be written, posited two major features. The first was that the essay should reflect the experience of a professor in a state university where the study of religion is accepted as a responsibility of the institution not to be shared by the churches. However, I should state at the outset that any generalizations made here are derived from fairly wide knowledge of the situation in the country as a whole. My analysis, I think, is more true than, with equanimity, I care to accept of any private university or state university in the country. Moreover, it is, alas, the graduate schools of these institutions which largely create the contours of our present thinking as it shapes the ethos of our smaller colleges.[1] The second feature which should set the contours of discussion in this essay was that a particular effort should be made to raise what was called "the question behind the question." In short, somewhere in this volume an effort should be made to call into question two far-reaching assumptions which dominate most thought in this field. The first assumption is that liberal education in the arts and sciences as normally construed in private university, state institution, and church-related college alike, can somehow constitute an adequate foundation for the professional education in theology of the future minister as it does for the professional education of the other two of the—classically considered—learned professions, law and medicine. The second assumption is that therefore the essential problem becomes: How and when shall we fit the study of "religion" into this picture?

By liberal education in this context is meant that aspect of education which is addressed to man as man. So considered, liberal education can include religion, just as (in theory) it can include jurisprudence or bacteriology; but, so this view of the matter contends, it must be regarded as education whose purpose lies not in the acquisition of professional skills, however profoundly understood, but in fulfilling and in realizing man's essential humanity in giving him breadth of outlook, etc., etc. This view of the matter goes deep. It embodies the common point of departure both of those who, in the U.S.A., Britain, and Europe, accept what I shall call, to simplify the matter, the traditional seminary or divinity school approach and of those who, usually from the standpoint of membership of a department of religion, reject it.

The former position is the one which has for years been accepted in A.A.T.S. circles, and it is the one, moreover, which is usually urged by those to whom the future ministerial student comes for academic counsel. As normally expressed, for instance, by a college or seminary dean or Episcopal bishop or Presbyterian minister it runs as follows:

> Give the future minister not "training" but "education" during his formative undergraduate years. Teach him there how to think and appreciate. . . . As for the field of his aca-

demic concentration? Any "broad" major like English, philosophy, history, or the classics is excellent. Even mathematics
or chemistry can be used for this purpose so long as they are
not too "narrowing" or "professionalized" in their approach.
However, "religion" as a "major" should be eschewed.

The opposing position argues against the A.A.T.S. orthodoxy along two lines. The first is that as long as the teaching of "religion" at the undergraduate level in church-related
colleges, for instance, was in the hands of unsuccessful parish ministers and was virtually nonexistent in the big private or state universities, anything different was academically impossible. Today, however, it is maintained that this
is no longer the case. Now we have available—and this
has been true for at least a generation—the Ph.D. products
of Yale and Union, of Duke and Chicago. Religion—and this
is the second line of attack upon the traditional A.A.T.S.
position—is now well established as an intellectual discipline
in its own right as one of the humanities; it has its own
autonomy and appropriate subdivisions, and its exponents
can now, with proper academic humility, look their learned
colleagues in the face—those in physics or philosophy, in art
or anatomy, and in music or mathematics.

The Achilles heel for either of these two points of view
lies, I am going to urge, at the point where they agree. This
is because of the existence of a hidden premise that can
take two forms. One is that the study of "religion" (or
"theology")[2] can be best understood in the modern world
as an independent academic discipline in the sense that our
present departments of arts and sciences view the matter,
i.e. religion is like art or classics or chemistry or sociology.
The second is that at any level which really matters, academically (and not administratively) speaking, the relation of
a divinity school to the university can be construed in the
same terms as that of the medical school or the law school.

Acceptance of the premise in either form veils the reality of the situation in the contemporary university world. In any serious sense, words like "theology" and "religion" refer to that which has become academically irrelevant on the contemporary scene. Let me illustrate my thesis by considering any discussion about students, curriculum, and the like at a typical faculty meeting in any one of the large universities in America.

If a professor of political science gets up to speak and points out that the issue in question is one which should be considered "democratically," his colleagues, by and large, will listen with both interest and a sense of relevance. If a professor of philosophy then gets up to make his contribution and suggests that the issue is one which should be seen in terms of the "philosophical" issues involved, his colleagues will still listen with a sense of relevance, even if their interest tends to wane. The same would be true if a professor of mathematical statistics suggests that the "statistical" evidence for certain conclusions presented by the Dean should be more rigorously examined. Interest might be restored and a sense of the relevant still maintained if a professor of psychiatry speaks from the standpoint of the "emotional" tangles which might emerge in the lives of the affected students. Yet we can be sure that if a professor of religion or theology were unwise enough to rise and suggest that the problem should be considered in its theological perspective, his enemies would be annoyed and his friends would be perplexed. They would all agree that he was introducing that which, even if it is intelligible, is irrelevant to the ongoing life and thought of a faculty meeting. Perspectives of the kind which he is urging might be relevant, it would be thought, in discussions among faculty members of a divinity school or a department of religion, but certainly they are not relevant, so it would be taken for granted, in the discussion of any question outside such walls.

By way of mitigation or excuse some might seek to explain this disturbing but, I am convinced, valid description of the situation by saying that Americans cannot be expected to think in theological terms. Church life is social rather than intellectual in its tenor; it is moralistic rather than theological in its emphasis. But such a line of argument does not justify the regrettable situation which I am seeking to analyze. It is agreeing with it and seeking to explain why it is so. Moreover, when we consider academic life at the center, i.e. in classroom, lecture theater, or seminar room, in those places where we seek to exhibit our attempts to make sense of human experience, the irrelevance of "religion" or "theology" is equally taken for granted.

Let me give two further illustrations. The first is drawn from my own institution where in all the literature dealing with an ambitious program in the field of international relations whereby the resources of all the social sciences and the language departments are utilized there is no mention (just as in the program itself there is no specific place for and consideration of the relevance) of "religion."[3]

And even if a specious justification for this policy is sought by way of quoting shibboleths about the separation between church and state, there are plenty of illustrations from the life of private universities. For example, two years ago Princeton University initiated a new approach to the problems of human relations whereby there would be created that which is the expression of an integrated rather than the specialized studies of the particularized social sciences. As described in the *New York Times*[4] this desirable end is to be achieved by a "Council on Human Relations" which will seek the fundamental principles in this field. The President of Princeton tells us that:

. . . the new council would bring together faculty members in history, politics, economics, sociology, anthropology and social psychology. All will be concerned with the study of human resources, human relations and human organization. Moreover, synthesis will be the dominating theme of these studies since the tensions in human relations in the world today no longer permit the slow accumulation of bits and pieces of research in the various specialized branches of social science. The findings of social psychology must be put to work immediately in political science, and sociology must help enlighten economic analysis.

What seems to be quite clear is that there is no point at which "religion" or "theology" is construed to have any relevance in the intellectual consideration—*even when synoptically undertaken*—of the relations between human beings and their behavior.[5]

Thus we arrive at a tragic conclusion. Theology, which, whatever else it may be, certainly involves a consideration of man, his place in the universe, and his relations with his fellows, in terms of his ultimate loyalties and ultimate principles of interpretation, is construed as being irrelevant to the intellectual purposes of the modern mind.[6]

But the consideration of these issues is not so much a *part* of liberal education. They are what gives it meaning. These are the issues in terms of which the very idea of liberal education arose in the academic scene of classical Athens and its intellectual offshoots in the museums of the Hellenistic world and Cicero's Rome. Clearly something of profound moment must have happened to Western thought. The temper of our universities is a reflection—indeed it is its most vivid expression—of this strange paradox: What in spite of all their many and profound differences was axiomatic to Socrates, Plato, Aristotle, Isocrates, Cicero, Virgil, and Marcus Aurelius, has become irrelevant to the life of the mind in the contemporary university.

How did it all happen? This is no easy question since

there is a good deal of history between the beginnings of liberal education in the Western world and where we are now. The classic expression of the essence of it is Aristotle's famous distinction in his *Politics:*

> There is a distinction between liberal and illiberal pursuits, and it is manifest that only such knowledge as does not make the learner "mechanical" (vulgar) should form a part of education. By mechanical pursuits we should understand all arts and studies that make the body, soul, or intellect of free men unserviceable for the use and exercise of virtue. This is the reason why we call "mechanical" such arts as produce an inferior condition of the body, and all wage-earning occupations. They allow the mind no leisure and degrade it to a lower level.

Such a statement has many serious deficiencies. It reflects Aristotle's incapacity for human feeling in his attitude towards slavery. It puts in his own words why Aristotle's influence on an emerging experimental science was calamitous.[7] Yet notwithstanding these inadequacies, Aristotle summons any teacher to his need for an educational theory which recognizes that man shall not live by bread alone but that he is a creature for whom life is more than livelihood. It reminds the teacher and scholar alike that in standing for that which is intrinsically (as distinct from instrumentally) worth while he is standing for that which is ultimately worth while and not for the immediately useful, not for that which is a utilitarian means but for that which refers to the final end or ends of human existence. Here the New Testament scholar can remind us that when the Greek talks about the "ends" of human life he is using essentially the same word, *teleoi,* that the author of the Matthean account of the Sermon on the Mount used in the sentence which in the King James Version runs: "Be ye, therefore, perfect." But it is only perfect in the sense in which for a human being we use the word "whole" or "integrated" or "com-

plete." Indeed, the New English Bible, under the direction
of C. H. Dodd, finds itself driven to paraphrase to the point
that the sentence ends up as: "You must, therefore, be all
goodness."

Aristotle's appeal for a sense of the wholeness of things
dominated the most famous book on higher education in
the English language, *The Idea of a University*. For New-
man, too,

> . . . what is merely professional, though highly intellectual
> . . . is not simply called liberal, and mercantile occupations
> are not liberal at all. Why this distinction? because that alone
> is liberal knowledge, which stands on its own pretensions,
> which is independent of sequel, expects no complement,
> refuses to be *informed* (as it is called) by any end, or ab-
> sorbed into any art, in order to present itself to our contem-
> plation.

In the period between the Athenian tutor and the Oxford
don this distinction between means and ends, between the
useful and the valuable, has had a long and honored history
in the training of the clergy of the Christian church. Two
distinct convictions have become enshrined in our thinking during the centuries and they are still apparently accepted in each of the positions with which we began: what
was called the A.A.T.S. orthodoxy and its opposing concept.

The first of these convictions is an acceptance of the
clear separation between what is the "liberal" element and
the "vocational" element in education. The second of these
convictions is that there is no serious reason why the general attitude and most of the content of classical learning
should not provide the basic constituents for liberal education.

It is true that there is a good deal of evidence for the
belief that the Christian intellectual tradition could have
been radically different. Tertullian, one of the most powerful minds of the early church, would have set the course

of theological training along a diametrically different course if his standpoint had been accepted. Trained as a lawyer, equally at home in either Greek or Latin and well read in philosophy and history, he was not to be taken lightly when he developed with all the rigor of a disciplined judicial mind and with a profoundly Roman sense of order and authority, his particular side of the Pauline paradox that Christianity was a divine foolishness which enshrined the highest wisdom. But it was not for him a wisdom that could be squared with that of the philosophers. With the vivid literary style of an experienced advocate in a Roman court he rhetorically asks questions of the philosophers and declaims vehemently against them:

> What indeed has Athens to do with Jerusalem? What concord is there between the Academy and the Church? What between heretics and Christians? . . . Away with all attempts to produce a mottled Christianity of Stoic, Platonic, and dialectic composition! We want no curious disputation after possessing Christ Jesus, no inquisition after enjoying the gospel! With our faith, we desire no further belief.[8]

What was to become, instead of Tertullian's view of the matter, the classical Christian view, whereby the learning which we would now call the liberal arts became the foundation of theological studies originated, appropriately enough with a native-born Athenian, Clement of Alexandria. In the well-known words of his essay *Philosophy the Handmaid of Theology*, Clement wrote:

> Accordingly, before the advent of the Lord, philosophy was necessary to the Greeks for righteousness. And now it becomes conducive to piety; being a kind of preparatory training to those who attain to faith through demonstration. . . . For God is the cause of all good things; but of some primarily, as of the Old and the New Testament; and of others by consequence, as philosophy. Perchance, too, philosophy was given to the Greeks directly and primarily, till the Lord should call the Greeks. For this was a school-

master to bring the Hellenic mind, as the law, the Hebrews,
to Christ. Philosophy, therefore, was a preparation, paving
the way for him who is perfected in Christ.[9]

Students, therefore, under Clement and then under his
student, the even better known Origen, were rigorously
grounded in grammar and logic, in geometry and physics,
before they proceeded to the study of what we would now
call moral philosophy, comparative ethics, and biblical exe·
gesis.

In the succeeding centuries the ablest minds followed the
path blazed by the Alexandrians. Jerome in the East and
Augustine in the West struggled long and hard with the
problem of reconciling their Christian faith with their classical learning.[10]

Within this framework many problems appeared. There
was a time when it appeared that the theological question of
the place of classical learning in the Christian scheme of
things would be overshadowed by the more utilitarian
question of how the literary devices and the rhetorical mode
of expression of the pagan should be used in the Christian
cause. This was the period when Juvencus, for example,
wrote a paraphrase of St. Matthew's Gospel in terms of Vir-
gilian hexameters.

But it soon became clear to Christian and pagan alike that
there was a glaring need for a more thorough attention
to knowledge itself rather than to methods of persuasion.
In short, the neglected "liberal arts," as a synthesis of human
learning rather than rhetoric, as a method of presenting
what was believed and known, offered the most promising point of departure. St. Augustine (incidentally, a sometime professor of rhetoric) for one began, but never finished,
a comprehensive rewriting[11] of an encyclopedia, basing his
approach on the first attempt in this field, Varro's *Discip-
liarum libri novem,* a volume which had appeared in the

early days of the Empire. Augustine's contemporary, Martianus Capella, was more successful in at least the quantity of his output if not in its quality when he produced, in the form of an elaborate allegory, his famous Compendium, *Marriage of Philology and Mercury*. The first two books were introductory to the remaining seven, each of which treated one of what came to be the standard seven liberal arts. His work furnished the dominant foundation of the curriculum for centuries, even though little use was made immediately of his earnest but somewhat uninspiring effort.

The real advance came with Cassiodorus, a scion of the Roman nobility and a faithful servant of the Gothic conquerors, who in 536 A.D. suggested to Pope Agapetus the setting up of what we would now call a Christian university wherein, to quote from the preface to his later work, *The Institutes of Divine and Secular Letters,*

> . . . the unbroken line of the Divine Scriptures and the compendious knowledge of secular letters might with the Lord's beneficence be related.

From this time on there appeared to be no turning back. The monasteries and cathedral schools of the early Middle Ages, like the medieval universities at the time of Abelard and Aquinas, all operated in the light of the vision to which Cassiodorus had given concrete expression in the abbey which he set up on his ancestral estate at Vivarium in Calabria.

It is true, of course, that the early universities of Italy, France, and England during the intellectual renaissance of the twelfth century went much beyond the Roman patrician and the monks who followed his lead. As long as knowledge was limited to the seven liberal arts as they had been understood in the early Middle Ages, there could be no universities in the medieval or modern sense of the term.

Moreover, the far-reaching vision of Cassiodorus itself had

given way and, as so often has happened in the history of education, the stimulation of new ideas got lost in veneration for the written word. It is true, alas, that there was not a great deal to venerate—there was little more than the Latin grammars of Donatus and Priscian and a few accompanying simple reading texts; the arithmetic, music, and logic manuals of Boethius; and a rudimentary collection of elementary propositions in geometry, together with a simple textbook in practical astronomy usually attributed to the Venerable Bede.

But by the end of the twelfth century Ptolemy's astronomy, Euclid's geometry, and Aristotle's logic in a more adequate form began to be known. Avicenna's medical treatise and Arabic textbooks in algebra, trigonometry, alchemy, and astronomy were translated by the score into Latin. Moreover, the whole social and economic situation was radically different. The expansion of trade and commerce led to the rise of the towns and the recognized need for professional training in the other two of the learned professions, medicine and civil (not canon) law. Salerno led the way in the one and Bologna in the other, and by 1231 in the greatest of all universities, that of Paris, there were four faculties, each with its dean: arts, medicine, law, and as "Madame la haute science," theology. It is to this period that the contemporary university owes its debt for the idea of a systematic curriculum of study tested by examination and leading to a degree with its rights and duties.

Thanks to the pioneering genius of Abelard in the twelfth century and Thomas Aquinas in the following century, the terms of the relations between the liberal arts had been transformed as the result of a complete revision of the status of what up to then had been almost the Cinderella of the trivium, logic. Indeed, by the next century, Chaucer, when speaking of the clerke of Oxenford, could refer to the study of logic as implying membership of a university: "That un-to logik hadde longe y-go."

Like "science" in the twentieth century, logic became, not only the most important subject matter to study, but the method par excellence whereby the truth in any field could be investigated or, at least, exhibited for all to see. Valid knowledge of any realm, in earth, or in hell, or in heaven, as man understood it could be best understood, in fact could only be understood, by the human mind so long as it was expressed in the form of propositions logically related with each other in a systematic whole. Such knowledge, incidentally, was not to be discovered so much as expounded. In that sense "rhetoric" and "grammar" still had their parts to play.

This understanding of learning and scholarship ruled, too, in the professional schools of law, medicine, and theology. Justinian in law, Constantinus Africanus in medicine, and the Scriptures and the patristic writings in theology, furnished the prescribed texts which were to be mastered by the student in the light of his professor's commentary.

In short, what we previously saw as the Greek view of liberal education was basic to professional education all through the stormy period during which Europe, and therefore Western civilization, was being forged out of the impact of the barbarians from beyond the Rhine and the Danube upon the peoples who carried the spiritual and intellectual treasures of Palestine, Greece, and Rome. Thus, for a period which was twice as long as that which separates us from Christopher Columbus, the liberal arts were construed as the foundation of professional education for the future servant of the church.

Nor did Christian thought in the Renaissance and in the Reformation initially suggest a radically different view of the matter. In their differing fashions each of these two revolutionary movements of the human spirit as time went on increasingly challenged the medieval syntheses of classical learning with Christian thought. Each in its own way, like similar revivals over the centuries from the beginning of the Christian era, built upon what had gone before. But this time there was a difference; seeds were to be sown whose fruit was to become bitter indeed, for it is nothing less than the "humanities" with all their pathos in the contemporary academic scene. Indeed, the word "humanities" is the key to what happened. To an explanation of that process we must now turn.

Originally the word was used in the singular,[12] "Humanity," as the English translation of the Latin *humanitas*. By the time of Caxton it had been pluralized and it came to be contrasted with "Divinity," which oddly enough was not pluralized. The former was supposed to refer to knowledge on the human level and the latter was regarded as embracing the whole scheme of revealed Christian truth. Thus what began as a promising compromise whereby a dual frame of reference for a Christian humanism was to take the place of wrecked Scholasticism, ended up as a disaster. But that is to overrun my story.

Originally Roman writers like Cicero had used the word *humanitas* as the nearest Latin equivalent to the Greek *paideia*. It was, however, no longer the *paideia* of the Athenian city-state but this idea as it has been transformed by the life, thought, and feeling of the Hellenistic world. In the realm of the mind an ideal, that of belonging to the *oikumene*, the inhabited world, had now become operative, and this Alexandrian ideal transcended in its comprehension all loyalties to a city-state and its way of life. *Paideia* was therefore no longer schooling in the sense of preparation for life; it had become "culture" in the sense of that which gives meaning to human existence in a universal society. Its end product was not, therefore, a learned individual but a cultivated human being. Its antithesis was—as it still is to-day—"barbarity," one of whose acceptable translations, if we would use classical Latin, is *inhumanitas*.[13]

To Cicero, being the complete Roman that he was, *humanitas* meant that human beings were to be seen in a context more than their individual selves, and it was a context of which the Roman law was its most noble expression. But law, too, was only to be understood in a context wider and deeper than—and going beyond—itself, the ground and being of God.

> There is in fact a true law—namely, right reason—which is in accordance with nature, applies to all men, and is un-changeable and eternal. By its commands this law summons men to the performance of their duties; by its prohibitions it restrains them from doing wrong. Its commands and pro-hibitions always influence good men, but are without effect upon the bad. To invalidate this law by human legislation is never morally right, nor is it permissible ever to restrict its operation, and to annul it wholly is impossible. Neither the senate nor the people can absolve us from our obligation to obey this law, and it requires no Sextus Aelius to ex-pound and interpret it. It will not lay down one rule at Rome and another at Athens, nor will it be one rule today and an-other tomorrow. But there will be one law, eternal and un-changeable, binding at all times upon all peoples; and there will be, as it were, one common master and ruler of men, namely God, who is the author of this law, its interpreter, and its sponsor.[14]

Thus for Cicero, as for all the sages and scholars whose contribution to the liberal arts both before and after him we have considered, the humanities are to be seen as in-volving what one can only call a recognition of the "theo-logical" dimension of human existence. That this is true, even if we bear in mind the tremendous differences between Christianity and pagan thought which so bewildered such a soul as St. Jerome, would not be denied by the leading figures of the Renaissance even though they rejected in their various ways the particular formulation of this dimension which the medieval church in its setting of feudalism presented to them. The bankers, lawyers, and merchants of Venice and Milan, of Bruges and Amsterdam, when they sought to create a culture of their own, were willing to bypass both the chivalric culture of the feudal lords and the scholastic learning of the ecclesiastical authorities. Before their hopes and demands were met, their urban society had thrown up new methods of understanding the riches of Greece and Rome. Petrarch led the way in popularizing the idea that original sources are more valuable to the scholar than the most rigorous logic of an argument. And this historical insight arose from his sense of belonging (with all the difficulties involved in so doing) to the thought-world where both Cicero and St. Augustine somehow lived together.

Moreover, those who, like Lorenzo Valla, Nicholas Cusa, and Erasmus, saw even more clearly that the way to an understanding of a writer, once the relevant documents had been collated, was through an appreciation of his historical setting, illuminated by an analysis of his language and style, could join Petrarch in that conviction even if they would not use either his style or his language.

When we pass on to the Reformers, we appear to be moving to another world. No one was more aware, for example, than Luther was of the tremendous gulf between himself and, say, Erasmus. Yet in a sense their quarrel was a family quarrel. Indeed, on occasion Luther kept his criticism of Erasmus to himself lest those who did not value, as Luther did, the study of the literary sources and original languages in which the Bible had been written would misunderstand the situation. He was a typical Renaissance figure in that his passionate concern for literature and language led to a

complete incapacity to understand what Copernicus was doing in astronomy[15] just as in his rejection of Scholasticism
he tended to disparage all philosophy. Yet, granted the temper of his day, one can hardly blame him for the fashion
or the extent to which he emphasized the relevance of literary, linguistic, and historical studies to the achievement
of what we would still call a liberal education.[16]

Calvin was even more than Luther a product of the
Revival of Learning, in every meaning of that term. Indeed,
in a sense he was an intellectual child of the renaissance of
the twelfth century, for not only did he view Aquinas with
genuine respect, but in his love for intellectual system, which
he learned at the University of Paris before he left in 1528
to study law in Orleans, he was one of the Schoolmen sufficiently to justify the remark of my old teacher, R. H.
Tawney, who once said that John Calvin, if it had not been
for the later arrival of Karl Marx, would have been the last
of the Scholastics. But Calvin had appropriated, too, while
in Paris a mastery of the Latin classics, and when he left
Orleans for Bourges to study with the Italian jurist Alciati
he did so because the latter was leading the way in interpreting civil law in the light of the history, languages, and
literature of antiquity.

It is no easy task so to interpret the Renaissance and the
Reformation to the modern university mind. Most professors
still entertain the nineteenth century verdict of George Voigt
and Jacob Burckhardt: The Renaissance is a break with
the Middle Ages in the name of the individuality of the self
and the rejection of Christianity. Popularized in the English-
speaking world by John Addington Symond's *The Renaissance in Italy*, this view of the matter still largely dominates
the contemporary situation. But from early in this century
a steady stream of contributions from scholars like Ernst
Walser in Switzerland, Francesca Olgiata and Guiseppe Tof-

fanin in Italy, together with Douglas Bush and Hiram
Haydn in North America, leads us to the conclusion that
such an interpretation is historically inadequate and philo-
sophically naive.

But—and this is the crucial point of this historical analysis—
what is certainly clear is that if the humanists of the so-
called end of the Middle Ages and the beginning of the
modern world laid emphasis on the values of this world
rather than of the next,[17] they did so, not because they
were humanists in the sense of "scientific humanists" of the
twentieth century, but because they wished to see this world
as good.[18] In short, it was not because they wished to affirm
the world-view that in the contemporary university mind is
entertained by the typical practitioner of the liberal arts and
sciences. The sources of this *Weltanschauung* lie deep in all
that is meant by the modern world when we think of the
free enterprise system, the natural sciences, and the Enlightenment.

Let me emphasize here that I am not arguing in any sense
for a going *back* in scholarship to the Middle Ages, any more
than I think that we can go back in economics to the nineteenth century. Indeed, on the contrary, I am urging that
we must go forward *beyond,* e.g. the Enlightment. Here I
can only say that I personally feel convinced that the insights
we must embody in our future thinking will come from the
two latter-day Jewish "prophets," Karl Marx and Sigmund
Freud. The older I get the more convinced I become that
these two thinkers, irrespective of how their respective followers might upbraid each other, are the correctives sent by
God to an intellectual world which when the "chips are
down" prefer Greece to Jerusalem.

Each age, then, must seek its own synthesis. All previous
syntheses, being human, break down. We are witnessing
such a one on the contemporary academic scene as we see

the fulfillment of the attempt to build a world upon experimental science, capitalist economics, and political democracy.[19]

Each of these liberating movements of the human spirit has helped to form a "mind-set" which is the more potent because it is not recognized. Thinkers as different as T. E. Hulme, Emil Brunner, T. S. Eliot, and J. H. Oldham have each sought to emphasize how this mind-set, like any other, becomes that *through which we see and in terms of which we judge* all else in such a fashion that we cannot see how much we are conditioned by it unless we know in an existential fashion *where we stand.* And it is precisely this step which the contemporary university or college on the American scene refuses to take, except at the point of trivialities —intellectually if not politically speaking—such as whether students and faculty members should be allowed to listen to Communists.

And if one seeks for the roots of our contemporary confusion and the powerlessness of professors before politicians and the public, one does not have far to seek. It is that higher education, insofar as faculty members are concerned, oscillates between two inconsistent positions: on the one hand, college and university stand for an objectivity which tries to be neutral on all questions involving the sense of meaning by which mankind can integrate its individual and collective life. On the other hand, explicitly believing themselves to be without presuppositions of value, they preach implicitly a very definite faith. In essence, the major doctrinal tenets of this faith are that human nature, if not perfect, is, like the world as a whole, slowly getting better, and that if we can only have more research foundations spending more money on more research schemes so that professors can have more frequent and longer sabbatical leaves in order to publish more books and monographs, then, sooner or later, we shall not only control the weather and get to the moon, but even get rid of death!

We have come a long way from the insights of the tradition of the liberal arts and sciences. And there is no simple going back to them. At each stage in their emergence and development, if we could have explored them more fully, their deficiencies would have been seen as glaringly evident again and again as new occasions taught new duties and time made ancient good uncouth.

However, through all the centuries until the Enlightenment certain insights were painfully retained, but over the last two centuries they have been increasingly ignored. Let us explore some of them and indicate what we have lost.

(1) Liberal education stood for the wholeness of things. We leave our students to fend for themselves between the optimism of our classes in biology and sociology and the pessimism of physics and astronomy. And we treat attempts to relate, say, one of the humanities to one of the natural sciences (to quote from a resolution passed unanimously— with the exception of the chairman of the philosophy department who sardonically smiled upon the intellectual naiveté of his colleagues—by a committee on humanities in one of America's leading universities) in the following terms:

> As a matter of principle, without regard to any individual who might teach a course of this kind (on *The Bible and Science*), it seems to us that such a course is not one to be taught disinterestedly by anyone primarily concerned with the prestige of religion; and it is equally clear to us that it is not the kind of course to be taught disinterestedly by a pure scientist interested in the prestige of science. A course of this kind, in any but the most disinterested hands, endangers the integrity of a university curriculum.

(2) Classical liberal education stood for the notion that man should know *where* he stands and *for what* he stands.

We so make objectivity our ultimate rationale that we fail to make clear to our students that in the search for truth, objectivity is meaningless except in relation to commitment. We forget, too, that truth is not a self-explanatory absolute, for man neither has the right to pursue the truth in any way he sees fit nor can he use the truth once he has got it in any way that he sees fit.[20] Thus, there are grades of significant truths.

(3) Classical liberal education stood for the conviction that what is significant is most worthy of attention by the human mind. We stand for the conviction that whatever we can measure is therefore significant. What it is that is being counted does not matter so long as we can count it.[21]

(4) Classical liberal education stood for the notion that the community of learning is human and universal. Even Isocrates, the legatee of Sophist teaching, could say that "the people we call Greeks are those who have the same 'paedeia' as ours, not the same blood," while Eratosthenes, the famous geographer of the museum at Alexandria, could go further: "It would be better to make divisions according to good and bad qualities: for not only are many of the Greeks bad, but many of the Barbarians are refined—Indians and Arians, for example, or Romans and Carthaginians." Yet how many would say, in spite of centuries of Christian teaching since the time of Isocrates and Eratosthenes and in spite of the witness, too, of the medieval universities with all their faults and failings, that their successors in the form of the liberal democratic universities—any more than those of the Communist countries—are able to deal with the ill effects of narrow nationalism. How few professors would bring the Alexandrian savant up to date and add Cuban Communists to the list of those among whom may be found the "refined."

Perhaps now my initial thesis can be better seen and understood even if not accepted. *It is that through the liberal arts and sciences as now understood the future ministerial student is taught a confused world view which challenges the basic tenets of the Gospel which he will be trained to preach.*

Whatever else the Christian faith is, it certainly involves both a sense of man's finitude and yet a sense of the wholeness of things. The fact that the "autonomous subject" (or "academic discipline") has become both the sacred cow of the soul and the basic category of thought of our colleges of arts and sciences means that the concept of the whole is denied.[22] The Christian faith stands for the need for decision and a sense of the tragic element in human existence. If a student gets either from the contemporary academic scene, it will be because of the grace of God.

At this point the reader will be asking the writer when he is going to get "practical." Here the latter can only reply in the words of G. K. Chesterton in his essay *On Business Education,* "when a problem is really bad and basic, we should rather wail and pray and cry aloud for an impractical man." As Chesterton goes on to point out, the more serious the trouble, the more certain it is that some knowledge of "scientific theory" will be required. The practical man can deal with a machine only when there is something not too seriously wrong with it. A garage mechanic can mend a flat, but he cannot design a new car.

Thus the essential point is not whether what I have said above is "practical" but whether the analysis is true. In short, we should begin by being "theoretical" in the original sense of the term; we should see things as they really are. Only when that issue is settled—and we are far from that state of affairs today—can we go on to consider means and methods.

Certain conclusions or rather starting points, however, are clear once the dire straits of the present situation are accepted.

The first is that, contrary to what perhaps the former analysis might lead the reader to believe, I am convinced that we must look for enlightenment to a source other than the classical learning of Greece and Rome.[23] I suggest that just as the book of Genesis was a prolegomenon to the Exodus so we might notice that its first eleven chapters are a most complete prolegomenon to liberal education. These chapters may not give all the answers in terms that will satisfy the modern Christian mind, but they certainly raise them. Who was man? Where did he come from? Whence arise pain and suffering? What is the meaning and significance of knowledge? How shall we interpret the significance of sexuality or of language or of work? Why are there nations and rainbows and different modes of locomotion for living creatures? Why is there a division of labor between men, some of whom are farmers and others work in metals? Why do civilizations rise and fall?

If the influential figures in the councils of the Christian churches and their theological seminaries and divinity schools will only goad the deans and professors whose names appear on church rolls (even if their minds are back in the graduate school of twenty years ago), then perhaps in God's good time a framework of thought for liberal education will appear which will be more adequate for the needs of the present times than any return to either St. Jerome or St. Augustine, to Abelard or St. Thomas, to Erasmus or Luther, to Calvin or Schleiermacher could provide.

We might begin by recognizing that truly biblical thinking will learn from the Old Testament that there is no word there for religion and that the word "theology" is Greek in origin and not biblical. We might then see that what is required is not a dialogue between *disciplines*, but between *persons* who are identified with their particular disciplines. We deceive ourselves even if we think that a conversation between "theology" and "sociology" or between "religion" and "literature" is what is needed. Not only does this view of the matter rest upon the hypostatization of two abstractions, but it misses completely the point of what constitutes biblical thinking. The latter is not a body of thought like sociological theory (this is the weakness in all our talk about biblical theology), but it is thinking about *anything* (and not only about a particular realm of "biblical" data[24]) from a specific standpoint.

Let me hastily add that I am not denying that "religion" *can* be a field of study, and I am not denying that "theology" can be regarded as an autonomous discipline. I am not saying, therefore, that in a college of arts and sciences in a university or in a liberal arts college, "religion" has no place "in" the humanities or "in" the social sciences. I would be flying in the face of empirical fact if I did. What I am saying is that if we try to take a biblical framework of thought seriously, the specific witness of "religion" (to use in the absence of any alternative such a non-biblical term as "religion") is lost if it is seen as essentially that which can be localized in a course or curriculum rather than as a "standpoint" or a "perspective" from which knowledge in any field is seen and understood and appreciated.

Such a view of the matter, I recognize, needs some elaboration, an elaboration of which only the bare outlines can be presented here.

We can begin by recognizing that the word "knowledge" has no meaningful plural. Monotheism at that point is still accepted by the university world. Yet man cannot deal intellectually with everything all at once. Even a metaphysician in the classical sense, who, to use A. N. Whitehead's phrase, seeks to synthesize the knower and the known, has to abstract from the total given situation presented by experience before he can do anything.

Thus from man's earliest ventures in the field of education in institutional terms of school (as distinct from family and tribe) he has sought consciously to understand his world, sometimes, on the one hand, by dividing the *content* of his knowledge into what we now call fields of study, and sometimes, on the other hand, by adopting different *methods* of studying the data given in his experience. As illustrations of the former fields of study we have, for example, in the medieval universities the trivium and the quadrivium, and then law, medicine, and theology, mental, moral, and natural philosophy, while in the modern university we have the familiar "Art to Zoology" departmental pattern. As an example of the latter methods of study we have all that is indicated by a word like "scientific" or "historical" or "sociological" when what we have in mind is not so much a particular body of data but a method whereby we can seek to make sense of any particular body of data from the standpoint of the particular method in question. Moreover, this distinction between a field of study and a method of study is not absolute. Thus we can have history as a field (and this usually means political history) or we can have history as a method, and so we get the historical study of art or the historical study of music.

Religion is so ubiquitous and so significant in human affairs that we mislead ourselves in thought if we regard theology as one field among others, just as we misinterpret it in life if we view religion as one interest among others and, hence, particularly in a fragmented world like that of the twentieth century, we should put our stress on religion as that which holds things together, rather than as a substantive field of study. It is in this sense that we must bring back (if that is the right phrase to use) theology to the field of liberal education. It is in this sense that theology is like charm, as Maggie defined it to her brothers and father in J. M. Barrie's *What Every Woman Knows:* Charm is such that if a woman has it, it doesn't matter what else she lacks, but if she doesn't have it, it doesn't matter what else she possesses. So, too, for theology. If in the contemporary academic scene the future minister can be taught to understand theology during his undergraduate years as a context of thought in which he can understand all the arts and sciences, or as *The New Yorker* puts it, "everything has some theological angle"[25]—it will not matter whether the student has majored in religion or not.

FOOTNOTES

1. The damage there is not always as serious as at first sight might appear since these are the institutions where what little of genuine creative thought about higher education *which is of any "political" effectiveness,* so far as I can see, is now taking place.

2. As it would be called in England.

3. I write, incidentally, during a week when a U.S. President has received a diplomatic setback of the first order arising, among other things, from his incapacity to deal with a Roman Catholic government faced with Buddhists whose political theories are based on *samsara, sunyata,* and *nirvana.*

4. September 11, 1961.

5. And it is no reply to suggest that religion is not "in" the Social Sciences but "in" the Humanities. It is "how" it is in the Humanities or anywhere else which is the question at issue.

6. I do not have the space at my disposal to give further evidence for this conclusion. I must therefore restrict myself in reply to those who would reject it to the suggestion that they should also bear in mind while doing so that they must also deal with such singularly diverse confirmation of my thesis as they will find in, for example, the weighty words of William G. Pollard (Executive Director of the Oak Ridge Institute of Nuclear Studies) in his essay "Dark Age and Renaissance in the Twentieth Century" in *The Christian Idea of Education* (New Haven, 1957), or of the distinguished English educator and historian, M. V. C. Jeffreys who points out in his *Education: Christian or Pagan* (London, 1946), speaking of the British situation, that "it is impossible to introduce any specifically religious conceptions such as sin or salvation into a modern discussion about education without producing the sort of impression that one would create by going out to dinner clad in a bear skin" instead of a tuxedo, or of a former president of the American Psychological Association, Hobart Mowrer, in his recent article in *The Christian Century,* "Science, Religion and Student Values" and in the Harvard Report on General Education, especially Chapters II and III. Last, but by no means least, for those concerned with the relevance of liberal education to future theological studies, my critics will have to explain on *their* grounds why in our departments of classical languages Hebrew has no status; yet no less a figure than Erasmus could regret to the end of his days that, as he pointed out in one of his letters to Colet, he was too old after his years in Oxford to learn Hebrew when he got to Paris. Here I can only explain what has happened by saying that even in the minds of our professors of classics, the Renaissance has been conquered by the Enlightenment, so aptly described by the Aus-

trian epigrapher and linguist, Ernst Doblhofer, as the "tireless search for knowledge and truth, allied to an uncritical contempt for everything which had for so long been considered the sole refuge of this truth."

7. As I have tried to show in another place. See *The University and the Modern World* (New York, 1943), pp. 57 ff.

8. *De Praescriptione Haereticorum*, Chapter VII, E. T. by Peter Holmes in *The Writings of Tertullian*, Vol. II of *Ante-Nicene Christian Library*, Vol. XV (Edinburgh, 1870).

9. Opening paragraph of Clement's essay on "Philosophy the Handmaid of Theology." E. T. by William Wilson in *The Writings of Clement of Alexandria*, Vol. IV of Ante-Nicene Christian Library (Edinburgh, 1867).

10. St. Augustine went so far as to discuss whether one could be really free and happy to the greatest extent in heaven if one did not know and appreciate the liberal arts here on earth! See *De ordine* II.26 (Note also II.44 for a more "modern" defense!).

11. None of Augustine's attempts to write a treatise on each of the liberal arts survived except *De musica*, but we have his excellent discussion of the teacher in *De magistro*.

12. As it still is at the University of Glasgow where the title of what we would call the professor of Latin is "Professor of Humanity."

13. Uses that we still have in mind when we refer to the Nazis as "inhuman" or when Mr. Nehru, the product of Harrow School and Trinity College, Cambridge, tells engineering students at an Indian University that the way to become an integrated human being is to aim at the possession of those "essential cultural features which make a man a man."

14. Cicero, *On the Commonwealth*, Sabine and Smith, tr.(Indianapolis, Ind., 1959), pp. 215-216.

15. Luther died in 1546, three years after the one which saw both the death of Copernicus and the publication of his *On the Celestial Orbs*.

16. In his well-known letter to Eoban Hess, Luther says that "the remarkable disclosure of the word of God would never have taken place had He first not prepared the way by the discovery of languages and sciences."

17. And with the humanists we must include here the Reformers. Luther once told a farm maid that "God through you milks the cow and does the most servile work," and for Calvin the Christian can only overcome the world by recognizing at the same time the value of its life.

18. Although I doubt whether any one of these thinkers, other than the Reformers, was conscious of what he was doing, I venture to suggest that here they were much nearer then they thought to the Hebrew than to the Greek emphasis in thought. To the Old Testament mind, nature is good, whereas the Greek philosopher—in the last resort —entertained contempt for the world of time and space in preference for one of pure and rational being. Incidentally, when I say that any of these writers see the world as good, I do not mean that they saw it as "secular," i.e apart from God.

19. Perhaps I can refer any reader who wishes for an expansion of the line of thought in this paragraph to the introductory chapter, "America at the End of the Protestant Era" of *Protestant Thought in the Twentieth Century*, edited by Arnold S. Nash (New York, 1951).

20. The Nazi experiments on human beings have been a terrible price to pay for the lesson at this point to the liberal world of scholarship.

21. Perhaps a personal note from my own field, the sociology of religion, may not be out of place here.

A few years ago it was my privilege as Chairman of the Section of the Sociology of Religion of the American Sociological Association and on another occasion as the Chairman of a similar section of the Southern Sociological Association to read a score or more papers which would-be authors wished to have considered for presentation at the annual meeting of the appropriate learned society. With one or two exceptions the writers failed to see that the fact that people go to church is not necessarily *religiously* significant. People go to church and synagogue for all manner of profoundly different reasons. In fact, many of them are quite *irreligious* ones, just as many other people stay away for genuine *religious* reasons. This aspect of the matter is, of course, an old story. It goes back at least to the horticulturist Amos, who uttered his religious protest from out-side the temple at Bethel to those who were entering it. It is a sorry but true comment on a great deal of contemporary sociology of religion on both sides of the Atlantic that the crowds who flocked to the temple would be statistically significant, but Amos would be ignored except as a defiant deviant.

22. For a brilliant delineation of the situation see Section II, "Specialization and Its Consequences" in the chapter "Religion and the Mind of the University" in *Liberal Learning and Religion* edited by Amos N. Wilder (New York, 1951).

23. I suppose that here I am "going back" to the unknown author of *The Apostolic Constitutions* who in Syria at the end of the fourth century summoned his readers to recognize that "if thou wilt explore history, thou hast the Books of the Kings; or seek-est thou for words of wisdom and eloquence, thou hast the Prophets, Job, and the Book of Proverbs, wherein thou shalt find a more perfect knowledge of all eloquence and wis-dom, for they are the voice of the Lord, the only wise God. Or dost thou long for tune-ful strains, thou hast the Psalms; or to explore the origin of things, thou hast the Book of Genesis. . . ." (I am indebted to my former teaching assistant, Miss Mary Ann Brown, for bringing this quotation to my attention.)

24. Or "revelation" so far as that goes.

25. September 2, 1963, p. 184.